Free Cyntoia

Free Cyntoia

MY SEARCH *for* REDEMPTION *in the* AMERICAN PRISON SYSTEM

CYNTOIA BROWN-LONG
with Bethany Mauger

ATRIA BOOKS
New York London Toronto Sydney New Delhi

An Imprint of Simon & Schuster, Inc.
1230 Avenue of the Americas
New York, NY 10020

Photos courtesy of Ellenette Brown, Cyntoia Brown-Long, and Jaime Long, unless otherwise specified.

First Atria Books hardcover edition October 2019

Interior design by Joy O'Meara

Manufactured in the United States of America

10 9 8 7 6 5 4 3 2 1

Library of Congress Control Number: 2019948672
ISBN 978-1-9821-4110-3
ISBN 978-1-9821-4112-7 (ebook)

This publication is a memoir. It reflects the author's present recollections of her experiences over a period of years. Many names and identifying characteristics of individuals have been changed. Some dialogue has been re-created from memory. Some scenes are composites of events. Events have been compressed and in some cases their chronology has been changed.

This book is dedicated to all the women, men, and especially juveniles serving time in the American prison system. You may have lost all hope and feel like your voice has been silenced and your life doesn't matter. Know there's ONE person who sees you.

You, who have shown me great and severe troubles,
Shall revive me again,
And bring me up again from the depths of the earth.
You shall increase my greatness,
And comfort me on every side.

—PSALM 71:20–21 (NKJV)

CONTENTS

Introduction xv

1. The View from the Outside 1
2. Tales of a Displaced Princess 15
3. Longing for a Happy Ending 25
4 Trying for Normal 37
5. Going for Grown 45
6. Damaged 51
7. Powerless 59
8. Self-Defense 77
9. Trapped in a Cage 95
10. Facing Life 107
11. Spared 117
12. Fighting for My Life 127
13. Two Paths 139
14. Self-Destruction 151
15. Proving My Worth 161

16. The Hands and Feet of Christ 173
17. "The Chick in the Box" 189
18. Memphis 197
19. Finding My Way Home 211
20. Burned Letters from Texas 223
21. Last Resort 235
22. Going Viral 249
23. Asking for Mercy 263
24. Finding Home 277

Epilogue 291
Acknowledgments 299

Free Cyntoia

Introduction

AUGUST 26, 2006

My knees shook as I stood in the courtroom. Any moment now, the jury would file in. Twelve men and women had spent the last six hours debating whether I should spend the rest of my life behind bars.

I'd sat in the Davidson County Courthouse holding cell, staring at the cinder blocks, reading the names of men and women etched on the walls. The metal bench pressed into my back, but I barely noticed. My mind was busy playing the same scene over and over . . . The last five days of testimony went by in slow motion. *Did that juror smile at me?* I wondered. *What were they thinking then? Are they on my side?*

I didn't expect to walk out of that courtroom a free woman. That doesn't happen when you kill someone—especially when you're a biracial girl who shot a white man. But I did hope for some sort of mercy.

I was sixteen years old, just a kid, when I thought I'd fallen in love. In my crazy, teenaged head, we were building a future together. He wasn't a pimp selling my body to fund his lifestyle. Our arrangement was only temporary, just until we could run away to Vegas and start our life. I thought I was making Kut happy when I climbed into a middle-aged man's truck and agreed to have sex with him for $150. But when the night dissolved into a nightmare, I panicked and shot a man. It was self-defense, I reasoned. I wouldn't get in trouble.

I had no idea how wrong I was.

Maybe I would get fifteen years, I thought. Almost as long as I'd been alive, but better than a life sentence. Fifteen years and I could be back in my mommy's house, ready to make a fresh start.

Without warning, the courtroom door burst open. The jury strode in silently, their heads down. I stared at them desperately, hoping someone, anyone, would make eye contact with me. Only one man looked up. We locked eyes for a split second. My heart pounded as he shook his head slowly, imperceptibly, before he looked down again. Maybe he was ashamed of what he had done. Or maybe he'd fought the battle for me and lost. Whatever it was, I knew right then and there I was getting a life sentence.

I stared at the jury, my chest heaving as I tried to slow my breathing. *Whatever you do, don't cry*, I thought. I wanted them to feel my anger.

My attorney Rich McGee leaned forward in his suit, his blue eyes boring holes through the jury. *He knows it too*, I thought.

"Has the jury reached a verdict?" the judge asked the jury foreman.

"We have, Your Honor."

Tension radiated through the room. I stared the lady down, waiting for her to read the words I'd dreaded for months. *Why does she gotta pause like that?*

"We, the jury, find the defendant, Cyntoia Denise Brown . . ."

She paused again for what seemed like hours. *Just do it already*, I thought.

"Count one, guilty, first-degree murder."

I flinched. Her words carried the weight of condemnation. I felt like she'd just confirmed I was a monster, a murderer, a whore.

"Count two, guilty, felony murder."

Pause.

"Count three, guilty, especially aggravated robbery."

I didn't have to wait for the judge to read the sentence. I already knew. Everyone did. First-degree murder carries an automatic life sentence in the state of Tennessee.

I was still just a teenager. I'd never had a driver's license, never been to prom, never voted.

"God," I said, back in my cell, curled up in my yellow jumpsuit, "if you let me out of here, I'll tell the whole world about you."

1

THE VIEW FROM THE OUTSIDE

When I was a little girl, I would do anything to make my mommy proud. We were attached at the hip, walking around as if it were the two of us against the world. I was a princess in my parents' eyes, and even though I'd have rather climbed trees and made mud pies, I let them doll me up in frilly dresses and clip bows in my curly black hair.

My big brother and sister, Chico and Missy, were already grown and out of the house, and Chico always complained that I was spoiled. Looking back, he was probably right. Mommy and Poppy ate up every second of having a little kid in the house again, and whatever I wanted, I got. When I begged for my own swimming pool, Poppy made sure my wish was granted. While Chico and Missy had had a whole list of chores when they were little, my only job was to load the dishwasher.

I didn't have many friends, but I didn't need them. Mommy was my only playmate, plain and simple. I spent most of my time working to keep us safe, especially from the house fires I was sure would strike as we slept at night. Ever since I heard a boy down the street's house had caught fire after he put Kool-Aid in an iron, I was terrified that my little brick one-story house would be next. I kept backpacks stuffed with extra clothes and toys, ready to grab at a moment's notice, and I even held my own fire drills. Mommy and Poppy laughed, but I wasn't messing around. I wouldn't let anything hurt my family.

When it was time for me to start kindergarten, I clutched Mommy and Poppy's hands as tight as I could. I wasn't scared—after all, school meant I'd finally be able to read my beloved books all by myself. But I was nervous. My parents walked me into the classroom, helped me hang up my Care Bear backpack, and got me settled at my table with crayons.

I was happily scribbling away on construction paper until I noticed my classmates walking in with their parents. Everybody was the same color as their parents, shaped with Momma's nose or their daddy's eyes. Not me. My five-year-old world was rocked as I realized my light skin didn't match my dark-skinned parents. I didn't look like their princess. I looked like I didn't belong at all. And everybody noticed.

"Your skin looks funny," a little boy said, pointing.

"Yeah," a little girl chimed in. "Are you white or are you black?"

I stared at them, confusion clouding what should have been a happy first day of school. "I . . . I don't know."

"How do you not know?" another kid asked.

My stomach felt sick as Mommy buckled me into my car seat that afternoon. The question swirling through my mind felt stuck in my throat as Mommy carefully backed out of the parking lot and turned toward our home.

All my life, I'd thought nothing of the fact that most of the people around me were black. Now I felt like the guy in *The Emperor's New Clothes*, after somebody told him he was naked.

Finally, the words tumbled out. "Mommy, why don't I look like you and Poppy?"

Mommy was quiet as she paused at a red light. "Well," she finally said, her eyes on the road, "you're adopted, baby girl. Poppy and I brought you home when you were only eight months old."

My brain tried to process Mommy's words.

"Your momma was so young," Mommy continued. "She was only sixteen years old. She wanted you but she just couldn't take care of you."

My mind raced, trying to take in information too complicated for me to possibly understand. In a way, the news didn't change anything. Mommy and Poppy were still my parents. I had no doubt they loved me. But who was this lady who somehow belonged to me too? "Who is she?" I asked.

Mommy hesitated. "Her name is Gina. She's a white lady who used to be a friend of Chico's."

I frowned. "So that's why I don't look like you?"

"You are your own unique person. You're mixed, and you're beautiful," Mommy said firmly. "Gina is white, and your daddy was black. That makes you special. Just like Mariah Carey."

Mariah Carey's music was the constant soundtrack of my childhood bedroom. *Music Box* blasted from my little stereo over and over as I serenaded my toy poodle Fefe with "Hero" and "Dreamlover." I couldn't help but smile. "Yeah, she's beautiful," I agreed.

I HAD NO MEMORIES OF GINA, KNEW NOTHING BEYOND WHAT MY mommy and poppy told me—which wasn't much, at first. The Browns had taken me into their home before I could walk, and they gave me their family name shortly after I could talk. I never wished I could meet Gina or wondered what she was like. I never quite understood why she didn't want to meet me or come to visit, but I always pushed the thought aside. As far as I was concerned, the Browns, my mommy and poppy, were my family and that was all that mattered.

In his heyday, my father was an army first sergeant and paratrooper with the 101st Airborne Division. On the weekends, he sat in his chair soaking his feet in peroxide, regaling me with another tale from his days in the Vietnam War. My mother managed a local furniture store until she quit her job to take care of me. By then, my father had retired from the military after twenty years of service. For most of my childhood, Poppy was a long-distance truck driver. Mommy and I were on our own during the week as he drove up and down the southeast states, making it home only on weekends.

Mommy spent most of her days tending the peonies and bleeding hearts in her flower beds—I swear she had at least fifteen different gardens.

I can still smell the Avon Skin So Soft lotion Mommy would smooth on her hands in the car before church Sunday morning, popping in a stick of Winterfresh gum and brushing burgundy lipstick on her lips before she drove us to Ogburn Chapel Missionary Baptist Church. I didn't pay attention at church much, but our lunches afterward sweetened the deal. Every week, Mommy took me to Ryan's Steakhouse, where I would tear up the buffet like I was a grown man and not a stick-skinny little girl. I'd load up my plate with a huge helping of spaghetti first, then circle back to the buffet for turkey, chicken, and green beans before heading back for soft-serve vanilla ice cream. Going to a restaurant with Mommy felt like a little date. I felt special as I sat across the table from her, like there was no one in the world but us.

Anybody would have thought I was headed for success. When I was in second grade, my teacher called Mommy to my school to tell her they'd identified me as gifted and wanted her permission to place me in the Program for Academically Superior Students, or PASS, as everyone called it.

"Toia, you should feel so accomplished," Mommy said, beaming. "You really can excel at anything you put your mind to."

Mommy's words made my heart swell with pride. I just knew I'd grow up to be a fashion designer, or a doctor, or whatever struck my fancy that week—my dreams changed all the time. I had it all figured out. I'd get married, get a house down the street from Mommy, and we'd play with my babies on the front porch. But when I looked down at my light skin, I wasn't so sure. I saw a girl who didn't belong. Not in our black church. Not in my class. Not in my community.

"You're white," someone would say in a tone where I just knew it wasn't a simple observation.

"Look at her hair," someone would sneer.

It all reached a boiling point when I was cast in an elementary school production of *Tom Sawyer and the Whitewashed Fence*. Everybody in my class had to participate, but I had to admit I was a little excited to stand under the spotlight, even if I was only cast as one of the kids who assisted in painting the fence. Mommy even helped me fix up my face, smudging dark makeup on my cheeks. I looked exactly like I'd been playing in the mud. It was perfect.

The audience roared with applause as we took our final bow that night. I curtseyed with a grin and beamed as Mommy applauded, that look of pride I loved so much on her face. Then I noticed a little white boy standing in the audience, pointing right at me. "Look at that dirty white girl," he said loud enough for me to hear.

My cheeks burned as I clenched my fists and glared. Here I was, trying something new, and still no one saw me as anything but the white girl who didn't belong. I was furious with him for ruining the moment. I would have loved nothing more than to punch that boy in the nose then and there. Standing onstage, though, with everyone looking at me, I sucked in my breath and told myself not to cry. I wanted to shrink into the floor and disappear. Instead, I stood firm. *Don't let him know he got to you*, I thought.

More than anything, I wanted to belong. I wanted to sit down with a group of friends and feel like I was accepted for who I was, that I didn't have to try to fit in. But it didn't happen. I felt awkward and alone.

"The other girls don't like me," I'd cry as Mommy held me on her lap at night. "Why do I have to be different? I wish I was just like everybody else."

Mommy wiped the tears from my cheeks and looked me deep in my eyes. "You listen to me," she said firmly. "There's nothing wrong with you. You're perfect just the way God made you. You just let those girls know, *I am who I am, like it or not.*"

Her words comforted me in that moment, but they didn't stop me from plowing through a whole list of extracurricular activities, looking for some place I was accepted. I swung at baseballs. I strapped on cleats and kicked a soccer ball down the field. I waved pom-poms and tied a bow in my hair on a cheerleading squad. I even played the trombone in the band for a few weeks. But I never found a place where I felt like I truly fit.

Sometimes, I'd do something that made other kids not want to play with me anymore. Like the time our neighbor's granddaughter came to visit. She was just my age and I couldn't wait to spend the week riding bikes, exploring the neighborhood, and coming up with games off the top of my head.

"Let's play war," I said one day. "My poppy told me about it."

It's possible the game I described to the neighborhood kids slightly resembled something Poppy had described to me, but I'm sure when he said it, he never pictured me and the other kids standing on opposite sides of the street, throwing rocks at each other. Everyone was running and laughing, having a grand old time chucking stones. I was running along the sidewalk looking for rocks when I spotted it—a giant red rock just begging for me to pick it up.

Wow, I thought. *I wonder if I can throw that all the way across the street.* Without another thought, I clutched the rock in my hand and hurled it across the street as hard as I could. It hit our neighbor's granddaughter square in the forehead. We stared at her as blood immediately poured out of the wound.

Uh-oh. In the moments before I threw the rock, it had never occurred to me that anyone could get hurt. I felt sick as I watched the girl stand frozen to the sidewalk without making a sound—that is until she reached up and touched the blood.

Her bloodcurdling scream sent just about every adult in the neighborhood running into the street. Our neighbor grabbed her granddaughter in her arms, holding her close to comfort her before demanding, "Who did this?"

Everyone looked at me. I hung my head. I knew how badly I had messed up and I wanted desperately to fix it. But the damage was already done.

Needless to say, I wasn't allowed to play with that little girl anymore.

Mommy and Poppy were beside themselves. They paced up and down the room, yelling and hollering, telling me about the butt-whooping that would follow their lecture. I stared at the floor, wishing with all my might that I'd never picked up that dang rock.

"What were you thinking?" Mommy asked in frustration, shaking her head. "Why would you *do* that?"

I gave them the only honest answer I could. "I don't know." Afterward, I replayed the scene over and over again in my head. I didn't mean to hurt that girl. It was like the idea to throw the rock popped into my brain, and before I could think through what would happen, the rock was already sailing through the sky. *Why did I do that?*

It was the same when I ripped all the letters off a brand-new sign in the park, and Mommy and Poppy had to foot the bill. And the time when I snatched a friend's mom's jewelry—that one cost Mommy and Poppy $500.

"Why would you do that?" was the constant refrain I heard from Mommy and Poppy. And every time, my answer was the same: "I don't know."

Why can't I just be like everybody else? I constantly asked myself.

I was sick of standing awkwardly on the fringes of groups of kids, pretending like I was supposed to be there when everyone knew I wasn't.

After a while, I stopped trying to fit in. If they wanted me to be an outsider, that's exactly what I'd be. Slowly, a chip the size of Texas formed on my shoulder. When somebody called me white, I didn't sink into the floor anymore or wait until I got home to cry into my pillow. I snapped my hand onto my hip, looked them in the eye, and told them I thought they and their smart little mouth were stupid.

When I was seven years old and in the second grade, Mommy got used to the almost weekly notes and phone calls from my teacher, all about me disrupting class or disrespecting her. Every note brought another whooping, another lecture. But the worst came when I was kicked out of PASS. The teacher didn't like the fact that I refused to work in groups, I did my work before it was assigned, and I absolutely did not want help from the teacher. She told Mommy I was downright rude when she dared to stop by my desk.

I could see the disappointment written all over Mommy's face. That program was everything to her. She'd told me all the time how proud she was that I was chosen, and I knew she'd bragged to all her friends that I might as well be a genius. In that moment I understood what I'd done. All my life, I'd done everything I could to make Mommy proud. Now letting her down felt horrible. I wished that I could go back and just shut my mouth in class.

"But I don't understand it, Toia," Mommy said. Her face was desperate, like she really wanted me to give her some kind of insight into what was going on in my brain. "You never act like that at home. Why are you doing this?"

I shrugged. "I don't know." I didn't know how to explain what it was like to feel constantly on the defensive, like everyone was looking for a reason to pick on me. I don't know that I understood it myself.

Everyone knew I'd been kicked out of PASS when I returned to the regular classroom. I could feel them whispering about me as I leaned over my desk to solve math problems, the weight of their judgment heavy on my shoulders. No one said it to my face, but the message was clear: I was no good.

Their judgment became a self-fulfilling prophecy. If everybody thought I was bad already, what was stopping me from doing what everyone thought I was doing?

It started small. I grabbed a two-dollar choker off a Walmart rack when Mommy wasn't looking, after she told me it was too grown-up for me. I made the rookie mistake of stuffing it in my puffy coat pocket right before Mommy decided to wash it. She marched me right back to Walmart and made me put the choker back, the whole time telling me I was about to get arrested.

I could see Mommy and Poppy's dismay and confusion give way to helplessness each time I got caught in another lie. They were well beyond asking what I was thinking at this point. Worry lines were etched in their foreheads, constant tension in their voices. I noticed Mommy and Poppy didn't talk as much as they used to. Looking back, I knew I was the cause of their stress, but I never admitted it to myself at the time. I was too absorbed in myself and whatever I could get away with next.

Of all the mischief I got into, I never thought a bottle of NoDoz could send me past the point of no return. Missy and her husband lived a few blocks away from Mommy, and I'd found it snooping through my brother-in-law's truck one afternoon while they were visiting, not looking for anything in particular. I was just nosy and liked to snoop where I wasn't wanted.

I couldn't wait to show off my latest find at school the next day. You couldn't pass me in the hall without me sticking the bottle in your face.

Then, toward the end of the day, the school resource officer motioned for me. "Ms. Brown, you need to come with me," he said. I'd barely walked into the principal's office before the officer was frisking me like I was a city crack dealer. He never let on to what he was looking for until I saw him smirk, the NoDoz in his hands.

"What are these doing in your jacket?" the principal demanded, holding up the container the officer had handed her.

I stared at her. "They're caffeine pills," I said. "I found them."

The principal and resource officer exchanged glances before they both turned to me sternly. "Cyntoia, we take drugs very seriously here. We've expelled kids for less."

"But . . . but these aren't even drugs!" I sputtered my words as I tried to make sense of what was happening. I felt like I was caught in a trap, like I was being set up. The whole school thought I was the bad kid. Now this seemed like their chance to prove it, to get me off their hands, to let me be somebody else's problem. I knew this lady wasn't going to listen to a word I said.

When Mommy walked through the door, I knew I was really in trouble. This was beyond PASS-level anger. This was a new low. Mommy gripped my shoulder in her hand as we walked together into the conference room, where the principal and other angry-looking adults were waiting for us. Their decision, they said, was final. I couldn't come back to school for the rest of the year. I was expelled. Kicked out of sixth grade for a few caffeine pills.

Mommy barely said a word the whole ride home. Her lips quivered in fury, her disappointment and frustration now turned to anger. Poppy, however, had no shortage of things to say when he learned what I'd done.

"What the heck are you thinking, getting kicked out of school?" he shouted. "Girl, you are twelve years old. You want to be like your birth mother Gina? Keep right on doing what you're doing." He shook his head, disgust written all over his face.

A pit formed in my stomach. We never talked about my birth mother. I knew nothing about her except that she was young when she had me. For the first time, I wondered what might be lurking in my genes. Who was this woman who was part of my blood?

"Well, what was she like?" I finally asked cautiously.

"You wanna know?" Poppy was so livid he could barely speak. He practically spat out the words just to get them out of his mouth. My heart pounded as I waited for him to continue.

"That woman," he hissed, "ain't *nothing*. She was a drunk. A drug addict."

I swallowed hard, forcing down the lump in my throat. I knew he was trying to scare me straight, but hearing that I came from trash made me feel like I was trash too. And he wasn't done.

"She was so addicted to drugs that she had sex for money just to get it. Gina threw her life away." He paused and glared at me, pointing his finger at my chest. "And if you don't shape up, you're going to end up just like her."

I stood rooted to the ground as Poppy turned around in disgust. My whole life, I'd felt that I wasn't like anybody else. Was Gina the reason? I wondered, my mind racing. Was she behind every piece of candy I stole, every smart remark I shouted at a teacher? Was she my future? What if it was only a matter of time?

Getting expelled wasn't the get-out-of-school-free card I thought it would be. Mommy refused to let me sit at home idle all day. Instead, she enrolled me in our only remaining option—Greenwood Alternative School.

The school was on the other side of Clarksville, so far from our house I'd have to ride the city bus every day, since Mommy couldn't drive me and make it to work on time. Mommy took a day off work to help me get a bus pass from the depot downtown and decipher which routes to take on my daily commute.

Calling Greenwood a school was a stretch. Imagine a large group of teenagers all deemed too dangerous, too rebellious, too incorrigible to be around other students in the public school system. These teens were left to their own devices several hours a day, without adults or any supervision. Alternative school was not a place where behavioral health specialists or special education instructors cared for kids with special needs. Instead, you were told to tuck your white T-shirt into your blue jeans, tighten your belt, and sit quietly with your back to the teacher as you worked independently through a list of assignments in a textbook. The teachers didn't teach, and questions weren't welcome.

If alternative school was supposed to turn me around, it had the opposite effect. Inside the school walls, I was surrounded by an eerie quiet, the silence practically ringing in my ears as not even a whisper was allowed. Outside, it was a free-for-all. The kids who surrounded me had been expelled for far more serious infractions than carrying NoDoz. Before and after school, they roamed the streets, raiding nearby stores and abandoned houses. Once, a group of boys who claimed to be in a gang met up in a parking garage under the bus terminal and took turns beating the hell out of one boy. I helped him dust off shoe prints from his blood-speckled T-shirt. Compared to these kids and their rap sheets, I was practically a good girl by comparison. But that wouldn't last.

I spent more and more time with a girl named Sarah, who introduced me to Nick and Brett. Nick could have been the twin of Fred Durst from Limp Bizkit, while Brett walked straight out of the pages of *The Outsiders*, complete with slicked-back hair and a black leather jacket over a white T-shirt. I asked him once if he knew what a greaser was. He just stared at me.

My new friends and I walked from the bus depot to school together almost daily. Sarah suggested we head to her house in Woodlawn one day, about an hour's walk from the closest bus stop. When we finally arrived, she dug around her purse and cursed.

"I forgot my key," she said. "But I think my bedroom window is unlocked."

Seconds later, I was being hoisted through her bedroom window so

I could unlock the door from the inside—I was chosen since I was the smallest. Nick and I searched the house for a few hours while Brett and Sarah had sex in another room.

Suddenly, a noise stopped me in my tracks—keys jingling in the front door. Nick and I didn't have time to move before a forty-year-old white woman opened the door and screamed.

"Get out of my house!" she shouted, frantically grabbing the phone.

Sarah darted into the living room, smoothing her disheveled hair and tucking in her shirt as she tried to explain. Her mom wouldn't listen. I heard her say her address to the person on the other line and realized she'd called the cops.

I've got to get out of here, I thought. I took off running as fast as I could, throwing open the door and sprinting across the lawn. I heard feet slapping the ground behind me before someone grabbed my purse. It was Sarah's mom.

Tug-of-war over the purse quickly escalated to us swinging fists. Clawing. Screaming. A woman driving by the house even pulled into the driveway to stop the fight. Sarah's mom didn't care. She clung to my shirt as I swung and squirmed from her grasp.

I never thought my first fight would be with a forty-year-old white woman. I certainly never thought I would face charges for a fight I didn't start. Yet a few days later, there I was, sitting in a juvenile detention cell, Poppy's words echoing through my brain. *If you aren't careful, you'll end up just like Gina.* I stared at the cinder blocks of the cell surrounding me as if I could see my future written on the walls. I'd never felt more like Gina than I did in that moment.

2

TALES OF A DISPLACED PRINCESS

Poppy could barely contain his fury as he picked me up from the juvenile holding cell. The look in his eyes said it all—I hadn't listened to his "scared straight" speech. I'd taken another step down the very path he'd told me not to go down.

"Do you have any idea how much your attorney is gonna cost me?" he muttered as we walked to the car. I knew better than to give him an answer.

I had no idea what my charge was until I sat down before a judge. But it was all I could do to keep from popping out of my chair when he said I was charged with breaking and entering, and theft of property over $1,000. I don't know what that lady claimed to be missing but I knew I didn't take it, and I was sure nothing in that house was worth $1,000. The judge never mentioned the fact that the woman assaulted me and grabbed my purse. As much as I protested, my attorney thought it would be inappropriate to bring it up. The whole thing felt like a setup.

The judge ordered me to undergo a psychiatric evaluation before he pronounced the disposition of the case. That meant I'd be sent to a Nashville facility called Crockett Academy for thirty days. My attorney explained to me and Poppy that this was standard procedure for a juvenile's first time in court. But nothing about the word "psychiatric" seemed standard to me. I pictured crazy people roaming the halls, doctors in white coats wrapping me in a straitjacket, injecting me with God knows what. I was terrified.

Crockett Academy may have looked like a campus, but life inside those tall metal gates was like living in a tunnel. The staff led me down a long hallway to my new home for the next thirty days, the walls seeming to grow closer together with every step we took. This was no detention center. This was a full psychiatric facility filled with patients ranging from kids there for the same reason as me to girls who carried on conversations with the air or rocked in their chairs staring blankly ahead of them. One girl seemed completely normal aside from burn scars covering her body. *I am not like these girls*, I thought. *I shouldn't be here.*

I was assigned to a cinder-block room with one window covered in mesh. Two wooden beds filled most of the floor space—one for me, one for my roommate. I sat down to test out the mattress and made a face as I felt springs poking my backside under the thin, scratchy blanket. To make matters worse, they handed me a bottle of soap that was also supposed to function as shampoo. That mess wasn't going to work for this curly haired girl. Everything in my room seemed designed to remind me that I didn't deserve the good stuff anymore. I was a delinquent. What did I expect?

This was my first dose of facility life, and it was entirely its own beast. Every morning we had to walk down the hall to rooms that functioned as a school. We had two hours of class before a one-hour break in our dorms, and then we were back for two more hours of class in the afternoon.

No one was allowed to go back to their room unless the staff said you could. The academy had a gym, but we were only allowed there once in a blue moon. On the off chance we got rec time, a doctor or counselor almost always pulled me out to ask me how my meds were working or put me through another analysis. That left us with nothing to do all afternoon but sit in the common room, where a TV played nothing but cartoons all day long.

One day I overheard Miss Diane, a lady on staff, teaching other girls how to crochet. I never had much interest in learning, but now that I was required to sit in the common room from 3 p.m. to 6 p.m., it suddenly seemed interesting. She brought in yarn and needles and taught us the classic granny square pattern. From then on you never saw me without a ball of yarn and a needle. I kept my hands busy stitching granny squares into a little blanket for Mommy, just big enough to cover her lap. I wanted her to see I could make her proud again.

Every time I turned around, some staff person was looking over my shoulder, telling me I couldn't go back to my dorm or take a second helping at dinner. Getting away wasn't an option. So I learned to work the system. If I smiled my sweetest smile and promised not to tell anyone, I might get an extra snack or time to myself.

But it turned out I wasn't the only one who'd learned how to play games inside. I learned that the hard way, when someone set fire to paper towels in the bathroom. Academy staff yanked us out of our rooms and marched us right into the hallway while they ransacked our rooms searching for matches. I leaned against the door frame and jiggled my knee waiting for them to hurry up and finish so I could get back to my granny squares. I could hear the sound of rustling sheets as someone lifted the mattresses. Then suddenly, the noise stopped. My heart dropped into my stomach as the counselor stomped into the hall and thrust a box of matches in my face.

"Those aren't mine!" I cried. "I swear. I did not start that fire and I know nothing about those matches!"

The teacher stared me down. "Then explain to me what they were doing under your mattress."

"It wasn't me!" I could hear the pitch of my voice rising the more I protested. "You've gotta believe me!"

I glanced around the hall, looking for someone on my side. All I saw were accusing, disbelieving eyes until my gaze fell on the girl covered with burns. The corners of her mouth turned up as she tried to stifle a snicker.

In that moment, everything clicked. The burns that scarred her body after she set her house ablaze. Her love of playing with fire. *That chick set me up*, I realized.

Something swelled up inside me that I had never felt before. I thought of the NoDoz incident, the theft charges. No one listened to me. They just assumed I was guilty without giving it a second thought. My reputation as the bad kid took away any credibility in their eyes. This was one setup I would not let stand. My legs seemed to move themselves as I stomped across the hall and punched her in the face. Again. And again. I couldn't stop myself, even as she screamed and the staff pried me away from her.

I screeched like a wild animal as the staff wrestled me to the ground in the padded time-out room. With restraints around my body and a shot of Thorazine coursing through my veins, all I could do was cry at the unfairness of it all. I was trapped, and it had nothing to do with the locked door. I was helpless, with no control over anything that happened to me.

My thirty days could not have ended soon enough. With the evaluation finally complete, my attorneys asked the judge for a pretrial diversion, where I would be placed on probation for a certain period and, upon completion, my record would be wiped clean. It sounded easy enough.

They released me to go home a few days before Thanksgiving, with instructions to see a therapist and keep popping the psychotropic pills they put me on. The more that doctors experimented on me with different pills, the deeper I slipped into a mental fog.

I wasn't allowed back at New Providence Middle School until March, when my expulsion was finally lifted. The moment I walked through the door I realized something was different. The kids walking past me in the hallway wore football jerseys and cheerleader uniforms. They carried science projects to the lab and pulled Nano pets from their pockets. After surviving Crockett Academy and alternative school, their little school activities and projects just seemed foreign, like I was an extra in someone else's movie. I was the same age as all these kids, and yet I felt years older after a few short months away. I'd seen the inside of a juvenile detention cell. I'd even spent a month in a psych facility. You just don't walk away from those facilities as the same person.

I'd always felt like a stranger among my classmates. Now I felt like an alien who had landed on another planet. It felt more natural to smoke cigarettes, talk on the phone to boys, steal candy—basically anything else. Sometimes I did try to find my old self, my old way, but now my name carried a reputation. I was the girl no one wanted their kid to hang out with.

My only friend was Marissa, who I'd known my whole life. We walked to school together and sat at the same lunch table. She didn't smoke, and she still cared about school, but I made it my personal mission to change that. I'd offer her cigarettes as we walked to school, and coax her into skipping class with me. She was the only person who treated me as if nothing had changed, like I was the same girl sitting in the PASS program all those years ago. To everyone else, I was invisible.

Fine, I thought. *I'm not like y'all. I'm better*, I told myself. Their rejections only made me more determined to find my own way. But I felt lonelier every day and more and more out of options.

Even the school wanted to hide me. They stuck me in a behavior modification special education class, along with kids suffering from mental and developmental delays. I couldn't even sit next to my classmates. I was required to sit behind a screen in the back of class, where no one could see me. I didn't switch rooms at the end of each period.

I just stayed in the same room all day, like I was back in elementary school. I couldn't talk to a soul even if I wanted to. *Does anyone in this class know I'm back here?* I wondered.

The principal told me I had to stay in behavior modification until I could prove that I could behave. How was I supposed to do that, seeing as I was sitting alone behind a screen all day?

Frankly, sitting behind that screen was embarrassing. *They're doing this just to make me look stupid,* I thought as I slouched in my chair. I had no intention of filling out the worksheets the teacher, a white lady with dark curly hair named Miss Burnes, handed me. I was too advanced for those sheets, and she and I both knew it. I sat back there crocheting all day, not paying attention to one word the teacher said. They could stick me in that class, but they could not make me learn. All I wanted was to finish the school year, get the heck out of this class, and pray that they let me out of behavior modification the next year.

The only time I was allowed to get up each day was for lunch. The last thing I wanted was for anyone to see me coming out of that room, so I had it down to a system. The room was right by the cafeteria, so every day I'd throw down my yarn, hop out of my seat, and run to the cafeteria before anyone else had time to get there. Then, it was my routine to stop by the vending machine for a pack of SweeTart Minis before heading back to class.

It was during a lunch break one day that I realized I'd left my little black purse in the classroom. I figured I'd run out to get it and loop back to the vending machine. All the students had already left for lunch, so the classroom should have been empty. But it wasn't. I walked in the door and saw Miss Burnes standing at her desk, my purse in one hand and my yarn in the other. That lady was going through my freaking purse.

Not only did I not have any rights at school, but now I had no privacy. I could feel it rising—that feeling I experienced the day the girl with the burns framed me for burning paper towels at Crockett Academy. I spat the words out—"Give me my stuff."

Miss Burnes didn't bat an eye. "You're not supposed to be crocheting in class."

I stared her down, rage coursing through my body. I felt violated, disregarded, as I watched her pawing through my bag and my granny squares like they were nothing. "Well you're not supposed to be going through my stuff."

She didn't argue, but she wasn't giving in. Miss Burnes raised her hand behind her back, like she wasn't going to give me what was rightfully mine. She couldn't take my bag away from me. My crocheting was mine. Mine and Mommy's. I locked eyes with her as I marched to her desk and snatched it out of her hand. She let out a scream like I had just smacked her across the face. I didn't care. I took off with my little black purse to get my SweeTart Minis like I wanted in the first place.

I thought that was that, until the school resource officer pulled me out of class. We sat in the same principal's office where I was busted for NoDoz just months before. I stared at their serious faces as they explained Miss Burnes had accused me of assault.

"We have to call the police, Cyntoia," the principal said. "Miss Burnes is pressing charges."

My pulse raced and I closed my eyes. It all came back to me. The cinder-block walls of Crockett Academy. The mesh-covered window. Sitting in the common room watching minutes tick by. *Aw nah*, I thought. *I am not going back there.*

As soon as the school resource officer turned his back, I bolted out of there like someone was chasing me. I darted and dodged kids milling around the halls and pushed my way through the front doors. Kids waited on the sidewalk for bus rides and parents picking them up. I tried to blend in, like I was one of them. It didn't work. Everyone stared at me like I forgot my pants that day. I wasn't one of them, and I hadn't been for a long time.

"I'm trying to hide from the police," I loudly whispered at them.

They shrugged. "What police?"

I cursed under my breath as a cop car pulled into the parking lot. *I cannot believe this*, I thought. I booked it across the parking lot and to the sidewalk that led to my house, certain the police were hot on my trail. I don't know if anyone chased me. I never looked back. You take the time to look back, it'll slow you down. You can only look forward when you're running from something.

When I finally made it home, I slammed the door shut and leaned against it, my chest heaving as I tried to slow my breath. I hit the floor, ducking beneath the windowsill and peeking under the curtains. I was a fugitive on the run. It wasn't long before the police showed up, and I was back in the juvenile detention cell. Back in the place I swore I'd never be again. I felt like the system was rigged against me. No matter what I did, everyone in charge went out of their way to make sure I was someone else's problem, to get rid of me. And I was getting sick of it.

I spent about a week in detention before a guard woke me one morning to inform me I would appear in court that day. No one told my parents it was happening.

The judge decided I could go home after my hearing and had his staff call my parents to come pick me up. Mommy was teaching by then and couldn't leave her class, so she gave them Poppy's number. Poppy had already left in his truck to pick up a load out of state, but he promised he would send someone to come get me.

I was sitting in a glass box in the back of the courtroom, swinging my feet and waiting for someone to get me out of there, when I saw him grinning at me. Big John. *Of all people*, I thought.

Poppy's best friends at M. S. Carrier were both named John—he called them Big John and Lil' John. Lil' John's parents, Mike and Gail, were Poppy's age and lived just a few houses down from us, and Poppy took me up there with him regularly. Mommy only went once or twice before she decided they were all a little too drunk and redneck for her liking, so it took quite a bit of convincing before she let me stay with them at a cabin on Kentucky Lake while my parents enjoyed their anniversary trip. I remember her saying multiple times that she didn't feel comfortable leaving me there, but Poppy assured her I would be fine. What twelve-year-old wouldn't have fun in a cabin on a lake?

At first, he was right. Within an hour of getting there I was on the back of a four-wheeler, speeding through dark wooded trails along the lake. I learned to drive a four-wheeler on my own, ate as much ice cream as I wanted, and stayed up too late. It was like a big family affair with the whole crew, and I had the best time I could imagine.

Mike had just finished grilling steaks for dinner one day and sent me outside to get Big John. I found him sitting in his pickup beside the lake, talking on his cell phone, with one of his legs dangling out of the open door. I didn't want to interrupt and waited patiently for a stopping point to let him know dinner was ready.

Finally he looked up and noticed me. "Oh hey, Cyntoia," he said before turning back to the phone. A look crept over his face that I would come to know all too well, before he kept talking with a sleazy drawl. "Yeah, that's my homeboy's daughter," he said to whoever was on the other end of the phone. "She's one of those young girls who are developed in all the right places."

My cheeks flushed as I suddenly became very aware of my 34D chest streaked with stretch marks from rapid growth. Every Lifetime movie I had ever seen came flooding back to me—along with Mommy's disgust at unwelcome leers from creepy men. I grabbed the open truck door and slammed it on his leg as hard as I could. I could hear him cursing as I ran back to the cabin.

I burst in and announced to everyone gathered in the front room what Big John had done. I expected them to be just as outraged as I was, to take up their torches and pitchforks and run him out of town. Instead, Mike handed me a plate of steak.

"I'll talk to him," he said simply.

I was sitting on the cabin floor with my plate when Big John limped in, looking just as angry as I was. I stared at my steak, listening for the big lecture I was sure would come Big John's way. But Big John and Mike just talked about how good the steak was between swills of beer. No one said anything. No one cared about protecting my body.

Mommy was beyond pissed when I told her what Big John had said. But Poppy just didn't get it. He thought I was overreacting. Mommy was the one who declared she didn't want me around that creep anymore.

I never wanted to see that man again. Yet now here he was, standing on the other side of the glass, expecting me to get in his truck.

The court clerk popped her head in the glass box. "You're free to go," she said.

I shook my head. "I will not be leaving with that man."

She looked confused. "But you get to go home, honey," she said. "He's gonna take you there."

"I am not going anywhere with him," I interrupted before she could finish speaking. "I will not be alone with him like that."

I watched the clerk motion for Big John to step into her office while I stayed put in the glass box. A few minutes later, he stormed into the courtroom, glaring at me as he stalked across the room. I didn't care. I glared right back at him.

It was the first time anyone had stood up for me when a man made me feel uncomfortable. But if I felt relieved, it was only for a moment. The court clerk stuck her head in the box again. "The judge changed his mind about releasing you," she said. "DCS is picking you up. You're heading to state custody."

I groaned. State custody was dreaded among kids in alternative school. This was more than the thirty-day stint I'd done at Crockett Academy. The Department of Children's Services could keep you for an undetermined period, even up until your nineteenth birthday. And I was only thirteen. I was getting locked up for real this time. This whole speaking up thing didn't seem to be working out for me.

3

LONGING FOR A HAPPY ENDING

My first stop in state detention was a facility called Clarksville Diagnostic Center, or CDC as most people called it, to be evaluated for my final destination. They needed to consider my charges and flight risk before deciding how much security I needed. The level two facility housed around twenty-five kids in a small building surrounded by a fence, with blacktop and basketball goals for recreation. Each room had two sets of wooden bunk beds, and we were assigned shirt colors depending on our behavior. We wore green shirts when we were well behaved. Kids in sky-blue shirts were being punished, and they couldn't speak to anyone or associate in any way with the rest of us. (Thankfully, I never had to experience life in a sky-blue shirt.) My hope, at this point, was to stay green. To complete my treatment program and get back to Mommy as soon as possible.

After Crockett, I considered myself a woman of the world. I thought I had seen everything. The kids at CDC proved me wrong. They were a step beyond anyone I'd encountered at alternative school or even Crockett Academy. I met kids who lived on the streets, who sold crack, who spoke with no emotion about how they shot someone. One seventeen-year-old girl had a thirty-five-year-old fiancé. They lived by a different set of rules and they weren't shy about teaching them to me. It wasn't that I only fit in among the juvenile delinquents. But the kids at CDC never made me feel like I had to act a certain way or do a certain thing to be accepted. I could just be me—they weren't too picky. I had to admit that felt good.

I'd only been at CDC for a few weeks when a girl named Pat shoved her way in front of me to jump in the shower.

"Don't get in that shower," she said, her hand on her hip. "This is mine. You best find another one or wait your turn."

I stood there wrapped in a towel, my soap and washcloth in my hands. I'd heard Pat was in a gang back in Springfield, and she had the attitude to prove it. But there was no way I was backing down. "I'm getting in that shower," I shot back.

She inched closer to me. "I don't know who you think you are," she hissed.

"I know I'm fixing to get in this shower."

Now Pat's nose was practically touching mine. Her squinted eyes were locked on mine, her face scrunched into her fiercest expression. I made up my mind this girl would not intimidate me. No one was going to tell me what to do, not the CDC staff and certainly not some chick named Pat.

"I'm getting in that shower," I said evenly.

I watched her mouth drop open as I pushed past her and pulled the shower curtain shut. My fists clenched. *Come at me*, I thought. *I'm ready.* Instead, I heard the flapping of her flip-flops as she shuffled away.

No one challenged me again in my sixty days at CDC. But that wouldn't last long. The courts decided I would be placed at a level three residential facility—the second-highest security level—and sent me to OmniCenter in Nashville. If I thought CDC was a different world, OmniCenter was another planet. I learned real quick I had to fight for my life every day.

The facility itself was better than I expected—it almost felt like a college dorm. The rooms were stocked with two wooden beds and the first fluffy comforter I'd had since I left home. I had a private bathroom with a shower, and two game rooms featured televisions, games, and couches. We were separated from the boys by two sets of solid double doors, but sometimes girls threw notes—and even themselves—over the adjoining group room's wall by moving the ceiling tiles. Downstairs, we went to school during the summer months and used computer labs to study for earning our driver's licenses or playing *Oregon Trail*.

The culture, however, did not match the facility. It was high school on steroids. Hostile, with fights every day. Back home in Clarksville, girls might shut you out or spread rumors about you if they found out you liked their boyfriend. Here, they would call you a bitch and punch you in the face. I got in the mix real quick—I was one of the smallest girls there, but I never backed down from a fight. I caught myself throwing fists over girls calling me white or claiming I stole someone else's lotion. Sometimes we didn't even know what we were fighting about. It wasn't unusual for girls to punch each other and grab fistfuls of hair in the afternoon and play Ping-Pong together by dinnertime.

Mommy came to visit every weekend. Her face was a relief, a reminder of a world where fists didn't fly over the slightest misunderstanding. She'd tell me about what Missy and Chico were up to, and I'd talk about math class, the food, anything but the turmoil I felt being locked up. I needed Mommy to think I was okay even if I wasn't. I'd already put her through enough. The last thing she needed was to listen to me complain about how horrible this facility was when I was the one who got myself locked up.

I didn't give much thought to the boys on the other side of the group room. I was too consumed with trying to survive to even look at them. Meanwhile, plenty of boys were looking at me. They didn't care that I was thirteen. I could see the older boys let their eyes linger on me as I walked past them. Men had looked at me like that for as long as I could remember.

Since the day I strapped on a training bra, I couldn't go anywhere without getting catcalled. I never minded, but Mommy would have none of it. Once, as we walked through the entrance of the Clarksville mall, a group of boys sitting on the planters whistled at me. I didn't look up, but Mommy stopped in her tracks. Their smiles disappeared as Mommy marched over to them, her finger wagging.

"Don't you disrespect my daughter like that!" she said. "You apologize to her right now."

Mommy didn't play, even when the attention was directed at her.

"Mommy, why does that make you so mad?" I asked once, when she'd finished chewing out a fool who had dared to approach her. "He was just complimenting your jeans!"

"No he wasn't, Toia," she said sharply. "You don't ever let someone treat you with no respect like that."

Truth was, I liked the attention from cute boys. That didn't go away, even at OmniCenter.

The more my thoughts lingered, the more my eyes drifted to the boys around me. My gaze eventually settled on a boy named Mike. I saw him roaming the halls of the Institute for Learning Research, which was basically where kids went when even the alternative school couldn't handle them. OmniCenter bused us there and locked us in classrooms all day, but some kids on probation drove themselves to school.

Mike was eighteen, the oldest boy in school, with braids in his hair, gold on his teeth, and fourteen tattoos. He looked like the kind of boy who could take me away from here, like he could be my runaway love. He wasn't in my class, but I caught his attention in the halls as I walked to the bathroom or to lunch. Before long, we passed each other notes back and forth and talked briefly in the hallway. I told him I was planning to run away from OmniCenter one of these days, trying to impress him.

"Well, if you ever make it out, hit me up," he said. "You can crash at my place."

That was all the invitation I needed. By Friday, I had my escape all figured out. A boy in my class who drove to school agreed to pick me up and take me as far as North Nashville. Another girl from the group home, Sparkle, gave me her mother's address and said I could stay with her until I caught a bus to meet up with Mike. I knew as long as I could make it to him, everything would fall into place. Sure, I'd taken a detour in life, but my happy ending seemed like it was right around the corner. We'd live in the shadows, away from OmniCenter, just him and me. Finally, I'd belong to someone.

When school let out that day, the boy from my class was already waiting in a parking lot next door. I sat next to the window, and when I was sure the teacher wasn't looking, I threw it open and leaped out. I ran through the grass and across a thin tree line separating the school from the lot, the thin branches scraping my legs as I jetted through them. I was undeterred. I never slowed down and I never looked back. I could feel freedom waiting just ahead of me.

My body shook as I jumped in the boy's Oldsmobile.

Sparkle's mom lived on Joe Johnston in Nashville, but the boy told me he had to stop at a house on 28th first. We pulled up in front of what can only be described as a run-down trap house and went inside. A heavy dark-skinned man with a mouth full of golds sat at a kitchen table counting money, while someone stood at the stove stirring something in a measuring cup. Standing in the kitchen, my excitement evaporated, leaving nervousness in its place.

Without saying a word, the boy from my class motioned me into a bedroom across the hall. I stepped inside, and as he closed the door, he pulled a condom out of his pocket. Instantly, I felt a sense of obligation I couldn't explain.

He didn't ask if I wanted to. I didn't say yes or no. An unspoken understanding hung in the air—he'd helped me escape, and now I had to pay the price. *Fine*, I thought, resigning myself. *It's not like it's your first time*.

Mommy never talked to me about sex beyond the basics. My education came from a 1970s porno I found when I was ten. After looking around to make sure no one was there, I popped it into the VCR and watched the screen, my eyes wide. *This is what Mommy's trying to hide from me when she covers my eyes watching HBO*, I thought. I felt like I was getting away with something, with no one around to force my hands over my eyes. It was my first exposure to sex, and as far as I knew, it was perfectly normal. Where some kids might have been horrified, I was fascinated. It was like the curtain was pulled back, like I got a glimpse at a secret.

Soon, that tape wasn't enough. I sat down at our family computer, waited impatiently for the old desktop to connect to dial-up internet, and punched in Poppy's credit card number to prove I was eighteen so I could watch all the porn I wanted. Sometimes I skipped school, playing movie after movie all day long. I still have Poppy's old credit card number memorized.

Behind the bad acting and terrible lighting, each porno carried a message, at least to my young brain. Sex with strangers was normal, they told me. I watched women walk into a room and immediately start having sex with whoever was there. *That must be how it happens*, I thought. Had Mommy known what was going through my head, she would have been horrified. I pretty much didn't connect any consequences to sex itself. It was like that game of war all over again, picking up the rock and throwing it as hard as I could, without ever thinking of where it might land.

That's how my brain worked the day I'd lost my virginity one year earlier. At twelve years old, I was waiting at the bus stop to travel to the alternative school when I decided to use the pay phone. Before I could drop in my coins, I heard someone call "Hey!"

A man stood in the doorway of a nearby apartment. I guessed he was nineteen by the looks of him.

"You can use my phone," he said. "It's too cold for you to stand out here."

I walked in without giving it a second thought. Alarms should have sounded in my head, screaming at me not to go in some stranger's apartment. I didn't know that part of my brain wasn't working.

The man told me I was pretty and moved in for a kiss. I didn't push him away. A kiss led to his hands on my breasts, my shirt being pulled over my head. I let him keep going until we were rolling around on his floor, having sex next to a car seat and a package of diapers. *This is just what you do*, I thought.

I never made it to school that day, and I never saw him again. To this day, I don't know his name. It was like a scene straight out of the pornos I used to watch when my parents weren't home. I didn't stop to think about what could happen if I let this man lay me on my back. I didn't even understand why I did it.

Now, in this boy's bedroom, trading sex for a ride to the projects was just what I had to do. I felt nothing as I lay on my back, waiting for it to be over. I was on autopilot, almost as if I weren't there at all.

When the boy was done with me, I made it to Sparkle's mother's house, which turned out to be just a few doors down from a police precinct. The woman welcomed me inside but asked me where her daughter was. She had expected Sparkle to run too. I didn't want to tell her the truth—that I'd refused to wait on Sparkle to find a way out of the group home.

"I think she's on her way," I said.

The woman didn't have a phone, so I walked down the street to call Mike from a pay phone. He instructed me to take the bus to a shopping center and he'd be waiting there to pick me up. He was there all right—on his bicycle. Not exactly what I had expected. *Where the heck am I supposed to sit?* I thought.

We walked together to his cousin's place, where we spent the next few days having sex all over the apartment, to the music of "Differences," by Ginuwine. "I love you," he'd say as he held me in his cousin's bed. "We gonna get married. We'll get our own place. It'll be just you and me."

I looked into his eyes and saw a boy who would love me, a boy who wanted me around, a boy who would protect me.

It all came crashing to an end on Monday morning with possibly the worst breakup line ever. "Do you have bus fare?" he asked out of the blue.

"Um . . ." I didn't know what he was getting at. "I'm not staying here with you?"

Mike rubbed the back of his neck and avoided eye contact. "Nah, my cousin ain't going for that," he said. "She was cool for the weekend but you gotta go now."

"Uh, okay." I stared out the window, watching sunlight stream through the glass, my mind too confused to be heartbroken. Mike's words didn't make sense. What happened to getting our own place, to running away and getting married? I thought Mike had this all figured out. If we weren't going to be together then what did I escape for? This didn't exactly fit my concept of runaway love.

"I could see you next weekend if you want," he said.

I stared at him. *Well where the heck am I going to go until then?* I thought.

Embarrassed, I took the bus back to Sparkle's mother's house. I had just walked in the door when she informed me I couldn't stay there either.

"DCS was here looking for you an hour ago," she said. I knew that was a lie. Everyone knew no one looks for you when you run from state custody—they just wait for you to get caught doing something stupid, which almost always happens. I got the message, though.

"Fine," I said. "But can I use your bathroom first?"

I went upstairs determined that no one would find me. I took out a pair of scissors to cut my hair into a bob, put on dark red lipstick, and took off walking with my grocery bag of belongings. I had no clue where I was going, but I wanted to look grown when I got there.

By the time I ended up on 8th Avenue, I realized my sister worked on the corner of 8th and Broadway. I strolled into her office like I was a grown woman there for a casual visit, not a juvenile on the run.

Missy seemed happy to see me at first. She hugged me and let me fix a cup of soup in the break room. We were chatting when I saw the police walk in. *You've gotta be kidding me*, I thought. *My own sister turned me in*.

The police took me to a medical center for a checkup before hauling me back to OmniCenter. An older lady took me into a room to interview me before she sent me back to my room.

"Your exam shows you were having sex," she said bluntly. "We need to know with whom."

My mind raced to come up with a good lie. Mike may have thrown me out, but I wasn't about to give him up. Protecting him seemed noble, like these people trying to keep us apart were the problem, not the relationship itself.

"It was my boyfriend, Smoke," I said.

The look on the woman's face told me she knew I was lying. I didn't care.

When I returned to OmniCenter, I was known as the resident escape artist. I soon met a girl named Bonnie, who was back in custody after being on the run for more than four years. She was referred to me for help with escaping.

"I'll help you," I told her. "But only if you take me with you and help me find a place to stay."

This time, we took off running as we were being loaded into a van. She zigged and zagged across the street and around trees. *This chick is trying to lose me*, I thought. Unfortunately for Bonnie, I was a great runner. I was right with her as we ran to a Save-A-Lot parking lot and waited for her boyfriend. He drove us to the Haynes Gardens Apartments, where I was introduced to her friends, LaRonda and Shay.

For a while, it seemed like I might actually make it on my own. I ended up staying with a girl named Peaches and running with her, Bonnie, and their group of friends. I was with them when I smoked weed for the first time on Halloween night. I inhaled the smoke and instantly I was relaxed, as if nothing mattered. I wanted to feel that way all the time, and getting high became a way of life.

I was on my own, no rules, no one telling me to wear a T-shirt under my tank top or that the cigarettes in my purse would give me lung cancer. I could stay out as late as I wanted, smoke whatever I wanted, say whatever I wanted. I was free. I may have been only thirteen years old, but in my mind, I was grown.

I pushed Mommy out of my mind. Going back to Mommy's house meant living under her rules again.

Besides, I couldn't go home even if I'd wanted to. She would have called the cops as soon as I walked through the door.

I tried to make Peaches, Bonnie, LaRonda, and Shay my new family instead. We made sure everyone had food in her belly, a pillow under her head, and a blunt in her hand. I thought that was all I needed. That is, until Christmas came. These girls who I thought were family went home to their moms and dads, brothers and sisters. They bragged about the hoop earrings and jeans their parents were getting them, the cash their grandmas always stuffed in envelopes for them. I felt a pang of jealousy as I watched them head out the door for the holidays. For the first time since I'd run away, I was lonely. Rules or no rules, I wanted my family. I didn't want to spend Christmas alone, no gifts under the tree, no parents to wish me Merry Christmas.

So I took off walking through the streets, my hands jammed in my pockets, feeling sorry for myself. The cold cut through my thin jacket, with no sun to offer warmth. Out of nowhere, the silence was shattered by gunfire.

I hit the deck, my heart pounding so loudly I thought for sure the gunman could hear it. I lay on the ground, jerking my head from side to side, trying to see where the shot came from. The eerie silence was terrifying. *Who is shooting at me?* I thought, convinced I was the target. Some Christmas. First I'm alone, then I'm getting shot at. I wanted to go home more than anything.

Finally, I called my brother. I needed to be with family. My friends planned to drive to a club in Murfreesboro and agreed to drop me off at my brother's house first. I had just fixed myself a big plate of food when sure enough, there were the police.

I whipped my head toward my brother and tried to kick him. "You turned me in?" I asked, astonished. "I could see Missy, but you?" My brother had always been the black sheep of the family and had his own share of trouble with the law. I thought if anyone would understand, it would be him.

"Mommy was worried, Toia," he said quietly. "We just want to know you're safe, and you're not safe on the streets."

I WAS BACK AT OMNICENTER SADDER, BUT CERTAINLY NOT WISER. All I could think about was getting out again. I made one last attempt, pulling the fire alarm and taking off running when they led us outside. But this time, I made a fatal error. I heard footsteps behind me and turned around to see who was following me. Big mistake. Turning around slowed me down enough to be caught.

This escape attempt was one too many. This time, it earned me a ticket to a level four facility called Woodland Hills—essentially a juvenile prison. There was no running away now. My only way out was to complete my treatment program, and with more than twenty assault citations in eighteen months, it wasn't looking good. I was staring down the barrel of staying in Woodland Hills until my nineteenth birthday.

But my fate unexpectedly changed when a former convicted dope dealer visited Woodland Hills. He'd graduated from barber school and gone on to make a name for himself. He and his stylists planned to treat us to makeovers, and the local paper wanted to take pictures. Our parents were required to give permission before our pictures could appear in print. Mommy said absolutely not. Under no circumstances did she want to draw attention to the fact that I was locked up.

When the article ran in the paper, there was my face, right in the middle of the spread. Mommy was furious. She got on the phone right away and threatened to sue Woodland Hills for ignoring her wishes. Like I said, Mommy didn't play.

The next thing I knew, my counselor handed me a stack of papers to sign. She told me I had completed my treatment program and would be released to my parents. I stared at her. She and I both knew I hadn't completed any program. Just a few weeks earlier, I'd thrown a plastic chair at this woman's head. Now all of a sudden, I was ready to get out. These fools didn't want to get sued.

But I didn't care how it happened. All that mattered was that after more than two years in custody, I would be free. I longed for the day when I would be on my own again, without guards breathing down my neck and telling me what to do or where to be. It didn't occur to me that home might be a new kind of prison to me—and that it was only a matter of time until I attempted another escape.

4

TRYING FOR NORMAL

I was finally going home. I took off my Woodland Hills uniform for the last time and sighed with relief as I slipped on my own clothes. No more guards. No more fights. I was free.

Mommy hugged me tight before she opened the passenger door for me. We took off, leaving the fenced facility behind me forever and taking the scenic route home. I leaned back in my seat and closed my eyes, the summer sun shining through the windshield.

Before I could fall asleep, I heard Mommy clear her throat. "Toia, there's something I gotta tell you," she said.

"What?" I asked, opening my eyes.

Mommy paused before she continued. "Poppy's gone."

I thought back to the last several months. I hadn't seen Poppy since I first got locked up. Every time I called Mommy and I asked to talk to Poppy, she always said he was at the store or driving his truck or anyplace but at home. A pit formed in my stomach as the puzzle slowly came together. "Gone where?"

"We got a divorce, Toia." Mommy's voice shook even as she kept her gaze steady on the road. "It just wasn't working anymore."

"Well . . . okay." To be honest, the news wasn't a complete surprise. It didn't take a genius to figure out Mommy and Poppy hadn't been happy for years. I remembered them laughing together with friends and holding hands when I was a kid, and Mommy planning elaborate birthday parties for him. Since Poppy started driving a truck, though, it was like a wall went up. They lived separate lives, and the few words they spoke to one another were laced with tension.

Our new reality sank in as I sat in the car with Mommy. "Why didn't you just tell me?" I asked.

Mommy sighed. "You were having such a hard time locked up at Woodland Hills. I didn't want to make it worse."

We sat in silence, staring at the road ahead of us as I tried to imagine the house without Poppy. I didn't think it would be that different, seeing as he was gone most of the time driving his truck anyway. I thought back to the weeks growing up when it was just the two of us while Poppy was gone, Mommy tending the peonies and bleeding hearts in her garden and watching her HGTV shows she'd taped. She may have been strict, but I always felt safe and loved when I was with her. *So it's just me and Mommy*, I thought. *Okay. I can get behind that.*

At first, I soaked up my new freedom like a sponge. Sure, it was a little boring—I didn't have the daily drama and fights to keep me busy. But I had no walls confining me, no guards watching my every move. I had my precious Dove soap back, and if I didn't like the shampoo and conditioner in our bathroom, all I had to do was ask Mommy to buy me something else.

I was supposed to be back in school, but I didn't bother to show up much. A girl who just served time in state custody isn't exactly welcomed back to public school with open arms. Teachers eyed me with suspicion as I slouched at my desk, my arms crossed. I felt like I was constantly under the microscope. Anytime they heard some whispering or passing notes, they whipped around and yelled at me, automatically assuming I was to blame. When I graced the school with my presence, I ended up suspended half the time anyway.

Any love I had for learning was long since gone. Juvy kids aren't provided the greatest education when they're locked up. No one bothered to teach me much. They just handed me a stack of assignments and told me to work my way through them. I hadn't sat in a classroom listening to lectures and taking notes in almost two years. I had no desire to go back now. I didn't see the point of trying. Everyone already figured I was doomed for failure. Sooner or later, they'd make sure they were right.

Eventually, I just stopped showing up. I walked out of the house each morning and waited until I was sure Mommy had left for her job as a special education teacher. Then I wandered back home. Sometimes I flipped on *The Young and the Restless* and relaxed on the couch. But most of the time, I smoked blunts with a girl down the street.

I hadn't been home from Woodland Hills long when I found a girl I'd known there lived close by. She was already eighteen and didn't have to go to school. She was also up for getting high. I spent my days smoking blunts with her, closing my eyes and letting the skunky smoke swirl around me. Being high made me feel good. These days, not much else had the same effect. School was a joke, Mommy tiptoed around me like I was a bomb that might explode at any moment, and endless days stretched before me with no drama, no fights, no entertainment. Getting high was all I had.

Once, I was so high I lost track of time and walked home just as Mommy turned her car onto our street. She took one look at me and knew I wasn't sober.

"Toia!" she hollered at me through her rolled-down window. "Get in the car. Now!"

I knew I was dead, but I was too high to keep a giggle from escaping my mouth. That didn't play with Mommy. She stormed out of the car, grabbed my arm, and threw me in the passenger seat like a rag doll, right in front of the whole neighborhood. Mommy didn't care who saw. Her chest heaved and I watched her draw in a deep breath, like she was trying to calm herself down.

The stench of weed filled the car, cutting through the usual Skin So Soft aroma normally attached to the vinyl seats. Mommy scrunched up her face.

"I know you're high," she said like she'd caught me in a big secret. "Why aren't you in school?"

I shrugged. "I don't know."

I should have known better. Nothing set Mommy off like those words. "Toia, you better check yourself," she shouted. "If you don't turn it around you're heading right back to Woodland Hills. You wanna get locked up again?"

"No," I said glumly.

"Then *why*?" I'd never seen Mommy so at a loss, so completely exasperated with me. "Why are you doing this?"

But the truth was, I didn't belong with the public school kids anymore. I'd spent the last two years plus living in another world, without parents, without school sports, without any of the things everyone around me seemed to care about. The adults who had decided I was too difficult to bother dealing with me stuck me in a virtual *Lord of the Flies* situation in state institutions. They call your sentence a "treatment program," like you're supposed to come out of those places a better person. But I learned way more from the other girls around me than I did from any counselor or psychiatrist they threw at me. Fighting isn't a choice there—it's a way of life. You don't just walk away from that kind of life and fit right back into normal public school. Before I got locked up, I'd never so much as raised my fist at another kid. Now that was my gut reaction anytime somebody called me white or looked at me in a way I didn't like.

I was managing as best I could. Life with Mommy was great, aside from some strict rules. It was just her and me again, just like when I was little. Our conversations may have been about whatever was on HGTV or the latest episode of *The Simpsons*, but just knowing she was there comforted me somehow.

Then came the phone calls. Normally Mommy never sat still while she talked on the phone. She was always washing dishes, folding laundry, or multitasking in some way. It wasn't unusual for her to put down the phone in the middle of the conversation, walk away, then come back and say, "Mm-hmm, I know that's right," as if she'd heard the whole thing. But now Mommy sat there not moving an inch. Her entire focus was on whoever was on the other end. I knew something was up.

"Who you talking to?" I asked suspiciously when she finally hung up one day.

Mommy looked startled. "Oh, just a friend," she said.

Eventually, she admitted the "friend" was a man named Frank. My parents knew him from way back when Poppy was in the military and they lived in New York. Chico and Missy even called him "Uncle Frank." Somehow they reconnected after the divorce. But it didn't take a rocket scientist to figure out he was not just a friend.

Before I knew it, this man was visiting my house, sleeping under our roof, even trying to tell me what to do. After what I'd been through, I already had no respect for authority. Now this dude was trying to act like some kind of stepdad, buying me gifts and setting rules I had no intention of following. The way I saw it, Frank was up in my territory and I was not having it. This was supposed to be me and Mommy, not me, Mommy, and Frank. *Oh no*, I thought. *Who the heck is this man? He is not gonna control me.*

I tried ignoring his pathetic attempts to make conversation. My crossed arms and eye rolls apparently didn't tip him off that I wasn't interested. I tried outright defying him. This so-called Uncle Frank could try telling me not to slam the door or leave dirty dishes on the counter all he wanted. I had no problem telling him that the last time I checked, he was not my daddy and he couldn't tell me what to do.

With one more authority figure in the picture, I found my thoughts drifting back to the streets of Nashville, in those weeks when I was on the run, living with friends, with no rules or responsibilities. Nobody in Clarksville wanted to live like that. Those weeks in Nashville made me feel like an adult—or at least, my idea of one. Every day I'd wake up and decide how I'd spend the hours ahead of me. No one told me to go to school or go to church. When I smoked weed all day, no one lectured me about how I was destroying my life. I thought I longed for Nashville because I wanted to be grown. But more than that, I missed our little family. With those girls, I felt like I finally belonged. They never called me white or gave me the side-eye for being locked up. *I gotta get back there*, I thought as I lay in bed at night. I just didn't know how.

Then I started talking to my old friend Bonnie from OmniCenter—the girl I helped escape—and her friends Trina, LaRonda, and Peaches, who I'd met while I was on the run. I couldn't pick up the phone without complaining about Mommy's rules or Frank's sad attempts to make me like him. These girls weren't teenagers like me. They were in their twenties, with their own places. More than once, they told me I was welcome to come stay with them.

That seed took root in my head pretty quickly. *What if I did it?* I thought. *What if I took off?* I could stay with Trina, pick up right where I left off. I'd be on my own, living like I was grown. I'd be accepted without having to jump through anyone else's hoops. As much as Mommy's rules and Frank's presence drove me crazy, that wasn't the real reason I wanted to run. It wasn't what I was running from. It was what I was running to.

So one day, when Trina made the offer, I jumped on it.

"Well how about today?" I asked.

Mommy was busy in the kitchen when I packed up a few outfits and toiletries in a garbage bag. I listened for her, making sure I heard the clinking of silverware and bang of pots and pans. My heart pounded, as if I were about to attempt an escape from Alcatraz. *I can't let Mommy hear me*, I thought.

When I was sure Trina was waiting down the street, I threw open my window and jumped out—not as dramatic when you realize our house was only one story.

Out of breath from my one-hundred-yard dash, I found Trina. The end of my escape, however, wasn't quite as dramatic. We got in the car, we drove to the mall, and picked up takeout. And then we headed to my new life.

5

GOING FOR GROWN

Trina showed me around her apartment, which didn't take long. Her place only had one bedroom, but I was welcome to the couch. She cleared out a drawer or two for me—more than enough, considering I barely had three outfits in the trash bag I was using as a suitcase. The couch was set up with blankets and a pillow.

Trina was a college student—well, technically she dropped out to be with some guy named Eric, but when that didn't work out, she pretended she was still in school. Looking back, I'm not sure how she paid her rent.

We spent our days driving around, with me mostly listening to Trina talk about what she called "the field." This girl's lifelong dream was to be a dope dealer's wife, and she had lots of elaborate theories and systems to make it happen.

Every man we encountered was categorized as either a major player or minor player, referring to how much money he made or how much drugs he sold. The major players were her target. She spent hours lecturing me about how to present myself, how to behave, and how to make myself appealing to attract a major player and entice him into making me his main chick. Men are never monogamous, she told me. As long as you're not their side chick, you're golden.

But the point wasn't a relationship. The point was what those men could do for you. No man should get to have sex with you without giving you what he owes you, she told me.

"You have God's gift to man, and you're just sitting on it," she said time and time again. "You can play with it, you can give it away for free, or you can get paid for it."

The trick was to get what you want before the time came to get into bed. Then, you can evaluate whether you're willing to have sex with them or if you'd rather split. Trina told me that the hook is the conversation, and the picture you paint for them. But at some point, every man decides he's spent enough money and it's time for you to start putting out. She said older men—and I'm talking forties—reach that point sooner. They don't play games. With younger men, you can stretch it out.

Trina walked the walk. Everything from the clothes on her slim frame to the weed she smoked was paid for by some man. I was cool with picking up men with her. I'd never had a problem getting men to talk to me. It almost felt like a game, figuring out how to say just the right thing and look just the right way until they were putty in your hand. She helped me sneak into clubs, and we'd give men our phone numbers, most of the time without knowing their names. Her game made me feel powerful, like I was in control.

But when it came time to ask for money, I balked. Mommy raised me to never ask anyone for a dime.

I may have strayed far from what Mommy expected of me, but this was one rule I couldn't bring myself to break. If somebody wanted to give me money, fine, but in my mind, there are some things you just don't do. I had already let Mommy down in pretty much every way. I didn't want to disappoint her in this way too.

The other girls thought I was crazy. "You can have sex with these guys and not get anything out of it?" they asked me like I had two heads. All of them felt the same as Trina. Peaches even had a rule that you couldn't have sex in her house unless you could pay a bill. There's no reason you should be broke if you're getting laid, she always said.

I found a loophole in their method by making up stories about why I needed money without actually asking men for it. I told them my rent was due, and if I couldn't pay it I'd be out on the street. Or, I was a college student from Indiana, and I would need to drop out if I didn't find money for tuition and books. Not once did I tell them I was fifteen. My entire persona was a lie designed to open their wallets.

Even without directly asking men for money, Trina's game still didn't feel right. I justified it by telling myself this was what it took to be on my own. It's not like a high school runaway can go get a job waiting tables. I had to have money to survive. Trina was telling me this was how I could get it. Otherwise, I'd be on the bus to Clarksville, admitting to Mommy that I couldn't hack it after all, that I was still just a kid who couldn't handle herself. I would call her from time to time from blocked numbers to let her know I was okay. She begged me to come back, but I couldn't. I'd already broken her heart by running away. I didn't want it to be for nothing.

But even I had to admit there were some major trade-offs. For starters, I didn't eat unless I was with a guy. We barely kept food in our house, not because we were watching our figures but because we'd rather spend every cent on weed. All I did was smoke. No book I'd ever read, no sport I'd ever tried compared to how good I felt when I was high. As soon as the high evaporated, I was already plotting how I'd get my next one. I was petite to begin with, but after a few months of living with Trina, my bones were visible under my skin, and my clothes hung on my body like I'd borrowed an outfit from my big sister's closet.

Our desperation for weed reached a low point one night when Trina stopped her car in front of an adult bookstore. This place had an upper level decked out with booths, where you could watch adult films right there. Not the classiest place, and yet Trina wanted to go in.

"I'm going to find a guy and make out with him," she said. "While I'm keeping him busy, you snag his wallet out of his pocket."

I nodded. I didn't have any men lined up at the moment I could ask for money. Obviously I didn't have a job. And I was hungry.

A bell jingled as we opened the door. Trina immediately zeroed in on a fortysomething white guy with a beard, glasses, and a trucker hat perched on his head. I looked at her as if to say, "Have you lost your mind?"

"Just play along," she whispered.

She and the white guy mumbled back and forth for a moment before they turned to walk upstairs. Trina motioned for me to follow them, and they led me to the attic with the video booths. It was everything you'd imagine a porn shop attic to be—dark, musty, littered with trash, and thick with smells I didn't want to attempt to identify.

The guy turned on a video as he and Trina started to do their thing. I sat on a stool, waiting impatiently. I did not want to be in this nasty place any longer than I had to.

Trina pointed at the guy's backside when she was sure his eyes were shut tight. "Get the wallet," she mouthed as he nuzzled on her neck.

But there was a problem. This dude's body was positioned in such a way that I couldn't pull the wallet out of his pocket. I had moved a little closer, waiting for him to move into a better spot, when I accidentally bumped him. At that moment he had the nerve to think I was joining them and pawed at me with his giant hands.

Aw nah, I thought. *I did not sign up for this.*

I moved across the room and cleared my throat. "So are you going to pay her?"

The man just stared at me like I had two heads. "Pay?"

I laughed. "You didn't think it was free, did you?"

"I don't have anything," he said, clearly uncomfortable. "I gotta get home to my fiancée."

Something bubbled up inside me. Trina had dragged me to this disgusting porn shop, made me watch while she made out with some creep, and made me an accessory to her petty theft. I had not wanted to be there in the first place, and I sure was not walking away from this place empty-handed after all that. In my mind I was ten feet tall.

"I tell you what," I hissed, "you're not walking out of here until you pay her what you owe her."

The dude freaked out. He pulled out his wallet and handed Trina a stack of cash. We turned and walked out of there without saying a dang word. It wasn't until we sat in her car that we counted the money—thirteen freaking dollars.

"You've gotta be kidding me." I leaned against my seat and shook my head. "You got me to freaking rob this man and all we got out of it was thirteen dollars!"

Trina didn't say anything. She just counted the money again, her mind in a different place.

"The way I see it, we have two options," she finally said. "We can go buy a few groceries that will last us. Or, we can spend ten dollars on weed and use the other three dollars to get some chicken at Krystal's."

"Uh," I said, the only word I was able to get out at first. "Maybe we should get some food? We got nothing."

"Nah." Trina shook her head. "We should get some weed."

I am over this. I am over this. My mind screamed the words over and over again. Sitting in that parking lot, I knew this was the lowest moment of my life—lower than Woodland Hills, lower than Crockett Academy, lower than alternative school. But what was I supposed to do? Trina was the only person standing between me and the street. I couldn't go back to Mommy. Not now. I'd dug myself into a hole I could never get out of. *Mommy wouldn't want me home if she knew what I was like now*, I thought. So I kept my mouth shut.

But it only got worse. Trina kept up her lectures as we drove around Nashville, but with a few new additions. She'd throw in sentences here and there about how I was adopted and my real momma didn't want me.

Sometimes I called Mommy just to hear her voice. I even told her I was thinking about coming home. But then I'd have a better day with Trina, or she'd apologize. *Oh, it's getting better*, I thought every time.

After dudes started wanting me instead of her, Trina had a sudden moral epiphany. "You know what, I really think you should be in school," she said with all the superiority she could muster. "I feel bad keeping you here when you're only fifteen years old. You need to go back home to your family."

But I wasn't ready to live with Mommy, so instead I ended up reaching out to my friend LaRonda.

6

DAMAGED

I hadn't seen LaRonda in about a year when she agreed to pick me up at the Greyhound bus station, my final stop after leaving Trina's. I squealed as I saw her standing next to her boyfriend, Andre, with a baby perched on her hip.

"This is Junior," she said proudly, nuzzling the four-month-old boy's cheek. "Well, that's just his nickname, but everyone calls him that now.

I hugged both of them and let Junior hold my finger. "He's so cute!"

Andre drove us to a North Nashville housing project called Andrew Jackson, where LaRonda lived. Andrew Jackson—AJ, as some called it—was mostly a place for old people and junkies. People only came to AJ to sell their dope or get high. You might see junkies fight one another every now and then, but for the most part it was calm.

I was relieved to find out Andre didn't live with LaRonda. Technically, he was on work release from prison, but he didn't have a job you could put on paper. He told the cops he worked for his sister's cleaning franchise, but really he roamed the streets selling dope. Every day he stopped by LaRonda's to cook his dope and eat, but then he was out the door again.

I didn't have a job, but LaRonda and Andre had plenty of ideas for how I could make some money. When LaRonda had somewhere to be, she paid me to take care of Junior. Eventually, she was gone so much that I was practically her live-in babysitter, which was fine with me—most of the time. Junior was a good baby and I didn't mind playing with him. But when I told LaRonda I was going out, she sucked in her breath.

"But I really need you to watch Junior," she'd say.

Not my kid! I wanted to shoot back. *How am I tied down with a baby when I don't even have one?* But, she *was* letting me stay with her for free. Most of the time, I sighed and gave in.

Meanwhile, Andre hooked me up with another gig, selling dope for him. After he cooked the cocaine into crack, I took out a scale and carefully weighed and measured it into dime bags. He taught me how to add just enough dope to make the scale blink between 0.1 and 0.2, then add just a small crumb to push it over the edge. Getting rid of the product was easy—LaRonda's back door led to a stairwell that connected right to a smokehouse's back door, where junkies sat around getting high. Anyone who wanted dope just knocked on the door to get what they needed or met me in the stairwell. I never even had to leave the building.

Selling crack doesn't exactly sound like an ideal job. In a twisted way, though, I felt more secure than I had in months. I didn't have to wonder where my next meal was coming from. I didn't have to run down my phone list looking for some guy to give me money or buy me weed. I was making money on my own. I was in control.

But I didn't trust Andre. At that point, I didn't trust anyone. I had a feeling he'd find a way to avoid giving me what he owed me, so I took out a little insurance policy by skimming a little dope off the top. I made my bags just a tiny bit smaller than I was supposed to and set the rest aside. I sold my cut and kept the money for myself.

Andre proved my suspicions right. On my first payday, he convinced LaRonda they couldn't give me the full $1,000 he owed me all at once or I would blow it. After trusting me with his stash and sales as he would another adult, he chose this moment to handle me like a child. He handed LaRonda $500, but I only saw half of that. Normally I would have blown up at him. Nothing got under my skin like being treated like a kid when in my mind I was grown. But this time, I shrugged. *That's fine*, I thought. *I already made that and then some.*

I never cared much for Andre—not for any particular reason other than he just rubbed me the wrong way. Then, the comments came. At first, they were subtle. He'd come to me after LaRonda and I got into it over her forcing me to stay home and watch Junior.

"You know, I got a house," he'd say when she wasn't around. "I got extra room. I can set you up if you want."

Something in his voice told me that room wouldn't be free—and he didn't want money. I brushed him off. But the comment opened a door he refused to shut. Every time LaRonda and I had an argument, he brought up that dang house again. He stopped hinting at what he wanted, telling me I could be one of his main girlfriends at the house. At that moment, I hated him.

I didn't walk away from our arrangement, though. I needed the money too badly. Instead, I took out my frustration on him by skimming even more dope off the bags I sold. I got reckless, not caring if I hurt his reputation or if he noticed that I was clearly shorting him. Sometimes when I handed him a bag, he picked it up suspiciously.

"This is a dime?" he asked, squinting.

I looked him straight in the eyes. "Yep."

I kept on bagging up his stash and selling dimes to anyone who knocked on the door. Eventually, I let another dealer named Kid share the spot with me. Andre wouldn't have liked it, but I was past the point of worrying about him. When I was done, I always hid his stash and money in the same spot under the stove top. Andre went straight for it each day when he came in for work release.

But one morning, I was asleep on an air mattress on the living room floor when I heard him banging around the kitchen in a full-on rampage. He swore under his breath.

"You stupid trick," he yelled. "Where's my dope at? I know you stole it. You took my money, too, didn't you, you little trick."

I rubbed my eyes and yawned. "What are you talking about? It's the same place it always is."

"It ain't there." He banged his fist on the stove top and growled. "Where is it, Cyntoia?"

"You know what, it's right where I left it." Never mind the fact that I really was stealing from him. It wasn't in the way he thought. I wasn't dumb enough to take his whole stash and think he wouldn't notice.

Andre laid into me, cursing at me, calling me names, and even threatening me. I let him have it right back. This man was not going to accuse me of something I didn't do and get away with it.

Finally I stomped over to the stove and lifted up the top. "I told you, it's right where I left it," I said, holding up the bag.

Andre shuffled his feet and looked down. "Oh." He silently took the bag, without a hint of apology on his face.

That night when LaRonda came home, it all came out. The names he called me. His accusations of stealing. His little comments about making me one of his girlfriends.

LaRonda stared at me in disbelief. "Why didn't you say something?"

"Would you have believed it?" I shrugged. "I didn't want to mess up our whole situation."

"Did you take his stuff?"

Now I was mad. "No, for the last time, it was right where I put it." I pulled up the stove top once again to show her. "He just didn't look good enough."

That night, I left, wandering the streets aimlessly and hitchhiking to nowhere. Eventually I found my way back to my friend Marissa's house, in Clarksville. Marissa gave me clothes and let me take a shower. I turned on the water and took off my slide wedges, finding my feet covered in black dust everywhere except for one stripe where the strap had been.

I walked over to Missy's house once I had myself together. Then, when I was ready, I walked up the street to Mommy's house—home at last.

Mommy's face lit up in a grin the moment she saw me. She was like the father in the story of the prodigal son, running down the sidewalk and scooping me up in a hug before I could make it to her porch. The burdens she'd carried on her shoulders fell away in an instant.

As she led me inside, everything I had willingly given up for the past several months smacked me in the face. I opened the fridge and stared at the fresh strawberries and grapes gleaming in a bowl. My mouth watered. Anything fresh was a luxury I couldn't afford when I was on the run.

"Can I have some fruit?" I asked Mommy, feeling bad about everything I'd put her through.

She looked at me like I'd lost my mind. "You can have anything in that refrigerator," she said. "You don't have to ask."

This should have been the moment I knew that life on the run wasn't worth it. I knew Mommy loved me and cried out to God every night for my safety, while those people in Nashville had shown their true colors. Yes, I had messed up, but Mommy would help me get my life back on track if only I let her. It wasn't too late for me. I was only sixteen. I could still turn around.

I wish I could tell you that's just what I did. Yet it wasn't long before I was calling Mommy from a Greyhound bus station just as I was about to board a bus. I didn't have the guts to tell her to her face that I was leaving. To this day, I'm still haunted by the sound of Mommy's voice shattering into a million pieces as she begged me to stay. I could hear her heart breaking through the pay phone. If I could go back, I would run back to Mommy's house right then and there. I would stop believing I was too far gone to save and let Mommy take care of me.

I didn't know that would be the last time I'd go home. My friend Peaches let me stay with her when I made it back to Nashville. Without my steady income from selling Andre's stash, I was back to my old methods. I sneaked into clubs, drank until I could barely walk, and handed random men my phone number. It wasn't unusual for the phone to ring with a number I didn't recognize on the other end.

But one day, when I answered, I heard a familiar voice.

"Hey," I heard a man's deep voice say. I knew right away it was Andre.

"I'm going down to Florida to pick up some kilos," he said. "I'll pay you $5,000 if you come help me."

While his call was out of nowhere, I wasn't surprised by his request. In the hood, everyone says the cops won't do anything to you if you're a juvenile. Drug dealers sometimes bring juveniles with them so that if they get caught, the juvenile takes the fall and they escape doing hard time. I knew the risk. I also knew I needed the cash. *I'll take that risk for $5,000*, I thought.

"Well, okay," I said. "What's the plan?"

Andre said he'd pick me up and we'd take a bus down to Atlanta. Then we'd meet up with three other people and drive to Florida.

When the day came, Andre pulled his car in front of Peaches's and I hopped in the front seat. I didn't say much until I noticed we were heading in the opposite direction of the bus station.

"I forgot something in my hotel room," he said. "We just gotta stop there and then we on our way."

Andre slowed to stop at the Days Inn. It was too hot to wait in the car, so I followed Andre as he took out his key and unlocked his room. I stood in the doorway, waiting impatiently, until Andre motioned for me to come in.

"Hang on," he said. "Let me call and make sure everything's straight."

He mumbled on the hotel phone for a moment or two before hanging up. "Ah, man, the bus got delayed a couple hours," he said. "Looks like we got to kill a little time."

He pulled out a bottle of Hennessy and two cups. "You want a drink?"

That's the last solid memory I have of that day. All that's left are flashes in no particular order, flashes of Andre and a gun.

I woke up what seemed like fifteen minutes later, half-naked under the covers on the hotel room bed. The room was blurry around me and my eyes struggled to regain focus until I saw Andre sitting on the edge of the bed. My brain raced, trying to process what the heck was going on.

What just happened? I thought. *Why am I here and where are the rest of my clothes?*

After gathering my clothes from the floor, I stumbled to the bathroom and locked the door behind me. I looked down and saw blood smeared between my thighs. A strange empty feeling gnawed in my stomach as bile rose in my throat. I could feel my cheeks burn as I scrubbed my thighs with a wet washcloth, trying to erase whatever just happened.

"Why am I bleeding?" I yelled as I burst out of the bathroom. It was far from the only question I had, but it was the only one I could vocalize at that moment.

Andre glared at me, as if he was furious that I dared to ask. He stood up from the bed to walk away but I wasn't done. I peppered him with questions about what he'd done to me, rapid-fire style, my voice getting louder by the second. Angry wasn't the right word. I'm not sure if the right word exists.

"I'm fixing to call Peaches to come get me out of here," I said, my back to the hotel sink.

Andre had enough. In an instant he was in my face, his lips curled tensely over his teeth. "You see that bathtub right there?" he hissed. "I'll lean you over the edge of that tub and pour your blood down the drain if you don't shut your mouth."

All I could think in that moment was *I am not ending up on* Unsolved Mysteries. If someone threatens to kill me, I am not sticking around to find out if he's serious. Somehow I pushed him off me. I may be small, but I tell you what, my fight-or-flight instinct is strong. I darted for the door and sprinted across the parking lot, yelling and hollering the whole way. "Help!" I screamed. "He's trying to kill me!"

Andre was right behind me, chasing me under the carport and all the way to the hotel lobby. "Cyntoia!" he yelled in that whisper yell you hear moms use on their kids when they act up in public.

If anyone heard us, they sure didn't say anything. No one tried to help me. Finally I made it to the lobby and threw open the door. A young white lady was sitting at the front desk, looking like she was staring at a crazy person.

"He's trying to kill me!" I screamed. "I need to call the police!"

The lady silently handed me the phone. Andre was at the door all the while. "Cyntoia!" he kept yelling in that tone. "Come here!"

But instead of calling the police, I called Peaches.

"Where the heck have you been?" she shouted as soon as I said her name.

"What are you talking about?" I asked. "I just left your house earlier today."

"No, Cyntoia." She paused. "You've been gone for two days."

"Two days?" I sputtered. "What do you mean two days?" I felt like I was in a movie. Two days of my life had disappeared, and I could not account for them.

I stood in the lobby, the phone in my hand, trying to piece together the blurred flashes of memory from my time in the hotel room after Andre poured me a drink. That's when it hit me. Andre had spent the last forty-eight hours repeatedly raping me as I drifted in and out of consciousness.

7

POWERLESS

The bathtub was my first stop after I made it back to Peaches's. I could smell Andre all over me. Every breath I took made me sick to my stomach. I let the water wash over me, rubbing soap over my skin again and again. But Andre was still there. Still coming out of my pores, still invading my nose. I lay back in the tub and closed my eyes, wishing the scent away.

My body was sore, my mind numb. As if my brain wouldn't allow me to process what had just happened. Like it would be too painful for me to really take in. I couldn't think about the two days that were virtually erased from my memory, except for pixelated flashes here and there. I couldn't think about how Andre had used my body as if it didn't belong to me. I'd had no say as he had his way with me over and over again. I felt used up. Discarded. Worthless.

Instead of thinking about myself, I remembered my childhood friend who was snatched as she walked home from school. Some man raped her right there in the ditch. The whole community was traumatized. "How can this even happen?" everyone asked. I remember being furious when I heard what happened to her, and determined that I would never let something like that happen to me. And now here I was. I felt stupid for walking into that hotel room in the first place, for believing Andre really had a plan that would make me $5,000. *This was my fault*, I thought. I should have hung up on him when he called. I never should have said yes. I should have known this would happen.

It would have been such a relief to tell one of my friends what Andre had done to me, to have someone be angry right along with me, to have someone demand revenge on my behalf. And yet I knew that was impossible. It was my fault. Andre was my friend's man, and I went to a hotel with him. I couldn't let them know how stupid I'd been. I couldn't give them a reason to throw me out on the street. I needed them. Even if that meant I'd have to keep the most horrifying thing that had ever happened to me a secret. Even if that meant I'd have to look Andre in the eye again knowing what he did to me.

You expect people to cry or fall apart when something horrific happens to them. Yet in that moment, the only feeling coursing through my body was rage. I was livid that he had violated me, that he made me feel powerless and stupid, that he had taken away what little say I had left over my life. *Andre's gonna pay for this*, I thought. *I'll get him. Even if I have to do it myself. He ain't gonna rape me and get away with it like that.*

So when Peaches asked me what happened, I told her a random guy from the club was responsible. She shook her head. "I told you it wasn't safe to hook up with guys you don't know," she said in an I-told-you-so tone. I sighed. No matter what I said, I was somehow to blame.

The next day I was in the car with my friend Kid and some of his friends when he said he needed to stop for gas. He pulled up to a gas station across from Tennessee State University and walked up to pay the gas attendant. I watched from the back seat as he approached a man standing on the dark side of the gas station. They struck up a conversation like they knew each other, but I didn't recognize him.

"Go ask that guy for a cigarette," one of Kid's friends told me.

"Okay, whatever." I crossed the parking lot to find the guy and get what I was looking for. As I got closer, I saw he was wearing a red T-shirt with a small cell phone tied around his neck with a shoelace. His hair was braided in neat cornrows, and gold gleamed from his mouth as he spoke to Kid. *He was older than me, probably in his early twenties*, I thought.

Oh he's cute, I thought. I took a deep breath when I was finally in front of him.

"You got any cigarettes?" I asked coyly.

His lips slowly curled up into a grin as his eyes took me in. "I don't smoke," he said. "But I'll give you five dollars to go in there and buy some if you give me your phone number."

It was all I could do to keep from giggling like a schoolgirl. Something about this man just drew me to him. The energy between us was electric, even though we'd only spoken a handful of words. My heart pounded as I tried to play it cool.

"You gotta tell me your name first," I said.

"Kutthroat. They call me Kut."

"Okay now." I smiled, taking a pen and a slip of paper out of my purse. "I'm Cyntoia. This is my friend's phone number, but you can get me here."

His hand brushed mine as he took the paper from me. I felt him look me up and down as he reached into his wallet. "I guess a deal is a deal," he said. "Here's five dollars."

"Hold up now," I said. "Ain't you gonna give me your number too?"

I walked away with his number in my pocket, feeling like I was walking on a cloud. I can't tell you how earnestly I wish I'd never taken up smoking. I might have left that day without ever speaking to the man with a cell phone around his neck.

I didn't wait long to call Kut. Before I knew it, he pulled up to Peaches's in his red Pontiac Grand Prix with dark tinted windows, Lil

Wayne's music blaring from the speakers. I smiled. Lil Wayne's *Tha Carter* was on constant repeat on my stereo too. *Looks like we've got something in common*, I thought.

"So what do you wanna do?" he asked in that deep, soft voice that made my skin tingle.

I shrugged. "I like riding around. Listening to music."

We took off, no destination in mind. The car's air-conditioning felt cool on my skin, a welcome break from the thick humidity and scorching heat. I leaned back in my seat and glanced at Kut, his hand resting on the steering wheel.

"So what's your story?" I asked him. I always asked the questions every time I was with a man. That's how the game is played—you get them talking and pretend to be interested. You tell them just enough to keep them wanting more. I'd spent every date with a man quietly pulling on a blunt while they droned on and on about themselves.

But Kut was different. He shrugged awkwardly, like he wasn't comfortable talking about himself. "Ain't much to tell. What about you?" Kut turned his eyes from the road and grinned at me. I felt my heart beat faster as my eyes met his. This was the moment I normally would have told him my go-to lie about myself. I always told men I was a college student visiting from Indianapolis. But when I opened my mouth this time, the truth poured out instead.

"I'm from Clarksville." The words just bubbled up, like my story was there the whole time, waiting for someone to care enough to ask. "But I took off. My momma was tripping. Making me follow all these rules even though I'm grown. So I'm staying with Peaches for now."

Kut glanced at me and smiled. "That's cool." I thought he'd jump in, start talking about himself. Everyone does eventually. Not Kut. *Is this man actually listening to me?* I thought. *He really gonna let me talk the whole time?*

So I kept going. I told him about Mommy and Poppy, about how they adopted me, about my birth mother, Gina. I told him about getting locked up, and how I didn't feel like I belonged at home even after I got out. And Kut listened to every word. He never gave me the side-eye or made me feel judged. He just smiled and laughed at all the right moments. Kut had this vibe where I just wanted to tell him my whole life's story, and it was addictive. I felt heard. I felt seen. And I wanted more.

I had no idea how trapped I felt in my lies until I experienced the freedom of being myself with Kut. I felt completely exhilarated as the walls I'd kept up around me for so long just crumbled down. I didn't have to pretend to be anybody else. I was no one but myself. Kut didn't say much in that sexy deep voice of his, but I knew right there in that car that he accepted me just as I was.

All my life, I'd heard that when you find The One, everything will feel natural. You won't have to try. The conversation will flow, you'll feel understood. *Maybe this is it*, I thought, feeling butterflies in my stomach. *Maybe Kut's the one*.

The only thing that threw me off was the bottle of Visine he kept in his car's ashtray. Every once in a while, he picked up the bottle and shot clear liquid up his nose. I stared at him the first time I saw him do it.

"Did you just put Visine up your nose?"

He grinned. "Yeah." I didn't find out until later that the liquid was actually laced with cocaine for what he called "instant drainage."

Kut dropped me off at Peaches's after making plans to meet the next day. And the next. By the third date, I was convinced we were an item. I usually didn't spend much time with guys I met. We rode around smoking and I called them again when I had nothing better to do. Kut was different. I wanted to spend more and more time with him, and at the end of the night, I didn't want to say goodbye. That third night, I didn't. For the first time in years, I didn't feel alone. I had someone who got me. A part of my spirit started to relax. We got a room at the Knight's Inn, where he convinced me to try my first bump of powder.

"It ain't even enough to do anything," he said, holding a card with a small corner of cocaine under my nostril.

It turned out to be just enough. In my eyes, our crappy hotel room might as well have been a palace. The dingy streets outside were like a meadow, the sounds of cars honking and roaring down the interstate like birds chirping. The world was a beautiful place on that perfect day. I hit the pillow with a smile on my face.

When I woke up the next morning, I had one question on my mind. "Where can I get more powder?" I asked Kut as we left our room.

AFTER THE EXPERIENCE I'D HAD WITH TRINA AND LARONDA, I DIDN'T like to spend much time at home, even though I wasn't living with them anymore. I kept a list of phone numbers from guys I met at the club, and when I felt like leaving, I'd call one of them up and ask him to take me out.

I called a guy from my list, and after we rode around snorting powder, he pretended to forget I wanted to go home and tricked me into sleeping at his house. I was so high I could barely argue. I fell asleep in his bed, only to wake up to find him on top of me. I felt like someone had hung a sign on me announcing my body was ripe for the taking. *How is this even possible?* I fumed. I was livid and demanded that this dude take me home. It turned out I was too angry to even sit in the same car with him. I made him stop the car and let me out right there on the highway.

Cars whizzed by me as I walked from the overpass to a Tiger Mart. The noise was a welcome distraction from my thoughts. I imagined calling Kut, telling him what this nameless man had done to me, and hearing his fury as he vowed to avenge me.

I found someone to let me use a phone and dialed Kut's number. He didn't answer. He usually didn't—he had a minute phone and almost always called me back from another number to avoid using his minutes. So I called the other number he normally used to call me back.

"What's up?" the voice on the other line said. It was Kut's friend T-Boy.

"Is Kut with you?" I asked.

"Nah, he inside the store."

I took a deep breath. I really needed to talk to Kut right now. "Can you tell him I need him to pick me up? I'm at the Tiger Mart."

"We'll be right there," T-Boy said.

I waited twenty minutes before T-Boy rolled up in his gray Caprice alone. "Kut had to take care of something," T-Boy explained. "He told me to pick you up." I was confused, but I was too relieved to have a ride back to Peaches's to ask many questions.

But on the ride to North 6th, I could tell T-Boy was messed up. Every other time I'd seen him, he was quiet and reserved. Now he was yelling and cussing at every cop we passed, and he swerved over the middle line more than once. I even had to talk him out of racing a police cruiser.

After a crazy sequence of events, we ended up in front of a house off Litton Avenue in East Nashville.

"You can sleep here," he said. "I'll take you back in the morning."

I stared at him, wondering if this had been his plan all along. *Was Kut ever with him?* I thought. *Did he even ask T-Boy to get me?*

"I'm not going in there," I said firmly. "I'll sleep out here in the car."

That apparently was not an option. The more I resisted, the more aggressive he became. We went back and forth, our voices growing louder by the second. Finally he changed his tactics.

"I got bunk beds. You can sleep on the top bunk. I swear I won't bother you."

I eventually gave in. I had no intention of staying with him, but I figured I could call Peaches to come pick me up.

Once we were inside, I headed straight for the phone. No dial tone. The line was disconnected. My stomach churned as for the first time I wondered if this whole thing was one big trap.

Through the dim lighting, I could make out a cramped room down the hall with bunk beds—the only thing T-Boy hadn't lied about so far. I made a beeline for the nightstand, where I noticed T-Boy's phone. But when I picked it up, the battery was missing. *I'm not getting out of here tonight*, I realized. I took a deep breath, pushing away that empty gnawing feeling in my stomach. If I was going to sleep here, I might as well make the best of it. I reached up to the top bunk, pulling clothes, shoes, and junk off to make room for me.

Suddenly I felt T-Boy's fingers curl hard around my arm. "You're sleeping down here tonight."

"What are you doing?" I demanded, as if I didn't know the answer. "Kut ain't gonna be happy when he finds out—"

"Kut?" T-Boy laughed. "He don't want you. He already got a family. That's where he's been this whole night."

My heart pounded as I yanked a blanket off the bed and pulled it over me on the floor. "You say whatever you want. I'm gonna sleep down here."

Now T-Boy was in my face. "You really want to test my gangsta? You gonna find out if I'm really about that life." In that instant I flashed back to the Days Inn, Andre leaning me against the sink, threatening to pour my blood down the drain. For a moment I thought I might be sick.

Maybe if I give in, it'll be quick, I thought. Maybe he won't hurt me. Just get it over with. Kut will get him back tomorrow.

He puffed out his chest, carrying on and yelling. For the first time I wondered just what else he might do to me if I didn't give in.

"Fine. Hurry up."

He did.

T-BOY HAD LONG SINCE FALLEN ASLEEP AS I LAY STARING AT THE ceiling. *First thing in the morning, I'm calling Kut*, I thought.

I couldn't think about the fact that I'd been violated not once, but twice in one night. One. *How does that even happen?* I wondered. My body felt numb, detached, like it didn't belong to me. I didn't want to cry. I wanted to get even. I lay there imaging all the things I hoped Kut would do to T-Boy as soon as he found out what he'd done.

I fell asleep that night sure I would be avenged the next day.

I DIALED KUT'S NUMBER AS SOON AS THE CLOCK STRUCK SIX THE next morning. He didn't answer but called me back from a number I'd never seen before. T-Boy bolted out of bed and grabbed the phone before I could, but I had already seared the numbers in my brain.

I finally got T-Boy to take me home, and I headed straight for the phone and called Kut at the number he'd used earlier. This time, he answered.

"Where did you get this number?" were the first words out of his mouth.

I did not know how to answer that question. Not without a long explanation. "You called me from it," I told him instead.

"I never called you from this number." His tone was angry, suspicious.

"Actually, you did," I tried to explain. "T-Boy—"

"I *knew* you were a slut."

I sat in shocked silence. "Wait, what?" I finally said. "No, you don't understand. I was trying to get home and T-Boy made me—"

"Oh, I understand. I understand you slept with my best friend."

"You think I wanted to?" Now I was angry. "I tried to get away but—"

"I knew it. I knew it all along."

I felt like I was in *The Twilight Zone*. Like the words I said weren't registering. I thought Kut knew me, that he understood me, that I was his girlfriend, even though he'd never called me that. He'd never spoken to me in anything but that low, quiet voice he always used. Now this man on the other end of the phone seemed like a different person. He was furious, snapping at me like I was trash. He didn't want to hear anything about what T-Boy had done. All the blame was laid squarely at my feet. Whatever had happened wasn't just the result of me making a bad decision in his eyes. That one night was who I was. I was a slut, he said. Always had been, always would be.

I wish I would have told him never to call me again and hung up. But I didn't. "Please, you gotta give me another chance," I begged. Kut was the one person who made me feel completely accepted for who I was. In those few nights we'd spent together, he made me feel like I mattered. I didn't think about the fact that he never told me anything about himself or his family, or that the only nice things he had said to me in the few days we knew each other were about what I did for him the night we had sex. All I wanted was to get that feeling again, that feeling of pure belonging. Of being heard. *I know we can get back there*, I thought. *I just have to make him understand what happened. I know he'll believe me eventually.*

As angry as Kut was, he still showed up a few hours later to take me out. I felt a glimmer of hope as I saw his red Grand Prix pull up out the window. *Okay, he's not done with me*, I thought. *Even if he thinks the worst, he doesn't care.* In that moment, that was good enough for me.

But something had shifted. I could tell as soon as I opened the car door. He still kissed me and kept up with the conversation like normal, but his attitude was detached.

Then, out of the blue, there it was.

"You know what, I always knew you were a slut," he said. "But it's cool. I ain't tripping. I like sluts."

I whipped my head around and frowned at him. Arguing with this man was pointless. That morning's conversation—or lack thereof—had made that clear.

"I mean, no I'm not, but whatever."

I thought that was it, but he was just getting started. With every lull in the conversation, he launched into his little observations again. "You know how I knew you were a slut?" he'd say. I tried to just shut it out. Sure, he might think that now, but he liked me. Eventually he'd listen. He had to see the truth sometime. I just knew it.

KUT GOT US A ROOM AT THE KNIGHT'S INN AGAIN—WE ENDED UP staying there a few nights. I didn't even know where he lived and I didn't ask. On a night I was at her place, Peaches asked me why he wouldn't take me home. I told her I didn't know, but Kut sure looked out the window a lot. She mentioned Bonnie's boyfriend did the same thing, and that he was nervous somebody was after him. *Maybe that's what Kut's afraid of*, I thought. I knew he was a member of the Bloods. Maybe a rival gang member was after him too.

The night was like any other—smoking blunts, having sex, over and over. I felt relieved. *He still wants me*, I thought. *This is just a fight. All couples have fights. We'll get past it.*

When we ran out of blunts, I walked across the street to the Tiger Mart for Swisher Sweets Cigarillos to roll more.

On my way back, I got that feeling like someone was watching me. I looked up and there was an older dude staring at me like he didn't care if I noticed. Wherever I went—crossing the street, in the hotel lobby, in the elevator—he followed me. He didn't say a word, just watched me with his hand in his pocket.

What the heck is up with this guy? I thought.

"There's this weird man following me," I told Kut when I made it back to the room. "He keeps staring at me like a freak and gawking at me. He even got in the elevator with me."

Kut smirked. "You know what he wants."

I was genuinely confused. "No, I don't."

"Yeah you do. Bring him up here."

"What the heck are you talking about? He's just a creepy man."

"Cyntoia." Kut spoke in this voice like he was patiently explaining something to a small child. "He wants to pick you up for sex."

My jaw dropped. "Why the heck would that man look at me and think I'm some kind of prostitute?"

"I told you. He could tell you was a slut," Kut said, pointing to my jean skirt, off-the-shoulder shirt, and wedge heels. "What you think is gonna happen walkin' around the hotel like that?"

He had a point. "Well, maybe, but it's still not like that," I said reluctantly.

"But he thinks you're a hooker. So pretend that you are. Bring him up here." Kut reached in his pocket and pulled out his gun. "And then I'll rob him."

"Wait, hold up," I protested. "I don't want him to get hurt."

"Well do you like sleeping in this hotel? Because we're out of money, and we gotta be out of here tomorrow."

"Fine." I picked up my purse and slid my wedge heels back on. "I'm just gonna take his money then. I won't bring him up here and be responsible for nobody getting hurt."

The guy was still outside in the parking lot when I walked through the hotel doors. I barely recognized myself as I strutted straight up to him with a boldness I never knew I had. "What do you want?" I asked him.

He looked me up and down, smiling, like he was appraising livestock. I felt my cheeks flush. "I pay you well," he said in a thick accent.

We climbed in his SUV and he put his arm around me. I cringed as I felt his fingers tighten on my arm. I told him I'd need fifty dollars up front. To my surprise, he took out his wallet and handed it to me without bargaining. *Dang, that was easy*, I thought.

I felt strangely proud as I handed Kut the money I took from that man. It was like I brought something to the table, like I truly had value now that I could bring money in. Kut smiled—the first time I had seen him smile that night. I wanted to see that smile again. Maybe money was the way to make that happen.

Picking up that guy wasn't so hard. It wasn't that different from what I'd done at the club so many times. Men had always been my ticket to all the weed, alcohol, food, and clothes I wanted. No one had ever asked me "how much" before this night, but deep down, I think I knew what they were getting in exchange.

Pretending to be a hooker seemed even easier. I didn't have to make conversation and pretend to be interested in what they were saying. I could get down to business and then take off with their money. It's not like I was dying to do it again. But I could if I had to. I didn't know I'd opened a door I couldn't close.

Paying for our hotel stay was a constant conversation. Kut had told me he sold guns, but I never actually saw him do it, and he certainly never seemed to have much cash on him.

He said he would buy some dope so he could start selling. He just needed a little money to get him started. That's where I came in. My job was to pick up men for sex, then take their money before we ever made it to the bedroom. Eventually, Kut would make enough money that I wouldn't have to go out. He didn't just want to be a small-time dealer. He wanted to be a major player, with an SUV with rims and the whole bit. Going out every night was never my endgame.

Only a day had passed since my first stint as a fake hooker when Kut told me he wanted to call someone over to rob him. "I'll take care of everything," he told me. "All you have to do is stall him for a few minutes."

I could do that. It wasn't my favorite thing to do, but it was easy money.

That night, a guy in a do-rag showed up with half a gram of cocaine on him. We both snorted it, but he was clearly already high, or just plain weird. He paced all over the room, occasionally taking off his do-rag and rinsing it in the hotel sink before putting it back on his head. *Where the heck is Kut?* I wondered, ready to get this creep out of my room.

"Are we gonna get to it or what?" the man finally asked.

"Uh, yeah," I said, looking at the clock. "I just need the money first."

"Okay, how much?"

"Um . . ." I threw out a crazy number to buy me more time. "I need $500."

"What?" The man was flabbergasted. "That ain't what I discussed with Kut."

"I don't care what you discussed with Kut," I shot back. "You ain't trying to get between Kut's legs." Hanging a price over his head made me feel powerful. It didn't occur to me that I was haggling with a man over the worth of my body.

My legs shook as I sat on the bed, the cheap polyester comforter scratching my skin. I looked toward the door, wishing Kut would appear. *What is this man gonna do to me if Kut doesn't show up?*

"You're tripping," the man said, storming out the door. "I'm going to get Kut." That was fine with me. I continued to snort his powder while he was gone.

When the door opened again, it was Kut. "Where the heck have you been?" I shouted. "What is taking you so long? This man is crazy, you can't leave me alone with him."

Kut crossed the room and put his hand on my shoulder. "Look, take care of my boy," he said. "Just hook him up. It'll be over quick."

The words didn't register at first. I thought for sure I must have misunderstood. *He cannot be asking what I think he's asking*. "What are you talking about?" I could hear the pitch of my voice rising right along with the panic inside me. "You told me you were gonna rob him!"

"Man, I can't rob my boy!" Kut protested, like this whole plan wasn't his idea in the first place.

"That is what you told me." I could feel my pulse racing as I realized he was serious. I looked at the door, the do-rag man undoubtedly waiting outside. There was no way I was escaping without giving up my rights to my body. Not with Kut standing there intent on selling me. I was trapped, and I knew it. Suddenly the hotel room felt smaller, confining, claustrophobic. For a moment I couldn't breathe. "I am not having sex with this man."

"Come on, don't fuck this up," he begged me. "We need the money. You'll be done before you know it. Just do this for me. Please."

I could not believe this was happening. Before I could even respond, Kut was out of the room, ushering in do-rag man. The man looked triumphant as he plunked down $200 on the nightstand.

I looked at him and laughed. "That ain't enough."

He sighed and reached in his pocket, pulling out another half a gram of cocaine and looking at me for approval.

"No," I said. "I need more."

The man stomped out to get Kut again. Kut was furious. For a moment, I wondered if he might actually hit me. Instead, he leaned into my face.

"You're gonna do this," he said between clenched teeth, "or you're gonna be out on the street. Get it done."

I couldn't even respond. By now, a dead anger had crept back into me. I felt the same defeat I felt that night with T-Boy. Once again, I had no control over my own body.

When the man came back, I asserted the only power I had left. "I'm gonna need your chain," I said, pointing to his chunky necklace with a "South Eighth" charm. "I'll keep that until you can bring me $300 more."

"Fine," he said. "Now are we gonna do this?"

We did.

When the man left, he sent Kut back in the room to fetch his chain. I threw it at him. I wasn't allowed the luxury of even thinking about how I felt about what just happened. Once again we were out of cigarillos, and Kut sent me out to the Tiger Mart to buy some. I needed air anyway.

As I walked back to the hotel, a white Nissan Maxima slowed to stop next to me and a man rolled down his window. "How much?" I heard him ask.

Hatred in its purest form blazed through my veins in that moment. Who decided the word "whore" was emblazoned on my forehead? Since when was my body chained to the auction block? It was bad enough that Kut had me selling myself without every man on the street assuming I'm up for the highest bidder. *I'm gonna teach this man a lesson*, I thought. *I'm about to take everything this man has to offer and leave him looking like the fool he is.*

"One hundred," I told him. He had the audacity to counter with fifty. *That'll cost you your car*, I thought. He handed me the cash and I jumped in the car.

After instructing him to drive to a construction site and get out of the car to climb in the back seat, I locked the door with his keys still in the ignition. I wasn't interested in his car. I wanted to embarrass him like he'd embarrassed me.

I dumped the car at a Jiffy Lube after searching it for anything valuable. Inside a briefcase was an envelope filled with cash. I didn't have time to count, but it had to be at least $1,000. Enough to make Kut happy. Maybe happy enough not to force me into enticing men for a while.

Kut promptly took the envelope from me with a smile—he always smiled when I gave him money. He counted it quickly and said he'd get us a room we could stay in for at least a week.

"Okay, but what about the rest of the money?" I asked him.

"What rest of the money? There's only $400 in there."

"No, there's not. I saw the envelope. I know there's more."

Kut's eyes narrowed. "You slut." In one swift motion he grabbed my hair and threw me to the ground, dragging me to the bathroom. I yelped as I felt searing pain shoot through my scalp. "Take a shower. You're disgusting."

I took a deep breath, forcing away the pain, and glared at him. "I'll take a shower when I want to take a shower." I pushed myself up, planting my feet, daring him to come at me.

Kut hovered over me. "Where do you get off thinking you can talk to me like that?" He laughed. "You're just a ho. You're nothing. No one will ever want you but me."

Before I knew what was happening, Kut's fist went flying into my face. It came again. And again.

I screeched as I flung my fists at him, trying to fight him off me. But it was useless. He was too big, too powerful. With each word, with each blow of his fists, I lost the will to fight back or argue. Slowly, my anger melted into a numb acceptance, like someone had crawled in my brain and flipped a switch to autopilot. My feelings meant nothing anymore. Only one thing mattered: survival.

8

SELF-DEFENSE

I'm not sure of the precise moment where I stopped feeling like I was pretending to be a prostitute, the moment where I accepted that as my reality. Even as I approached cars with rolled-down windows and negotiated prices, I told myself it was only temporary. But if I had to name a moment, it might be the day I saw an honest-to-goodness pimp in the hotel parking lot.

He looked nothing like the men you're warned to look out for. He didn't have a feather in his cap or a cane in his hand. He looked like any other middle-aged man you might run into at the grocery store.

I saw him standing outside his brown van when I was crossing the parking lot to the store. He walked toward me, but instead of propositioning me like everyone else, this man invited me to ride with him and his girls to a truck stop.

"No thanks," I said. "I'm good."

"Hold up now," he said, stopping me as I tried to turn around. "Do you know how to be a ho?"

"Of course I do!" I said proudly. I was just sixteen, with no idea what I was getting myself into and how close I was in that moment to being kidnapped. I went on my way to the store, where another guy picked me up.

Kut had used the money I'd brought him to buy us a week at the InTown Suites hotel. When we unlocked the door, I flopped on the bed and breathed in deeply. Moving into this room was a welcome break. It meant that at least for seven days, the pressure was off to earn money. I didn't have to go out or wait for Kut to bring some perverted man into my bed. This was a chance for us to spend time together, to rest, and just be normal together.

By now I felt sure that I was his girlfriend, even though he never called me that. He never even called me by my name. I was only his "bitch." To me, "bitch" meant I belonged to him. "Bitch" meant I had someone in my corner. Yes, I was angry about what he'd put me through over the past several days. But the way I saw it, every relationship has its rough patches. You just had to push through it. All we had to do was make it to Vegas. Kut would be a major player, he'd get his SUV with the spinning rims, and I wouldn't have to sell my body anymore.

No one had ever talked to me about what a healthy relationship looked like. Mommy and I had barely talked about boys at all. The only talk I can remember is during bathtime, when she used to tell me not to let anyone touch my special places. As I got older, she was so busy trying to figure out why I was beating everybody up that she couldn't fathom what was really going on behind the scenes. I was navigating the best I could, just hoping that eventually things would go back to the way they were. It didn't occur to me that a rough patch in a two-week-old relationship was a red flag.

With no work to do that week, Kut and I spent most of our time in the room. Our days were a haze of smoking blunts and having sex. But life in the InTown Suites wasn't the getaway I thought it would be.

Something inside Kut had snapped. Any illusions I'd had about us being partners were gone—he was in control and he made sure I knew it. As soon as we moved into our room, he instituted a no-clothes rule. I had to walk around completely naked as long as he was there, and maybe on a good day he'd let me wear panties. Sex was no longer optional. It was expected on an on-demand basis. I stopped arguing or putting up a fight. The sooner I gave in, the sooner I could roll over and fall asleep.

When he wasn't on top of me, he was pacing around the room frantically, a gun in his hand. Occasionally he raced to the window and cracked the curtain, like someone was after him. Before I could ask what he was doing, he was pacing in front of me again, launching into another lecture.

"You know what your problem is?" he said, turning to make sure I was paying attention. "You don't really understand you're a slut."

He talked at length about how much of a slut I was, and how no one would ever want me, which was fine, he said, because lucky for me, he happened to like sluts. Now I just needed to work on being a better one. One day, he even tossed me a piece of paper and a pen. "Here," he said. "Write this down. I want you to take notes on this." Inside, I was defiant. *I'm not a slut*, I thought. *I'm not the girl he says I am.* But there was no point in saying it. Arguing with him wouldn't get me anywhere. I just had to get through it. Get through this rough patch and come out on the other side.

I had to sit there and listen as he spelled out who I needed to be if I wanted to be a good slut. He told me how I should conduct myself, the age I should adopt and the name I should use if I was ever stopped by the police. Money was more important than anything else, he told me. No one cared about my feelings. It was my job to get out there and do whatever it took to get the job done.

You can only listen to so many of those speeches before you stop caring. At first I tried to shut him out. Eventually I told him he was right, that I had been tripping all this time.

But no matter how agreeable or obedient I was, Kut grew increasingly violent and erratic with each day that passed. The slightest word from me would send him into a rage that ended in him dragging me around by my hair. If I dared to get up, he shoved me back down on the floor. Sometimes I bucked back at him, but usually I rolled my eyes and tried to ignore him.

After a few days of this, he punctuated his lectures with screams. His .40-caliber gun became a permanent accessory in his hand, and more than once, he pointed it right at me as he yelled. I knew he kept a bullet in the chamber at all times. I learned to watch for the red dot on the side of the gun, telling me if the safety was on or if I was in real danger.

Yet as every chaotic day in that hotel went by, I didn't leave. I knew it was pointless.

I was Kut's bitch, and that's all I wanted to be. Yes, he might yell and scream and hit me, but he also wanted me around constantly. In my eyes, that had to mean we were a real couple. We spent every moment together, passing a blunt back and forth, rolling around in bed—sometimes I wanted it, sometimes I didn't, but it didn't make a difference to Kut. "You're so good, baby," he'd whisper. "I love how you ride me like that." That was the only validation I got from him, and I lapped it up like water.

Afterward, as we lay in a post-sex haze, Kut would tell me what I wanted to hear. "One day we'll get enough money to get out of here. We can go to Vegas. I'll get one of those SUVs with spinning rims. I'll be a major player and you can be my bitch."

There was no real plan, no steps for reaching our goal, not even a dollar amount we'd have to raise to get there. Still, I clung to every word in the hope that this was all temporary. *It's my fault we're still stuck here*, I thought. *I'm the one who needs to work harder.* If I could just hustle a little more, sell my body better, we'd be on our way to Vegas and Kut would be happy. He wouldn't need the gun.

Kut never told me where he was going when he left our hotel room, and I was afraid to ask. Whatever he was doing didn't matter. The minute he left, I felt relief wash over me. For a little while, it could just be about me. I wouldn't have to worry about messing up. I could just chill. I would slide on my favorite jean skirt, loving its comforting softness as it brushed against my legs.

I would sit on the bed, light up a blunt, and take a deep breath as the tension I permanently carried in my shoulders slowly slipped away. I was relieved for the break from another man forcing himself inside me. For a short while, my body was my own.

I was asleep, blissfully alone one night, when I was jolted awake by hot breath in my ear.

"What'd I tell you about these clothes?" I heard Kut whisper.

I sat straight up. My eyes adjusted to the darkness, as I made out the figure of him sitting next to me with his gun. I mumbled an apology and quickly stripped off my black top, my skirt, and my panties, feeling my power sliding off with every stitch of clothing.

Kut motioned with his gun across the room. I turned my head to see T-Boy sleeping on the polyester couch. Panic gripped my throat. I hadn't seen him since the night he'd forced himself inside of me, and now here he was, curled up like a baby, oblivious to the world. I had finally told Kut every detail of what happened that night, of how he hurt and humiliated me, but it didn't help. He still blamed me for the whole ordeal. T-Boy, apparently, was off the hook.

Kut saw me looking, and nodded his head toward T-Boy.

"Now go get in the bed with him." The gun was still pointed at me. I looked for the red dot, and my stomach dropped—the safety was off.

Kut's mouth curved into a hateful smile as I cried, begging him not to make me do it. Every tear that rolled down my cheek made him happier. I guess I had finally found the way to appease him, but it didn't make things better. It just hurt.

Satisfied with my reaction, he grabbed my ankles, pulling me to the edge of the bed and jumping on top of me. "Are you just gonna cry like that the whole time I'm fucking you?" he asked. I hid my face in the pillow. I didn't want him to see my tears. I felt so powerless, but I knew deep down that he loved me. He was just worried about money, I told myself. That's why he hurt me.

T-Boy, meanwhile, slept through the whole thing.

I just have to make us enough to get out of here and run off to Vegas, I told myself. *Then he won't do this anymore.*

Even in his darkest moments, I never thought that Kut would really kill me.

But all that changed the night Kut made me flirt with a pizza delivery guy over the phone to get a discount. The first time I did it, he couldn't have been happier when we ended up with two pizzas, wings, and two liters of pop for two dollars and some change. Then, we found out the guy lived with his roommate at the same hotel.

"He knows our room number," Kut said, pacing around the room. "He's seen you naked."

"Well it's not my fault you wouldn't let me put clothes on when you ordered pizza," I shot back. "No one made you bring him in our room." Kut had even boasted, "This is how we do it around here," as the guy gawked at my body.

Kut looked right at me when our room phone rang. I felt that sick empty feeling in my stomach when I heard the pizza delivery guy laughing on the other end, like it was some kind of game. "You gotta stop calling me," I told him. "I'm serious."

The guy could not take a hint. He called one night over and over again. Every time the phone rang, Kut pointed the gun at me.

"You touch that phone and I'll blow your hand off," he yelled.

I had no intention of picking up the phone. I just sat on the bed smoking a cigarette. But like I said, I still had some fight left in me. I let my elbow bump the phone, knocking it slightly off the receiver.

Kut was on his feet immediately. He stomped over to me and snatched the phone cord out of the wall. I sat on the edge of the bed, waiting for him to blow up. Instead, he returned to the couch. I could hear him having a little conversation with himself, shaking his head and growing angrier with every word he said.

"You think I'm a joke," he said. "You must really think I'm a joke."

"I don't see how it's my fault," I said. "I clearly told him to stop calling. I can't actually make him do anything."

Before I could say another word, Kut's hand was around my throat. I could feel his fingers constrict my air pipe. I gasped as he pushed me back into the mattress. My legs and arms flung wildly as panic rose up inside me, my mind focused on getting his hand off my neck. *Is this really happening right now?* I thought. *Are you really choking me right now?* I wondered if this was it, if this was how I was going to die.

The last thing I remember was him hovering over my face, smiling. "You don't think it's a game no more, do you?"

My mind blocked out what happened next. I woke up crying and hollering, lying on the floor in the fetal position with no idea how I got there. Kut gave me a sharp kick in the back.

"You slouchin'." He sneered at me with disgust. "Our week in this hotel is almost up and you don't even care. You ain't done nothing to earn your keep."

I looked up at him, motionless on the floor. I was too numb to apologize or attempt to make it right. I felt like I was hovering over our hotel room, watching from a distance.

Kut turned to walk away. "Get up," he said coldly. "It's time for you to go out. Time to bring me back some money."

I felt nothing as tears streamed down my cheeks that night. I was detached from my body, on autopilot. Kut watched, his arms folded, as I tucked his gun into my purse, the way I always did now when I picked up men. I threw on my jean skirt and black off-the-shoulder top and pulled my hair back into a ponytail. *All I have to do is pick up one man,* I thought. *Just bring back some money and Kut will leave me alone.* The only time Kut ever smiled anymore was when I slid a wad of cash into his hand. I wanted to see that smile again. To feel that he was happy with me, that I'd done something right. I wanted to feel like I was valuable to him, that I was bringing something to the table. A few minutes and it would be over. Just get it done. Bring back the money.

The night of August 6, 2004, I forced myself to put one foot in front of the other and make my way across the parking lot, walking nowhere in particular. A Sonic was next door. It seemed as good a place as any to walk. I tugged at my jean skirt, my wedge slides cutting into my feet. The hot night's humidity was relentless—I could practically feel my hair frizzing around my face no matter how many times I attempted to smooth it back. That was fine. I had long since stopped caring what I looked like. All that seemed to matter anymore was what I could do with what sat between my legs.

My neck ached where Kut's fingers had gripped it just a few minutes before. My whole body was sore. I couldn't see the bruises, but I could definitely feel their presence already. I wanted to be back in the hotel bed, watching BET videos, smoking a blunt, forgetting where I was. Instead, I was out here in the dark, cars whizzing past on Murfreesboro Road, one of them sure to stop at some point. I couldn't go back. Not without a little money.

Maybe he was right, I thought. *I ain't even thought about getting us money all week.* But then again, he didn't exactly do what he said he would with the money I brought him. He should have had enough to get out there and start selling drugs. *Why do I still have to do this?*

Maybe I wouldn't go back. Maybe the next person who picked me up could actually take me away from the misery that had become my life the past two weeks. Maybe I could actually go back to Clarksville, be with Mommy, and have a good life again.

I had barely reached the neighboring Sonic before someone stopped. My feet had just stepped onto the blacktop when I heard the squeak of brakes slowing to a stop ahead of me. I looked up to see a white F-150 idling loudly, a middle-aged man smiling at me as his window slowly rolled down. I knew the drill, but I didn't even bother to hide my tears. I was tired of pretending everything was fine.

"You need a ride?" he asked.

I closed my eyes and took a deep breath before I nodded. The fact that he didn't begin with "how much" seemed promising.

The truck unlocked with a click and I climbed into the cab. I could barely bring myself to look at him, but a quick glance revealed a thin brown beard covering the lower half of his face. A Sonic bag sat in his lap. He looked like a businessman, the kind of person who never worried where his next meal was coming from.

"You hungry?" he asked. I nodded. Tears were still pushing at the brim of my eyes.

We sat in silence as he pulled back into the Sonic, the man still glancing at me every now and then. "You okay?"

It was my opportunity. I didn't pussyfoot around. "No, I'm not." I let the tears spill over onto my face. I turned to him and explained my situation in no uncertain terms.

"I've been holed up in a hotel room with a man who rapes and beats me on a regular basis. He just put me out and I don't know where to go from here."

The man didn't speak but stared at me, his eyes wide open. I was hopeful as I watched him take in what I had said.

"Where are you from?" he asked. I didn't know how relevant that was, but I figured it was good I had him talking.

"Clarksville. I'm just up here for the summer while I'm out of school." He paused again. This was my Hail Mary. Everything was laid on the field, the ball hurtling through the air. I waited breathlessly for his response.

"Well," he started. The light streaming from the drive-thru bay cast an eerie glow on his pale face. A leer that I recognized all too well crept into the apples of his cheeks as his eyelids lowered at me. "Are you up for any action?"

Suddenly I was twelve years old all over again, sitting in a cabin at Kentucky Lake, a plate of steak in my lap, confused at the lack of indignation over a grown man lusting over a young girl. He's just like the rest of them, I realized, feeling sick under his gaze. All men are exactly the same. They use you, then they throw you away. There's no way out.

I looked back at the hotel where Kut was waiting for me to return with his money. It was so close he might even be able to see me from his window. I imagined his laughter at my stupidity, that I dared to think there was some way to escape.

I forced myself back to my mission. Play the part. Get it done. It'll be over quick. "Yeah, sure," I said, plastering a coy smile on my face.

Finally, the server made it to the truck to take our order. "You back already?" she asked him. She was perky, vibrant, playful, oblivious to the storm brewing in my mind. It took everything in me to muster a tiny smile as they bantered back and forth over the price of food.

"That'll be ninety-nine dollars," she announced with a laugh. When the man protested, she shot back, "Isn't she worth it?"

His lustful gaze was back on me. "We'll see."

After she came back with our order and he pulled out of the Sonic parking lot, I suggested a nearby hotel, but he shook his head. "Let's go to my house."

EVERYTHING THAT HAPPENED AT HIS HOUSE PLAYS IN MY MEMORY like a movie out of order. I remember a cabinet full of guns and fearing for my life. Then, a terrifying moment when my own gun fired. I had no idea what it meant at first. Three hours later, I just knew I had to run. Back to Kut. *He would know what to do*, I thought.

KUT JOLTED OFF THE BED AS I BURST THROUGH THE DOOR. I SLAMMED it shut, leaning against it as I tried to slow my breath.

"What happened?" he asked, more out of suspicion than concern for my obvious state of panic. "You don't look right."

I wasn't sure how to put what had just happened into words. I pictured the blood. The way he was slouched over on the bed. A cold realization washed over me. Whatever I said would sound fake, like I was lying. Finally I sputtered out, "I think I just killed somebody."

Kut shook his head. "You're playin'."

"I'm not playin'. I'm for real."

In a flash it all came back to me. The loud bang of the gun. My knees giving out, unable to support my body. The feeling that somebody must be chasing me as I forced my legs down the steps. The realization that I was alone. My memories were fuzzy, frozen, out of order. Like my brain wouldn't allow them to come together, like it was trying to protect me.

I'm not sure how long I stood staring into space before Kut scoffed. "Whatever," he said, walking to the window. I watched him take a hard look at the parking lot before he turned around. "Where'd that truck come from?"

"I just told you. It was that guy's truck." Kut didn't move as I told him what happened. I worried I might not get out of that house alive, I said. My fight-or-flight instinct has always been strong. This night was no exception.

"I don't know if he's dead," I said. "I wasn't taking any chances. I got the heck out of there."

I handed Kut the gun and watched as he opened the chamber. A bullet was missing, just like I told him. A look crossed his face I hadn't seen before—fear and maybe even a little respect? I couldn't be sure.

"And you brought his truck here?" Kut said, gesturing out the window to the white vehicle parked right outside. "You gotta dump that somewhere else. You might as well have called the cops and told them where to find you with that thing in the parking lot."

Kut instructed me to drive the truck to the nearest Walmart and wipe it down for prints. My mind was on autopilot as I climbed back into the truck with a pack of Lysol wipes, cleaning the steering wheel, door handles, anything I might have touched. The fact that I was trying to hide any evidence that I'd been there didn't register. I could only think about the man I was sure was fixing to kill me. Did he get hurt? Was he okay? Had an ambulance already found him? I couldn't process the idea that he might actually be dead, like my brain was trying to protect me. His cell phone was in the truck, along with an old phone book. Quickly, I flipped through the book, looking for the name I'd seen on his driver's license—I'd taken his wallet so I'd have something to bring back to Kut. I dialed his home number. *I just gotta know if he's okay*, I thought as I waited for someone to pick up. But nobody ever did.

Kut was watching the local news when I made it back to InTown Suites. That wasn't exactly on our regular viewing rotation, but I didn't have to ask why he was watching. He wanted to know the same thing I did—if this man was in fact dead, had anyone found him?

Soon enough, we got our answer. Every news station blared stories about the man found shot in his bed. Kut stared at me as the news anchor read the gory details. "Well, I guess you wasn't lying," he said.

I leaned back against the couch, my eyes locked on the screen. *It's real*, I thought. *I actually killed this guy*. My mind still struggled to believe it. The night had spiraled out of control so quickly. I felt distant, like I was watching a movie about someone else. This couldn't really be happening to me.

"You sure you wiped down the truck?" Kut asked.

I nodded. "Yeah, I did."

We passed a blunt back and forth as we stared at the TV. "Probably would be a good idea to move to another hotel," Kut said, glancing at the window.

"Why?" I crossed my arms and frowned. "I was defending myself. I didn't do anything wrong." The "kill or be killed" chant that thundered through my thoughts in the seconds before the fateful moment crept up from the recesses of my mind.

"Still. Tomorrow we gotta move."

"Fine," I sighed. "We'll move tomorrow."

I couldn't help but notice Kut was a little nicer to me that night. He kept his hands off me, his voice was quieter, and he didn't call me a slut for the first time since we moved into the InTown Suites. *He really does love me*, I thought as I laid my head on my pillow to go to sleep. *Maybe this rough patch is almost over*. Somehow, that horrible night earned me Kut's respect. I had proven my worth to him, proven he couldn't just push me around. My days as a ho were almost over. I just knew it.

I woke hours later to someone pounding on the door. I stared at it blankly. Despite what had happened, it did not occur to me that cops might actually be on the other side. I had wiped down the car. I had parked it at Walmart. No one knew I had been at his house. How would anyone find me? I pulled the covers over my naked body as Kut swung his feet over the side of the bed and stomped to the window.

"It's the police," he growled as he pulled back the blinds, his lips curled into a snarl. "I *knew* you was gonna get me fucked up."

I felt the blood rush to my ears as I raced to yank on my panties and black shirt. "No no no. I got this." *Kut can't get in trouble*, I thought. "I can fix it. It's fine. Everything's going to be fine."

"Don't let them know you're sixteen," Kut said, his hand on the doorknob. "You're nineteen. Your birthday is January 29, 1985."

I nodded impatiently. We'd been through all this before. "I got it, I got it."

Three cops dressed in black tactical gear pushed their way into the room as Kut opened the door. "Don't move!" their voices bellowed. "Put your hands up! Don't move!"

I froze, standing in nothing but my shirt and blue panties with the word "Aquarius" stamped on the butt, my hands in the air. My eyes locked on the three guns, all pointed right at me.

"Kut didn't do anything." I could hear my voice shaking. "I'll tell y'all everything. Just let him go. Kut didn't do anything."

The police stood stony-faced. No one responded to what I'd just said. If I was going to stand there with three cops staring at me, I at least wanted my clothes on. Slowly I knelt down to reach by the bed.

"I said don't move!" one of the cops shouted. I heard the unmistakable click of him pumping his shotgun at me. One wrong move and this man might actually shoot me. My heart raced as I realized how close I just came to dying right then.

"I was just trying to get my skirt," I explained. The cop wanted none of it.

"You can get it later," he barked, his gun steady. "I need both of you outside on the ground. Now."

IT WAS HOURS PAST MIDNIGHT WHEN THE COPS LED ME INTO THE police station and seated me at a long table. I wish I could tell you I was wracked with guilt over what I had done as I sat there, waiting for the police to grill me. Instead, my mind was focused on one thought—*I gotta make sure Kut doesn't get in trouble.* I wasn't worried about myself at all. It never occurred to me that I should be when I had just been defending myself.

I'd never encountered a situation where I couldn't find a way out somehow. I'm a hustler; I get through no matter what. I felt sure I was going to walk out of that police station that night. All I had to do was let them know what happened and they would let me go.

"We're going to ask you some questions in a minute," a cop, who told me his name was Robinson, said. "Whether or not you talk to us can mean the difference between nine years and ninety-nine years."

To me, that sounded like he was willing to make me a deal. I didn't think I had done anything wrong, but I also didn't like the sound of being in prison for ninety-nine years. There was no mention of calling my parents. I had told the cops I was nineteen, and they believed me without batting an eye. If I was nineteen, Kut couldn't be accused of rape. I was much more concerned with what would happen to him than what could happen to me.

"Okay, I'll talk to y'all," I said.

They told me they would take me to the interview room after they finished up some paperwork. I sat there staring at the door, wondering if I could make a run for it, when I noticed the other officer leaning over, like he was reaching for something. I followed his eyes to see what he was looking at, when it hit me. This creep was trying to look up my skirt. It didn't surprise me. His uniform might proclaim that he was dedicated to serving and protecting the public, but I knew better. No one helps you for free. There's always a cost. The previous night had solidified that for me.

If this man wants something, maybe I can use it, I thought. Robinson had left the room to get something. This was my moment.

"I'll let you see up my skirt if you let me out of here," I said.

The other officer jumped, caught red-handed. "I can't do that."

"Yes, you can. All you have to do is turn your head and I'll walk out."

Before he could speak, Robinson was back. "Are you ready?"

The other officer told Robinson what I had just said and he laughed it off. We sat down in the interview room and they slid me a soda before Robinson read from a sheet of paper. I realized they were my Miranda rights. But when he got to the part saying they hadn't promised me anything, I held up my hand.

"Wait a minute," I cut him off. "Yeah you did. You told me if I cooperate it will be the difference between nine years and ninety-nine—"

"I just meant we'll tell the DA you cooperated," Robinson interrupted. He kept stuttering and saying words that didn't make any sense to me.

Yeah, yeah, whatever, I thought. When they asked me to sign the paper saying I understood my rights, I crossed out that part. They knew what they'd said.

The cops launched into their questions about the night before.

They kept rephrasing questions, and I knew they were trying to catch me in a lie. But I told them the truth about what I'd done. The way I saw it, I had nothing to hide. All I'd done was try to protect myself. They even tried telling me they'd found my fingerprints on a night-stand drawer, and that a gun was missing. I knew right away that was a lie. I'd never even touched the nightstand. All my time was spent trying to find a way out of that house, not rifling through drawers.

The entire interview was clouded through the filter of making sure I didn't get Kut in trouble. I stuck to my story of being nineteen and meeting Kut in the parking lot. I even gave them my birth mother's last name—Mitchell. Everything I said was designed to steer attention away from him. All I wanted was to get out of there and back to him. In my mind, we were Bonnie and Clyde, and I had no doubt as soon as we had enough money, we would run off to Vegas, elope, and never have another care in the world.

"Were you a prostitute?" they asked.

"Oh, no, never," I responded flippantly. I wasn't fixing to call Kut out as my pimp. I had no idea that right at that moment, Kut was singing like a canary to cops in another room.

The night dragged on. At one point, I laid my head on the interview table and closed my eyes, seconds from sleep. Finally, the cops drove me to another location for night court and booking. Peaches and a few other friends were waiting on the sidewalk in front of the station when we arrived—when I called her earlier that night, Robinson had told her where we were heading.

"Oh my god, Cyntoia," she cried as the cops pulled me out of the car. Her eyes were puffy, her voice hoarse. "How did this happen?"

"It's fine," I said, trying to reassure her. "I just have to go inside for a minute. I'll be right back."

Peaches stared at me incredulously. "No, you won't," she said. "You ain't getting out."

A few minutes later, I sat on the other side of a glass wall, waiting to be processed into the jail, when Robinson came storming around the corner. His whole face had changed. This wasn't a man who wanted to work with me. This man was pissed.

"You're sixteen?" He spat out the words like they were venom. "You lied to me. You're a freaking teenager."

My stomach got that sick empty feeling again. Up until this point, I truly thought I would get out of this. The anger in Robinson's eyes now told me otherwise. Lying was clearly an unforgivable sin in his eyes.

"Now you're really going to do life," he hissed.

Wait, life? I panicked. You're not supposed to go to jail if you're a minor. Everyone says they can't do nothing to you if you're not an adult. Robinson's words cut through me like a knife. For the first time that night, I knew there was no way out.

9

TRAPPED IN A CAGE

I preferred to keep the lights off. It was the only thing I could control these days in my Juvenile Detention Center cell. I perched on the metal toilet, hugging my knees to my chest. It wasn't the most comfortable seat, but it was the one private spot I had left in my cinder-block cell.

The room was just big enough that I could lay on the floor if I wanted to. Everything was metal—metal bed, metal toilet-sink combo, metal door. The door had a window just larger than an eight-and-a-half-by-eleven sheet of paper, a pie slot underneath where trays of food were shoved three times a day.

My cell was one of eight set up in a semicircle around a guard's desk. The guard on duty watched television all day long, the noise of a local news station blaring through my door. Over and over again, there it was. "Teenaged prostitute Cyntoia Brown was arrested on first-degree murder charges," I heard condemning news anchors say. There was my mug shot again, my hair a mess, my dead eyes staring into the camera.

The desk guard outside my cell whipped his head around and peered through my window, just like everyone did when they heard my name. I crouched away from his view as the light from the television flashed through the opening, painting blue squares on the wall.

Sitting in my cell, I felt like I was stuck in a Chinese finger trap. It was more than the walls surrounding me, more than the heavy metal door. For weeks, I'd felt trapped by Kut's rules, by the men who claimed ownership over my body, by the feeling there was no way out. Now that feeling wasn't a metaphor. It was my reality.

There's something about being trapped that exaggerates the emotions and issues already inside you. The numb, autopilot state I'd been in for weeks melted away. Now I felt everything. Anger when guards shackled my hands and feet like I was some kind of dangerous weapon. Fear of what this murder charge would mean. Frustration at the guards who seemed to enjoy telling me when I could shower, eat, or call my mom. I felt like a wild animal trapped in a circus cage, and I would do anything to get out.

The court assigned me Kathy Sinback as my public defender. The first day we met, she handed me her card with her phone number. "You can call me anytime," she assured me.

Her first move was to file a motion to have me sent for a mental evaluation. The court had scheduled a hearing to determine whether I would be tried as a juvenile or an adult, so Kathy wanted to know if I had any psychological issues that could explain what had happened.

I knew it was coming, and that it was standard protocol. But no one told me about the plastic zip ties they'd strap me in for the transfer. These things are your worst enemy. They dig into your skin and leave you with absolutely no mobility. I grimaced in pain the entire ride to the hospital.

By this point, Crockett Academy, where I'd had my mental evaluation as a preteen, had closed, so I was taken to another mental hospital, where I'd done my intake before Crockett. Sitting in the lobby waiting to be processed, I could hear patients shouting nonsense words and moaning. I saw men and women rock back and forth in their seats, some even carrying on full conversations with the air in front of them. I shrank back in my chair, trying to distance myself from these people who seemed straight-up crazy. Sitting in the middle of a mental hospital, I was terrified.

I shouldn't be here. There ain't nothing wrong with me.

But I didn't exactly prove that to the staff. I had screamed like a lunatic as they dragged me into the facility. When the nurse told me I couldn't use the phone, I had to be forcibly removed and hauled back to my room. If I wasn't crazy before I got there, I certainly felt like I was heading in that direction now.

Each day, staff members told me what to eat, when to eat it, what to wear and where I could sit. I couldn't use the phone—they told me I hadn't been there long enough yet. I couldn't even use the restroom without someone standing there watching me. My throat constantly burned with acid reflux. Even when I was allowed to have meals, I could barely eat. Whatever I managed to get down my throat often came right back up anyway.

None of the staff were familiar to me until the shift changed. I couldn't believe my eyes when the woman assigned to watch me was none other than Miss Diane, the woman who had taught me to crochet years ago. I broke down crying when I saw her.

"You gotta help me get out of here," I pleaded with her. I lay in my bed, begging her to help me escape as she gently rubbed my head. The more she reassured me, the more I cried hysterically.

"I have to get back to Kut," I cried. "Please."

Miss Diane asked the medication nurse to give me an Ativan. I drifted off to sleep as Miss Diane stroked my hair. "It's going to be okay," she said over and over.

....

I HADN'T SEEN MOMMY SINCE I WAS ARRESTED. I HAD BARELY EVEN talked to her—they only allowed me one short phone call, where I had to break the news of what had happened. But when my first weekend at the mental hospital came, I was finally allowed to see her.

Mommy and Missy walked in as I was in the middle of chowing down on my second tray of Chinese fried rice. It was the first meal I had felt well enough to choke down, and I couldn't get enough.

My face broke into a grin as I saw them. For the last week, I was called "Brown," not Cyntoia, and treated like a dangerous criminal. I finally was with people who loved me and cared about me, and that felt good.

Mommy and Missy broke down crying as soon as they saw me. Immediately I felt self-conscious of my bony frame. All those months of choosing weed over food had caught up with me. My normally 125-pound body had shriveled down to just 98 pounds.

I could see heartbreak in Mommy's eyes as she gingerly touched the bones protruding from the top of my shirt. "Oh, Toia," she kept repeating.

"Quit crying!" I said. "I'm okay. Really I am." I needed Mommy to think I was okay, even though I most certainly was not. Her daughter had just been arrested for murder. She didn't need the added burden of my emotional breakdown.

We held one another as I saw my past clearly for the first time. *Why did I ever run away?* I wondered. My reasons at the time seemed so stupid now. I had a good life at home with Mommy. Sure, she was strict, but there was never anything I could have wanted or needed that she wouldn't give me if I only asked. I had it all and willingly threw it all away. All the while, Mommy had stayed up at night praying, wondering where I was and if I was safe. I thought of all the times she'd begged me on the phone to come home. *I did this to her*, I thought. *It's my fault she's crying right now.* A lump formed in the back of my throat as I realized the effect my actions had on the rest of my family. I wasn't the only one paying the price. My whole family was paying it right along with me.

I hung on to the joy I'd felt seeing Mommy. It was the only thing carrying me through. It didn't last long, though. A few days later, I was jolted awake by a staff member telling me I was being moved to a different facility. No one would tell me where I was going or why. When they refused to allow me to call Mommy and tell her I was moving, I screamed and kicked as the staff struggled to contain me. Finally they gave me more medication to calm me down.

Once again, thick, white plastic zip ties bound my wrists and ankles as they loaded me into a van for the three-hour drive. The counselor sitting next to me couldn't keep her eyes open. When I was sure she was asleep, I used my fingertips to rummage through her purse, searching for something that could cut through my zip ties. My fingers closed around a lighter. That was good enough for me.

"I need to pee," I told the driver. In the past, anytime I'd been transferred, the driver always stopped at a convenience store if any of us needed to use the restroom. This time, it was different. The driver told me to hold it for another hour until we got there.

I decided to hold on to the lighter just in case I had another opportunity to get away. When we made it to Timber Springs Adolescent Center in Bolivar, I was told I'd complete my evaluation here instead of in Nashville. My eyes took in our surroundings, plotting out where I could go if I managed to escape. I saw a shopping center across the street, and only a small fence I'd need to clear around the recreation area.

When I finally got to my room, I hid the lighter on top of a ceiling fixture over my bed.

I asked on a regular basis if I could go outside to the rec area. Finally someone told me we never went out there. The only hope of seeing the sky was if there was a fire drill. That was all I needed to know. I decided to play it cool until I saw an opportunity.

I didn't have a nurse watching me twenty-four hours a day, but they were always around somewhere. When I went to the dayroom that first night, the nurse told me we had assigned seating. That made no sense to me—I could plainly see five rows of chairs, and only one of them was taken. I walked past her and tried to sit down.

"You can't sit there," the nurse said, grabbing my arm to stop me. "You gotta sit over here."

I flopped down in the appropriate chair, fuming. I was in my own little world until I saw a girl walk to the nurses' station to call her mom—even though they'd already told me I couldn't. *Well that's not fair*, I thought.

I marched over to the nurse. "I want to talk to my mom too," I said. "She don't even know I'm here yet."

The nurse stared me down. "You haven't been here long enough," she said flatly. "You're out of place. Get on out of my office."

I could feel my blood pressure rising. "All I want to do is talk to my mom. Everybody else gets to. That don't make sense."

"I already told you no."

That was all she wrote. I lunged at the nurse as if I had no control over the matter. I could see my hands around her neck and could feel another nurse grabbing me from behind, trying to pry my hands off. It was like I had blacked out and someone else had taken the controls. I ended up stretched out on a bed, my hands and feet tied down in a four-point restraint for the rest of the night.

THE FACILITY PLACED ME ON ONE-TO-ONE WATCHES AFTER THAT, meaning someone was watching me every second of every day. I spent most of my days asleep, too doped up on Thorazine to stay awake. My butt cheek was so sore from the injections that I couldn't walk properly. They call it the Thorazine shuffle in the facility—your legs hurt too badly to do anything but shuffle along.

When I was finally cleared from one-to-one watches, I found myself alone in my room for the first time. This was my chance. I grabbed the lighter I'd hidden on the fixture and held its flame to the fire sprinkler. Immediately, alarms blared and sprinklers sprayed a black liquid all over the room. *All I have to do is get outside*, I thought. *Then I'll make a run for it.* I knew no one could catch me once I ran. I'd climb the fence and be on my way to freedom.

The nurse showed up at my door, and I waited for her to escort me outside with the rest of the girls. Instead, she held me by the arm. "You've got to stay in here," she said.

All the hope I'd harbored inside me sank into the ground. *I'm really trapped*, I thought. *There is no way I'm getting out of here.*

I went back to the Thorazine shuffle. Nurses shoved a needle in my butt cheek every time I was awake and moving. I didn't care anymore. I preferred sedation to reality.

Needless to say, I didn't leave the hospital with a good evaluation. I didn't even make it through the full thirty days. They kicked me out early. They said I was too much to handle. Let me tell you, being too much for even a mental hospital to handle is downright embarrassing.

BACK IN NASHVILLE, I MADE GOOD USE OF THAT CARD MY ATTORNEY Kathy had given me. When I wasn't visiting with her, I was on the phone with her, talking about everything from my case to any issue I had in the Juvenile Detention Center.

We met every other day to help her prepare my case for the transfer hearing. "I want you to take me through exactly what happened leading up to the murder," she had told me. "Take me through why you weren't living with your parents. Where were you staying?"

I told her about Trina, and how we'd made our living convincing men to give us money. To me, I was just explaining what happened. I didn't think I was saying anything out of the ordinary. But I watched as Kathy's eyebrows shot up to her forehead.

"What?" I asked her.

"That's not normal," she said. "That's not what a healthy relationship looks like."

"What are you talking about? That's just how it works. If you want to get something from these guys, eventually they're gonna want something in return."

She frowned. "Did they know you were fifteen and sixteen?"

"They didn't ask," I said. "I don't think they cared."

"Cyntoia," she said. "That's not okay."

Is she crazy, or am I? I wondered. *Is she just a white lady who doesn't understand?*

But Kathy wasn't just some out-of-touch white lady. Every time I called, she was there. Every issue that I needed her to fix, she fixed it. Any question I had, she answered it. And yet every time we talked, something I said completely blew her mind. Even things I accepted as normal, like being with older men, horrified her. I started to wonder if maybe Kathy wasn't wrong. Maybe it was me.

After years of keeping just about everything from Mommy, I started confiding in her. I told her about the long list of older men, the drugs, the philosophy of exchanging relationships with men for money. Mommy could barely speak. She just kept saying, "Oh, Toia."

"Where was I when this was going on?" she asked me. I reassured her that it wasn't her fault. She couldn't have known—I told strangers more than I told my mom at that time.

Mommy's reaction confirmed it for me. Something wasn't right. None of this was normal. But I still wasn't willing to give on one thing—Kut.

It didn't take many meetings with Kathy before she finally sat down her pen and looked me in the eye. "We need to talk about Kut." I stared at the floor, avoiding her stare. *Here it comes*, I thought. *Kut warned me about this.*

In my mind, Kut and I were still in love. The world was just trying to keep us apart. I called him as often as I could—he didn't answer the phone every time, but that was nothing new. Those conversations reassured me of his love—not that he ever actually said that. I hung on to the fact that he answered the phone as proof that I was still his bitch, and that he was still worth defending. I tried not to dwell on the fact that he never came to visit me. Once he showed up for a hearing. I only caught a glimpse of him in the parking lot, but it was enough to send me into a hysterical crying fit.

"They're trying to get me," he said when I asked why he hadn't come to see me. "I gotta be careful. I can't be coming up there or they might end up arresting me."

I wouldn't listen to a single negative word anybody had to say about him. Now I steeled myself for the attack on Kut I was sure Kathy was about to launch.

"Look, Kut is an important part of your case," Kathy told me. "What he did to you is relevant to the court. If you keep defending him, it's only going to mean more jail time."

"You're just gonna have to find something else to defend me, because I'm not gonna say one bad thing about him," I said coldly. "He's my boyfriend."

"Honey." Kathy put her hand on my shoulder, her face scrunched into a concerned frown. "He does not care about you. He doesn't care if you get in trouble. All he cares about is himself."

I shook my head firmly. "I'm not gonna do anything to get him in trouble. He would do the same thing for me."

Kathy sighed. "Cyntoia, Kut told the police everything."

The words didn't compute at first. I felt confused, like my head was spinning. Kut was the one who came up with our story. Why would he do that if he wasn't going to use it? I remembered how the police lied to me when they first took me to the station. *Kathy must be doing the same thing now*, I thought. *She's just trying to get me to talk.*

"You're a liar," I said. "Kut would never do that."

"He already did." Kathy dug into her briefcase, pulling out a copy of a signed document. "It's all right here."

The Metro Police Department logo was stamped on the official document I held in my hands. I could see his familiar signature at the bottom. "No." I threw it back at her. "Someone doctored this up. Kut would never do that."

"Let's call him right now and find out." I could tell by the look on her face that she was serious.

"Fine." I put him on speaker as I dialed from the office phone. Kathy stood next to me as I told him what she'd said.

"Man, you know they lying," he said. "They just trying to get you to turn against me."

"Yeah," I sighed. "I know."

Kathy was undeterred. One day, she sat me down and whipped out a sheet of paper. I watched as she divided the paper into four sections and wrote headings on each one—"Good things about Kut," "Bad things about Kut," "Things Kut does that make me feel good," "Things Kut does that make me feel bad." Even I couldn't deny that the bad columns had a whole lot more written in them than the good columns. I still had my defenses up. I still believed Kathy was just trying to get me to turn on Kut. But I was the one who wrote those things down. For the first time, I had to consider that maybe, just maybe, I was wrong about Kut. Maybe it wasn't as great as I told myself it was.

But I still wasn't ready to say anything against him until the day I sat down with Fakisha, one of the court social workers. Kathy had a tendency to sugarcoat my situation and beat around the bush. Fakisha told it like it was. This tall, beautiful woman wore her hair in a natural afro and pushed through work each day even though she suffered from Crohn's disease. She did not have time for nonsense.

"Look," she said, sitting down with me. "Here's the deal. You're facing life in prison."

"Wait, what?" Now she had my attention.

"You heard me. You're facing life in prison."

It was the first time anyone on my legal team had ever mentioned this as a possibility. "No, I thought I was facing eight years. Kathy told me if I got transferred to adult court, I'd get eight years for robbery and manslaughter. That's the worst-case scenario."

Fakisha looked at me sadly. "No, honey. You're facing life. This man Kut is not. I suggest you start talking and protect yourself instead of protecting him."

As soon as she left I went straight to the phone to dial Kathy's number. I could feel acid churning in my stomach like it had right after I was arrested. It couldn't be true. I had never heard of a juvenile getting a life sentence. That doesn't sound right. How could that even be legal?

I waited anxiously as I heard the phone ring on the other end. "Um, Fakisha just told me I was facing life in prison," I said without even saying hello.

Several seconds passed before Kathy spoke. "Well, yeah," she said, dragging out each word. "But we're not going to think about that. Not unless we have to."

"Why wouldn't you tell me that?" I exploded. "I kind of need to know if they're fixing to lock me up for the rest of my life."

"It's not gonna happen," she reassured me. "You have a strong case. We'll stay in juvenile court. Don't worry."

But I couldn't help it. Reality hit me for the first time. This was real. I wasn't getting out of this. And there was a very real chance I'd never be free again. I felt sick as I imagined my life passing by, every year within the walls of a cinder-block cell. For a moment, I thought I would be sick.

My transfer hearing loomed in the distance. One hearing stood between me and adult court. One judge. One prosecuting attorney. I couldn't believe the rest of my life could come down to this. I wanted to be strong, but the truth was I was tripping. I was only sixteen. I was supposed to have my whole life ahead of me. Now I wasn't sure what kind of life I'd be allowed to have.

10

FACING LIFE

From the first day I met Kathy, we started preparing for my transfer hearing. This was our first big legal hurdle, the hearing where a judge would determine if I should be tried as a juvenile or an adult. If my case stayed in juvenile court, I'd stay at a juvenile holding center, and my sentence would be lighter. Adult court meant moving me to the county jail and facing a longer sentence. The district attorney wanted to try me as an adult, but Kathy told me not to worry. She told me about cases in other states, where they'd determined that kids aren't as culpable as adults because their brains aren't fully developed. She kept bringing up this boy who was charged with murder but ended up being tried as a juvenile, like his case meant the same thing would be true for me. She never mentioned the fact that there were far more cases of kids who ended up being tried as adults, and I never asked. Looking back, I probably should have. By now I had decided to testify at the transfer hearing and tell the judge everything, including the parts that made Kut look bad. Mommy, Kathy, and basically everybody who cared about me practically staged an intervention to convince me that the way Kut treated me was not okay. Plus, Fakisha's revelation about me facing a life sentence scared me. I stopped calling Kut. For the first time, I realized I might be the one who needed protecting.

Kathy and I spent hours preparing me for my testimony. While we went over my answers to potential questions, our strategy hinged on one crucial point: don't lose your cool.

"The DA will try and press your buttons," she said. "You can't get upset. You can't be so aggressive, even if you think he's wrong."

We role-played court scenarios, with Kathy saying everything in the book that could possibly make me mad. I learned to resist the urge to yell "That ain't what happened!" and clap back at her. I learned not to roll my eyes or move my head. I practiced speaking without an attitude.

As Kathy prepared for the transfer hearing, she told me early on that she wanted to bring in my birth mother, Gina. She thought it might show the court that something hereditary was involved in my case—maybe Gina's issues gave me an excuse. Once, when I was just a few months old, Gina even kidnapped me and took me to crack houses and who knows where else, and Kathy thought that might have had a developmental impact. She was someone who abandoned me, who gave me up without even trying to be part of my life. She never visited. She never called. And yet, she was part of me somehow.

I had never had a deep longing in my heart to meet my birth mother. But I had to admit I was curious. I grew up hearing Poppy rail against how awful she was and warning me that I would end up just like her if I wasn't careful. But was there more to her than that? Part of me wondered if meeting Gina would be a glimpse into my future if I didn't choose a different path.

What does she look like? I wondered. *Where has she been? Does she still prostitute herself and do drugs?* I played it cool, but I was anxious to have the answers to these questions.

Before Kathy flew Gina in to meet me, I spent hours on the phone with Mommy reassuring her that I knew who my mother was. I didn't want her to think she didn't do something right, or that I was trying to replace her. Luckily, Mommy was never insecure about that. She wasn't tripping. Her only concern was my protection.

"I just don't want you to get hurt, Toia," she told me. I assured her I'd be fine.

Dan Birman, a documentary filmmaker, had reached out to me through Kathy to ask if he could film my story. Cameras had been following me since practically day one of my arrest. While at first it made me uncomfortable, I figured it could help other kids in situations like mine. Cameras were rolling when the day arrived for me to meet Gina, and I couldn't help but feel like we were both performing somehow.

Gina was waiting for me in the visitation gallery, next to Kathy, when I walked in. As I saw her sitting at the table, anger I didn't know was lurking inside me instantly rose up. I could feel myself getting a defensive attitude the moment I laid eyes on her. *I don't care what she says, this lady is not gonna be my momma*, I thought. She couldn't be bothered to call in all these years? She doesn't just get a free pass now. She was nothing like I imagined her. Her hair was braided to her scalp like Allen Iverson, she was short and squat, and she was just kind of there. Neither of us spoke as I took her in.

Finally, Kathy broke the awkward silence. "Why don't you give Miss Gina a hug?" she said.

It didn't seem like I had much choice in the matter. I gave her a quick pat, the way you hug people you don't feel like touching. Kathy and Dan left to give us some privacy.

"I like your braids," I told her. It was the only thing I could think of at first. But then I launched into my interrogation. "Where you been?" I demanded. "Where do you live?"

Gina didn't say much. She admitted she couldn't be around for my childhood, but she said she was ready now. This time she was sticking around for good. She told me she was staying overnight at a nonprofit hospitality house called Family Reconciliation that allowed people to stay for free when they visited loved ones in prison.

"I'll be back tomorrow," she told me.

True to her word, she stuck around—at first. But red flags were popping up all over. In the middle of a visit, she casually mentioned that Mommy stole me from her.

"Excuse you?" I protested, my hand on my hip. *No she did not just say that*, I thought. *She is not gonna disrespect my mommy like that.*

"I never wanted to give you up." Gina looked like she'd been backed into a corner. "She stole you from me while I was locked up."

"Okay, let me tell you something," I said defiantly, my finger wagging now. "Don't you ever sit here and lie about my mother. She did what you couldn't do. What you wouldn't do."

"But I didn't—"

"I found those letters you wrote to me. You said you were giving me to Miss Brown. You wanted to just lie around and get high. Mommy took care of me. Don't ever sit here and disrespect her."

Gina kept acting like it was Mommy's fault she wasn't part of my life. Our visit that day ended on a sour note.

"I'll be back for the hearing," she said, as she walked out the door.

To my surprise she did show up at the transfer hearing and even testified. For a while, she was happy to talk to Dan anytime he needed her. Then all of a sudden, she was gone. For the next several years, she'd disappear for six months to a year at a time, only returning when there was a TV interview or some kind of attention involved. I didn't get many letters in between those visits, and we certainly didn't talk on the phone often, if ever. Mommy, meanwhile, was faithfully there for me like clockwork. Mommy was my rock no matter what. I had always known I already had everything I needed in her. Now I knew Gina couldn't even be in the same category. I'd spent a full three months in juvenile detention before my transfer hearing. With nothing but time on my hands, I decided if I was ever going to get close to God, this was the time. I may not have paid attention all those Sundays I was dragged to church by Mommy, but now every snippet of a sermon I could remember came flooding back to me. I prayed fervently every single day.

Lord, please don't allow me to be tried as an adult, I prayed. *If you keep me in juvenile court, I'll never run the risk of facing life in prison. I'll be out by my nineteenth birthday. Please, God, I know you can do this.*

I truly believed that if I prayed enough and did the right things, God would protect me from being tried as an adult. As far as I knew, that's what the Bible said. God would keep up his end of the bargain, and I'd be out by my nineteenth birthday.

As the date drew near, Kathy's nerves sank to an all-time low. She tried to mask her fear, but Laura Dykes, the second attorney assigned to my case, didn't try to sugarcoat anything. She was already preparing for our defense in adult court. Every time she mentioned it, I felt that sick empty feeling in my stomach. It was like looking into a future that I never wanted to happen.

The morning of my hearing, I leaned against the sink in my cell, staring into the aluminum mirror and praying with all the sincerity I could muster. *Oh Lord, please deliver me from the threat of transfer*, I prayed.

Kathy had told me to make myself presentable—whatever that meant in my standard-issue orange jumpsuit and matching orange Keds. After thinking a minute, I combed my hair into two pigtail braids, tying the ends with torn-off sections from the finger of a latex glove. Looking in the mirror, I felt like an impostor. My braids made me look like a child, yet a judge was about to decide whether I should be tried as an adult.

In that moment, I longed for the days Mommy sat me beside the kitchen sink, a comb in her hand. Each time, she carefully combed my hair into the same pigtails I'd attempted to re-create. I'd squirm and pretend to be anxious to finish, but secretly, I wanted it to last forever.

Mommy, Gina, and my pastor, Reverend Brown, were seated together in the hearing room when I walked in. A pit formed in my stomach when I saw the people across the aisle, their faces shooting daggers at me. My victim's family. I recognized the man's fiancée from a picture in his house, and I spotted his brother in a leather jacket, staring holes through me. In that moment, I realized that what I'd done went far beyond that man I thought was trying to hurt me. All this time, I'd only thought about protecting myself, keeping myself out of adult prison. I didn't even consider what his family had gone through. They'd lost a fiancé, a brother, a son. I found out later that his dad died of a heart attack soon after that terrible night. These people hated me, and I couldn't blame them. And now they were sitting feet away from the witness stand.

Oh, Lord, I thought. *How am I supposed to testify now?*

Acid reflux burned the back of my throat as I watched witness after witness testify against me. Laura slipped me a Tums. Nothing could put out the fire. This hearing wasn't supposed to prove my guilt or innocence, but it sure felt like it.

A woman who had known me at Woodland Hills was one of the witnesses. This lady was always supportive when I was locked up, and everyone thought I was the teacher's pet. Now, though, she gave me this horrified look as she walked down the aisle, as if she was looking at a monster. I listened as Dr. Bernet, the psychiatrist who had interviewed me after I was arrested, announced that he thought I had a personality disorder. I tried not to roll my eyes when Gina took the stand, her sleeveless pantsuit showing off her tattoo. The court stared at the word "Suicide," in giant letters, as she attempted to explain my life. The police who had interviewed me testified. And then, it was my turn.

My mouth went bone dry the moment I opened it to speak. I could hear my voice shake as I swore to tell the truth. A sob was hanging out in the back of my throat, threatening to pop out at the worst possible moment. *Don't cry, don't cry*, I told myself.

All those hours of practicing my testimony with Kathy paid off. I kept my voice steady, my face straight. I forced myself to give simple yes or no answers, fighting the urge to explain myself. Kathy had told me under no uncertain terms that if you're only asked to say yes or no, you don't say anything else. I broke only once. I couldn't help myself. The district attorney (DA) wouldn't stop going off about how I must have felt comfortable in the dude's house if I ate food from Sonic and used his bathroom. Finally I couldn't hold back any longer.

"I'm sorry, have you ever killed someone?" I asked accusingly.

The DA's eyes popped out of his head, like he couldn't believe I just gave him a free shot. "Why no, Miss Brown," he said, a smug look on his face. "You're the only one on trial for murder."

"Okay then. I think I know what I'm talking about."

I could feel my victim's family glaring at me as I sat on the stand. I did everything I could to avoid looking at them. I couldn't handle the guilt—especially not while I was trying to defend myself. Every so often, the DA would stand next to them, so I had to look in their direction.

The whole time, my mind raced as I studied the judge's face. I wondered what she was thinking, whether she believed me. I clung to every breath and tilt of her head, anything to give me a hint of how this was going.

The DA never questioned the fact that a forty-three-year-old man was picking up a teenager for sex, and my attorneys didn't want to make the victim look bad. They never brought up Kut's age or described our relationship as statutory rape, or even thought it was strange that a grown man gave a teenager a gun. I was described as a teenaged prostitute, not a trafficking victim. The word "trafficking" wouldn't be used in connection with my case until many years later. In the eyes of the prosecution, I was a murderous whore, an evil, out-of-control teen whom they were dead set on locking up.

The whole ordeal lasted a few hours before the judge closed us out, saying the case was a tragedy on both sides. I hung on her every word, hoping that meant she would show me some level of mercy.

"I think that went well," Kathy said as we filed out of the room. I hoped she was right.

A transfer hearing is different from a trial, where you hear the result within a few hours. It could be weeks. Waiting was not exactly the best thing for my anxiety level. My nerves were on edge as I sat in my cell, replaying the judge's expressions and remarks over and over, analyzing what they meant. I memorized the state statutes involving my case and wrote down every single detail I could think of that related. My room was cluttered with documents detailing case law. Some nights I never slept, poring obsessively over them. It was as if I could worry my way into being tried as a juvenile. Kathy had told me about an intensive treatment facility where the juvenile court could send me if that's where my case ended up. I was willing to endure any treatment they handed me as long as I didn't have to face life in prison.

All the while, I prayed. I begged God not to let me be transferred to the adult system. A church volunteer who visited me in prison once brought me a mustard seed. He told me if you have the faith of a mustard seed, mountains would move. I believed with everything in me that if I kept praying, miracles could happen.

Kathy told me she would come visit me when the decision came down. I was so anxious to hear the ruling that I told Kathy I didn't even want to wait the amount of time it would take me to walk to the visitation gallery to see her. So she and I came up with a system. As soon as I turned the corner of the corridor, she would hold up a Post-it Note I could see through the glass. If it was a small Post-it Note, it meant I was staying in juvenile court. But if she held up a big one, I would be tried as an adult.

Usually, Kathy's visits weren't a surprise. I called her every day, and she told me which days she was coming up to visit me. Two weeks after the transfer hearing, an officer showed up at my cell door.

"You got an attorney visit," he said.

My head snapped up. We didn't have anything scheduled. A decision had come down.

My heart pounded as I turned the corner of the corridor. But before I could even look for the Post-it Note, I saw her face. Her mouth quivered, like she was trying to force the corners up. I froze.

Kathy fought back tears as she held up the large Post-it Note, and I felt my whole body cave in. Every ounce of strength I had evaporated as I forced myself to keep walking, to sit with her at the table.

"When am I leaving?" I whispered.

"Right now," she said, her voice breaking. "The transportation officers are on their way. They wanted me to tell you to go pack up all your things."

Neither of us could speak about what had happened. There were no words.

I was given a trash bag to haul the few possessions I had left. There was no time to think, no time to process the fact that I was facing a life sentence. Before, when I thought the most I would get was eight years, I knew it wasn't the end of the world. No one wants to go to prison, but I could serve my time and move on with my life. Now I couldn't begin to fathom what it would look like to grow old in prison. I'd never had a driver's license, never voted. I thought back to my dreams of getting married and settling down in a house in Clarksville, playing with my babies on the porch with Mommy, working at a career I loved. And now I faced the very real possibility that none of those things would ever happen. I was too young to buy cigarettes or alcohol, but now I was subject to prosecution under the fullest extent of the law. God hadn't heard me at all.

The transport officers shackled my hands and feet and made me carry my own trash bag of property. Already I could feel things were different. They weren't treating me like a child anymore. I was a prisoner for life.

As they led me into the hall, Glen Cook, the chief administrator of the detention center, stopped me. *What's he gonna say?* I wondered. Not two weeks earlier, this man had pepper sprayed me when I refused to exchange my clothes for a paper gown. But whatever anger or judgment he once had for me was gone. Instead, he put his hands on my shoulders and looked me square in the face.

"You're going to go home," he said, with deep conviction in his voice. His words were like a life preserver in an ocean of uncertainty. It may not have been my reality, but something told me there was truth behind it. The fear I'd felt since seeing the Post-it Note disappeared, and a glimmer of hope took its place.

11

SPARED

The transport van slowed to a stop in front of the CCA correctional facility. I shivered as the door opened. Instead of wearing a uniform, I was dressed in the clothes I was arrested in months before. The black top that had been appropriate for the August heat in Tennessee didn't offer me much protection against the cold November winds. By now, I'd gained a little weight, so I was allowed to wear the red sweatpants I'd received from the mental hospital. With my wedge slides and shackles, I was making quite the fashion statement.

Transfer officers led me inside the facility and we trudged down a long hallway yellow with the glow of fluorescent lights. My shackles dragged against the cold tile floor, clanking with every step and echoing off the concrete-block walls. A sense of doom hung in the air.

My first stop was a holding cell, complete with a concrete ledge that served as a bed and a metal toilet-and-sink combo. I could read the names of men and women who'd inhabited the cell before me etched in the concrete blocks. Everywhere I looked, dried boogers were smeared on the walls and concrete ledge. I had to be careful where I sat. The officers slammed the metal door behind me, woven with thin bars and a small rectangular slot in the middle I would come to know as the "pie flap." They slipped me a tray of food through the door as I waited.

I sat on the concrete bed, taking in my new surroundings. It was every bit as depressing as I had imagined. Scanning the cell, my eyes stopped when I found the light switch. I reached over and flipped it off. In the few hours that had passed since I left juvenile detention, I felt as if I had aged several years. I was a new person now, with only one thing in common with my former self—I still preferred to keep the lights off.

I hugged my knees to my chest as I pressed my face against the doorjamb, looking for faces to match the voices I heard echoing through the reception area. I could see the edge of a bench in a larger cell where a group of men sat waiting. A bald man leaned against the bars, talking loudly to the officer at the desk and bragging about the culinary arts certificate he'd earned while he was there. He was about to be released and was excited to use his new skills to make a fresh start, he said.

I wonder if I'll ever be in that position, I thought. My mind wandered as the man sat back on the bench and lifted his voice. I closed my eyes as his words soared through the metal bars, taking me back to the moment Glen Cook told me I would go home.

For the first time since I saw the Post-it Note, I stopped fighting the tears. I let them roll freely down my cheeks as I wondered what lay ahead of me. That uncertainty was my biggest fear, and it was sheer torture. Being a juvenile in jail puts you in a bizarre position. Although I was being tried as an adult, the jail had to follow certain rules until I turned eighteen. That meant no contact with any adult inmates whatsoever. My cell was in the G-Unit, the segregated area. Normally, no one goes there unless they're being punished for some kind of in-house offense. Each cell had bunk beds, but only one of my beds would be used since I couldn't have a cellmate. I didn't mind. I wanted to be alone.

My unit had twenty cells on two levels, all on one wall so that no cells faced one another. In the middle were four fenced-in areas that looked like dog kennels, where you could shower and use the phone. The whole place was pretty raggedy, but I hadn't expected much from jail. In theory, I was supposed to be out of sight and hearing range of any adult inmates, but that wasn't the case. Every day, when an officer led me to the kennel to shower, I had to take my clothes off, my naked body on full display in the cage until I closed the shower curtain. The ladies in the unit yelled at me through the cracks of their doors, hollering and calling me "juvy." Even in my cell, I could hear them shouting to one another. They didn't care whether it was morning or night. The noise was constant. I learned to sleep through it.

I was only in the CCA facility for a few months before they moved all of us to a brand-new jail right next door. The building was literally a two-minute walk away, but that didn't matter. Every single one of us was shackled and handcuffed to belly chains before we were loaded onto a prison bus. An officer stood outside the bus with a shotgun, ready to shoot anyone foolish enough to make a run for it. I gulped. This was one time that running away did not cross my mind.

The guard with the shotgun herded everyone into the new building—I was last, since I couldn't be in contact with the adult prisoners. My cell was the first one in the J pod, and I was its first occupant. I looked around at my new accommodations. It was still jail, still equipped with the typical metal bunk bed and a metal toilet-and-sink combo. But it was new, shiny, a far cry from the dingy, filthy cell I had before. It also had a desk where I could write and eat. In that moment, I was grateful.

The new building had a new routine. Every day when I showered, I was ordered to place my hands behind my back while a guard handcuffed me through the pie flap before opening the door. The shower had a metal door with a pie flap for the same purpose.

I was allowed one hour out of my cell every day to shower, use the phone, sit in the lobby, or play in the pod in front of my cell, on the PlayStation a counselor had brought for me. Mostly, though, I watched guards play on it instead, as I looked on from my cell window.

The jail's medical staff kept me on a steady diet of psychotropics. It seemed like the doctor put me on a new pill every other month, like I was some kind of guinea pig. At one point I was on Thorazine, Tegretol, and Prozac all at once. I was so doped up I could barely wake up to eat or use the bathroom. When I told a nurse I was having a hard time seeing, the doctor added Benadryl into the mix. If I was having trouble staying awake before, it certainly wasn't better after that.

Mommy worried that I would be lonely when she heard they were keeping me in segregation. She bought me a radio to help me pass the time. I kept the radio tuned to a local R&B station, but I didn't need the distraction. My mind was completely fixed on my case. Two months after I arrived at the jail, Kathy brought me my discovery packet with every witness statement and piece of evidence from the transfer hearing. She also gave me an LSAT prep book to help me better understand the case law.

I had barely cracked a book in years, but now I couldn't get enough of all things legal. I pored over law books, sometimes staying up all night. I took practice tests in the LSAT book and checked my scores, which I thought were decent considering I didn't even have a high school diploma. My transfer order was marked up with notes and symbols I'd made that today make absolutely no sense to me. I knew I couldn't just put my trust in a lawyer's hands. I was determined to find a way out.

I became obsessed with the idea that my transfer hearing constituted a double jeopardy, since the attorneys had focused on my guilt instead of whether my case was more appropriate for juvenile or adult court. The attorneys on my legal team exchanged glances as if I were losing my mind as I rattled off my latest theory.

"That's not double jeopardy," they told me.

"Yes it is!" I shot back.

I held up this tattered black law dictionary somebody had sent me. I'd flipped through it so many times the pages were falling out. "No, look here! Look what this says!"

I thought I must not be explaining myself well enough. I sat in my cell for weeks upon weeks, handwriting motions with instructions to file them immediately. "You work for me!" I shouted when my attorneys refused to file them.

"Why don't you want me to go free?" I begged my lawyers when they shot down my arguments. "Why are you fighting me?"

I just knew I had discovered a way out, and no one would listen to me. I could feel myself going crazy. I knew I'd developed an unhealthy obsession, but I felt powerless to stop it. I couldn't even sleep. In my mind, there was no time. My trial date was coming, and I had to figure out the perfect argument. In the end, they filed the motion, along with another motion saying I wasn't competent to stand trial at that point. I flipped out when I heard that. I screamed that I was competent. Why couldn't they understand?

When I wasn't obsessing over my case, I continued my quest to learn about religion. Back at the Juvenile Detention Center, I'd copied practically a whole ream of paper from an encyclopedia. I researched every religion I could think of—Buddhism, Islam, Judaism, Hinduism, you name it. Now, as I sat in my cell, I combed through those papers that I'd brought with me, searching for the truth. It didn't occur to me that maybe I wasn't in the best state of mind to recognize the truth. My search became just another obsession. I had no control over my life, no power, and I was looking for something, anything, to bring it back.

Mommy kept telling me everything I needed to know was in my Bible.

"It can't be that simple," I said. I'd heard about the Bible my whole life and nothing had worked out for me so far. I'd had faith that I wouldn't be transferred, and I'd asked God to deliver me, and nothing happened. Either I was doing something wrong, or the answers just weren't in there.

The only verse I knew was John 3:16, "For God so loved the world that he gave his only begotten Son, that whoever believes in him shall not perish but have eternal life." I started at the beginning and worked my way through, but I didn't get far. The book of Numbers tripped me up. All those names and laws and orders that made no sense to me were enough to make me give up.

I decided maybe I just wasn't doing this God thing right. I thought my prayers had the power to change the world, but maybe I wasn't praying long enough or hard enough. So I dove back in. I rebuked the Enemy and asked God to deliver me from the hold he had on my life.

One day, a Pentecostal lady who was a guard stuck her head into my cell window and told me that the men I'd slept with had spiritual ties on my life.

"You gotta pray off each and every one of them," she told me. "That's the only way to unbind their spirits from you."

I didn't exactly understand what she meant, but I was desperate. I took out a piece of paper and pen and sat at my desk. One by one, the memories came flooding back. That man at the bus stop. The boy who helped me escape Woodland Hills. Mike. My cheeks burned as I realized I didn't even know several of the names.

The list grew longer. And longer. Names of men who bought me weed after we slept together. Men who didn't ask how old I was. Men who knew but didn't care. Men who took my body without asking. Men who heard me say no and ignored me. Andre, who drugged me into unconsciousness so he could have his way with me. And Kut, who turned my body into something to be bought and sold.

I felt disgusted as I imagined each of these men still being tied to me. Still spiritually with me, even after they were long gone. *Oh*

God, please unbind these ties, I prayed. *I don't want these men with me anymore.*

I squeezed my eyes shut in the jail cell, repeating those sentences over and over. I waited for something, anything, to feel different. I wanted to feel set free. I wanted to feel healed. But I didn't. I just felt like a whore, with the list to prove it.

At my lowest point, I cut off my curly dark hair and shaved my eyebrows. I didn't want to be pretty anymore. Maybe if men didn't look at me like a sex object, I would be free.

Each obsession brought me closer to the edge. One reprimand from a guard or objection from an attorney was enough to send me into an all-out explosion of rage. Every day brought another outburst, another fight with a guard, another pill to help calm my anger. Once, I attacked a guard, after he took away my collection of *Seventeen* magazines, and ended up in a restraint chair for several hours.

I was in the middle of a nervous breakdown, with no way to process what was happening to me or why I felt the way I did. Anger coursed through my body, putting me through a mentally exhausting cycle that wreaked havoc on everyone around me. No medicine touched my mental state. If anything, it only made me crazier. One lady handed me a stack of coloring books and crayons as a way to calm me down. These were no adult coloring books. These were pictures of Tweety Bird and Jonah and the whale. Needless to say, that didn't help.

Mommy was my anchor. She was the only thing keeping me even remotely together. She visited me faithfully every weekend, and I called her as many times as I wanted. She always accepted my calls. She never acted too busy for me. Her soothing voice and calming words brought me down from the edge. When I felt like there was no point in trying to rein in my emotions, when I felt I had nothing to lose, she always brought me back to reality. Sometimes she told me to stop taking the pills prescribed to me. Other times she just broke down and prayed right there on the phone.

....

I WAS DEEP IN MY NERVOUS BREAKDOWN WHEN I SAT IN THE LOBBY one day during my hour I was allowed out of my cell. A newspaper sat on the table and I flipped mindlessly through it to pass the time. I was scanning through the local section when I found the police blotter. There it was, in black–and-white print, "Police identify man slain in parking lot as Garion McGlothen, 24." Garion McGlothen was Kut's real name.

My body let out a primal scream, the kind of scream where you don't realize at first you're the one screaming. I had never screamed like that before. I sobbed as I read the details of how he'd been shot in the chest, stomach, and face.

All the work I'd done to distance myself from Kut went out the window. I was right back where I was the day I got arrested, longing for a man who was never truly mine. Now he never would be.

An officer ran into the lobby and put her hand on my shoulder, asking if I was okay. I told her what happened and asked for some space. I needed privacy to grieve.

Without even thinking, I grabbed the phone in the lobby and squatted in the corner, dialing Kut's mother's phone number, which I'd had memorized from all the times I'd tried to reach him in different places. A woman who sounded tired and drained answered.

"I just gotta know," I sobbed hysterically. "Was he saved? Is he going to heaven?" As much as I doubted God's existence, I couldn't bear the thought of Kut rotting in hell. If God was real, I just knew he wouldn't hesitate to throw you into the fiery pit. It was easier to wrap my head around God's wrath than his mercy.

Although it was a horrible thing to ask a woman who had just lost her son, she was kind to me. "Yes, he was," she said simply. I slumped in the corner and hung up the phone as my body shook, tears streaming out too fast to wipe them up.

When the hysteria passed, the gravity of the situation sank in. If I hadn't been in jail, I might have been right there with Kut in that parking lot. That newspaper article might very well have said two people were shot and killed.

I was stuck in an awful situation, but the truth was that my life was spared. The fact that I was still breathing meant I had a second chance.

12

FIGHTING FOR MY LIFE

"I have some bad news."

Kathy had barely sat down in the visitation gallery for one of our regular visits before these words were out of her mouth. I took a deep breath. Things were already pretty bad. What could possibly be considered bad news now?

"What happened?"

Kathy sighed. "Well, apparently three girls who used to have a cell next to you are telling detectives you told them everything about the murder the first night you were in jail."

I snapped to attention. "What? I didn't tell anyone nothing! I didn't even talk to anyone that first night. They didn't bring me to my cell until eleven o'clock at night. I pretty much turned out the light and cried myself to sleep."

"I know, I know. But the DA wants to use their statement as part of the case."

"Of course he does." I rolled my eyes. "I'm sure they're getting some kind of deal out of it too."

"The problem is, two of them are represented by the public defender's office," Kathy said. "And that means I can't represent both you and them."

Her words slowly sank in. "So . . . you ain't my attorney anymore?"

Kathy shook her head sadly. "But don't worry. We're making sure you've got the best person on your case."

"Who is it?" I asked, eyeing her suspiciously.

"A man named Rich McGee has agreed to take you on. Have you heard of him?"

"Rich McGee?" I said incredulously. Everyone in jail knew about Rich McGee. He was famous for being the kind of lawyer who could get juries to find just about anyone innocent. *Man*, I had thought many times. *I wish I had Rich McGee so I could get out of this*. Now, without me ever asking, he was my attorney. I couldn't believe my luck.

Kathy continued to come visit me as a friend while Rich took over my case. I was excited for my first meeting with him and eagerly shook his hand. He was a distinguished-looking white guy with a thick head of perfectly coiffed hair, well dressed in an expensive suit. *This is the guy who's going to get me home*, I thought.

But I soon discovered that Rich is a man who doesn't take any crap. He didn't want to hear my double jeopardy argument, or any of my legal theories for that matter. He and his fellow attorney, Wendy, pushed me to my breaking point as they prepped me for my trial testimony, yelling at me when I offered a further explanation to a yes-or-no question.

"No!" he shouted. "You can't say anything else!"

"But I want to explain myself. I'm not going to just say yes or no."

"I didn't ask you to do that," he snapped, silencing me with a look.

Any questions that I asked infuriated him. I didn't care. It didn't matter to me if I had the greatest attorney in the world on my team, I wasn't going into my trial without knowing what was going on. Everybody says not to put your life in a lawyer's hands, and I fully believed that. That didn't exactly lead to the most peaceful meetings with him.

"I have over twenty years of experience with this," he exploded. "If I'm telling you to do something, you do it. It doesn't matter if you agree with it or understand it. If a surgeon tells you not to eat or drink before your surgery and you do it anyway, you could die on the table. He's telling you for a reason. You're not the surgeon, and you're not the lawyer."

That didn't sit well with me, especially when he and Wendy informed me that I shouldn't testify at my own trial. They said because I had initially lied to police, the court could charge me with perjury.

"But I was just trying to protect Kut," I protested. "I'll explain everything."

"That doesn't matter," Rich said. "The only thing they'll care about is the fact that you lied."

A sense of dread washed over me. My entire case revolved around self-defense. Who else would tell my story if I couldn't testify? I had to put my faith in the hands of Dr. Bernet, an old white guy with a doctoral degree. How could he possibly speak for me and convey what I had been through? Not only that, but the court had already banned us from using some of the witnesses we'd found, saying they were prejudicial. *How in the world are we going to convince this jury to send me home?* I wondered.

I MADE SEVERAL TRIPS TO THE ADULT COURTHOUSE FOR HEARINGS leading up to the August 2006 trial. Because I was a juvenile, that meant countless hours shackled in a small, dirty, concrete holding cell alone. The cells were so freezing that sometimes people would wet tissues and throw them over the holes of the vent to keep the air from flowing. I was always served the same lunch of sandwiches made from a mystery meat that might have been bologna, but also could have been salami or ham. It was hard to tell.

On the days I was seen by a judge, court officers who went by Big O and Tim D escorted me upstairs. They never made me sit in the upstairs holding cell and let me sit next to them. Unlike everyone else at the courthouse, they actually talked to me like a human being. Tim D even said he wanted his son to marry me one day. I laughed it off, but his words had a deeper meaning to me, like maybe I wasn't the monster the DA made me out to be. These days, that was a rare feeling.

By the time I'd been locked up a year, every inch of my character had been attacked from every imaginable direction thanks to my many court dates. The weight of judgment and ostracizing had worn my self-esteem down to nothing. Whether it was the degrading treatment of prison life, the news reports seemingly on repeat, or the whispered words I overheard in the courtroom, I felt that someone or something was always in the background telling me I was a horrible human being. After a while, you can't help but believe it.

The rumors swirling around me didn't help. My trial hadn't even started when I learned someone had started a rumor that I was pregnant by a prison guard. I was livid. Here I'd been living a nightmare, while someone's out there telling people I was here living it up, being promiscuous, and sleeping with officers?

"You might want to lay off the Doritos," said Wendy, one of my attorneys, as she broke the news of the rumor to me. "Try to lose a little weight."

I looked down at my swollen belly. I couldn't deny that the Snyder's of Hanover jalapeño pretzel pieces and strawberry Pop-Tarts had taken their toll. I comforted myself with commissary snacks, and other than pacing the eight feet of my cell, I wasn't exactly getting much exercise. Weeks away from my trial, I'd packed nearly sixty extra pounds onto my five-foot-two-inch frame. I already knew I looked like a different person. But I sure didn't appreciate anyone basically telling me I was fat. For once, I was speechless.

"You don't want to go into your trial looking like a football player," Wendy added.

Then there was the issue of clothes. Up until now, I'd worn my jail uniform to all my court dates. But the law says when a jury is present, anything that makes you look like you're incarcerated could prejudice them and sway their vote. Kathy brought me a few outfits to try on with the help of a lady named Judy Langston I'd met previously. Judy was a fiftysomething white lady, and the clothes she picked out looked every bit of it. Later, during the trial, it dawned on me that I was wearing the same freaking shirt as the court stenographer, who of course was a fiftysomething white lady too.

Mommy brought me clothes, too, but hers weren't much better. She picked out capri pants and a little top with beading around the neck like I was still fifteen. I couldn't even get the pants to button. Her clothes forced me to face the reality that I was no longer a child. Mommy might still see me as her baby, but now, in the eyes of the law, I was very much an adult. That mental space was a strange place to be.

STANDING OUTSIDE THE COURTROOM, I WAS DRESSED IN NICE PANTS and a blouse. This was it. After nearly two years of waiting, my trial was about to begin. Acid burned in my stomach and I chewed a Tums Wendy had given me in a futile attempt to put out the fire. I tried not to think about what the next few days would mean for my future. *Just get through today*, I thought.

I was as ready as I would ever be. Rich and Wendy had trained me to keep my composure no matter who was testifying or what they said. I knew the slightest eyebrow raise could turn the jury against me. I was instructed to keep my mouth shut as long as we were in the courtroom. Rich gave me a notepad and told me to write down any questions or points I wanted him to make.

But nothing could have prepared me for the moment we walked

into the courtroom for my first-degree murder trial. It was jury selection day, and men and women from all walks of life filled the room. To them, jury duty was a pain, and I watched them use every excuse in the book trying to get out of it. One lady with a skinny build and long brown hair was openly upset to be there, sighing and telling anyone who would listen that she didn't have time for this.

A court officer noticed she was being disruptive and asked her what was wrong.

"I cannot be here," she said indignantly. "I am biased and can't be an impartial juror. I was the victim of a home invasion." She spat out the words and looked at me with disgust. I was used to judgment by this point, but you never really stop being offended.

Everyone took a turn sitting in the jury pool so they could be questioned by my team and the DA. I watched as one by one they told the attorneys about their occupation and other personal information, every detail potentially revealing how they might react to me and my case. There was a defense attorney's wife. A woman who was a secretary at a police station. A black guy whose nephew was in trouble with the law. I studied each of their faces, trying to guess what they were thinking, wondering what they might do if they were selected. Without being obvious, I pleaded with them with my eyes, trying to send them some kind of vibe that would make them sympathetic and listen to my side.

Within a few hours, the final jury was selected, and we started the trial with our opening arguments. I listened to Rich speak, feeling better as he described me sympathetically to the jury. *This is good*, I thought.

But when the DA began his argument, I realized I was in for an emotional roller coaster. *No, no, no*, I thought, looking at the jury anxiously. *That ain't what happened. Please don't believe a word this man says.*

I turned my head toward Mommy to make sure she was okay. I knew it wasn't easy on her to hear people ripping me apart. Instead of looking upset, she caught my eye and smiled at me. Only Mommy would be worried about making me feel better when she's sitting at her child's murder trial.

The DA continued his attack, using his entire opening argument to paint me as a murderous whore. Tears stung my eyes as he told the jury I was dangerous, that the streets were safer without me. I inhaled sharply, trying to stop the sobs that were sure to come.

Finally they took a break, and court officers led me to the holding cell. I sighed with relief. Even in this nasty cell, it felt so good not to be the subject of disgust for even a few minutes.

The door clicked open and Wendy strolled in like she was on a mission. Her arms were crossed over her power suit, her mouth twisted into a scowl.

"Do you know what that DA just said?"

"No. What is it this time?"

She shook her head, as if the very thought of his words repulsed her. "He saw you crying in there and said, 'Oh, don't cry now.'"

My tears were immediately replaced with a steely resolve. That man would never see me cry again. I would make sure of it.

"Why does he hate you so much?" Wendy asked. It was obvious to anyone in the courtroom that the DA wasn't just doing his job. He had a personal vendetta against me.

I shrugged. "I have no idea. It ain't normal, I can tell you that."

The DA went on to prove my point when Rich showed the jury part of a folded-up picture Kut had taken of me while we were staying at the InTown Suites. "Look in her eyes," Rich told the courtroom. "Do you see the sorrow inside them?"

When it was the DA's turn, he snatched up the picture and marched right up to the jury. "Here's the rest of the picture," he said with a smirk. My attorneys watched in horror as he unfolded the picture and showed the jury my naked body. The DA looked smug, clearly enjoying himself. He might as well have announced "Look at this whore" to the whole jury. I felt dirty under the judging eyes surrounding me. Yet even in my embarrassment, I didn't change my expression. I was used to being torn down by now.

I sat stoically as the DA's witnesses were called one by one. I didn't move as the police who worked the crime scene gave their description of me, or when the same prison employee who told me to get rid of spiritual ties testified that I was dead inside the night I was booked. Detective Robinson was there, determined as ever to make sure I did life. I gritted my teeth and kept my composure as a girl from the same facility as me told the jury I'd confessed the whole crime to her and two other girls. It took everything inside me not to yell out, "You're lying! I know the detectives put you up to this!"

Reality came crashing down once again when the DA showed crime scene photos. The full impact of what I'd done sank in as I took in the graphic, bloody pictures, wishing I could look away but unable to do so. This man was gone. He had parents, a family who loved him. He didn't get a chance to change his ways. If I hadn't shot him that night, what kind of life could he have had? What if I had purposely aimed away from him just to scare him and then jumped out the window? My mind tried to rewrite history right there in the courtroom. I ached to undo everything, yet there was nothing I could do.

The trial was yet another reminder that nothing was private anymore. Even my most personal moments were displayed for all to see. The DA used the notes I'd taken back at the InTown Suites with Kut, when he'd forced me to write down how to be a good slut. They called it my "personality profile," saying I was planning to change my identity and run away. Hearing those words read in court was not only embarrassing, it was infuriating. I had no opportunity to tell the jury he was interpreting it totally wrong. Meanwhile, local news crews snapped photos and zoomed in on my face with their video cameras.

The only time I couldn't help but cry was when Mommy took the witness stand. The whole courtroom listened as the DA played a tape of one of our conversations, one of the few times I let my guard down and told Mommy I wasn't okay. Every time I used the phone in prison, a recording always said my call could be recorded or monitored, but somehow I still thought I had some semblance of privacy. Clearly that was not the case. During the call, Mommy had told me she still wanted me to have some kind of a life, and I broke down, telling her that was never going to happen thanks to what I'd done. "I'm not going to have an adult life," I said. "I killed somebody. I executed him," I said in the tape.

The DA locked in on those words, goading Mommy and trying to get her to say I'd confessed to killing an innocent man in cold blood.

"No, that's not what she was saying," Mommy protested. I choked back sobs as Mommy tried to defend me and explain my true intentions. *It's my fault she's even in this position*, I thought.

My shoulders slumped with shame, even as witnesses on my side testified. In addition to the self-defense argument, my attorneys brought out men and women to offer some kind of explanation for why my life turned out the way it did. Dr. Bernet told the court he believed I had a borderline personality disorder, which wasn't the most flattering description of me. While they didn't get any witnesses to say so, my attorneys were convinced I must have been abused as a child and tried to get me to admit it.

The overwhelming consensus among the world was something must be wrong with me. I was damaged. Defective. Broken beyond repair. Every mistake I'd ever made was now rolled out as more evidence that I was incorrigible, one big screwup. By the end of the trial, I felt like I was basically Satan's seed. The only question was whether I could be fixed, or if there was nothing left for me but to be thrown away in prison.

By the end of each day, I was emotionally exhausted. I didn't want to talk to anyone. All I wanted was to escape to my commissary stash of Snickers bars and Flaming Hot Cheetos. I didn't care how much it made my belly swell.

....

MY TRIAL LASTED AN EXCRUCIATING FIVE DAYS BEFORE EACH SIDE rested their case. I felt sick as I watched the jury retreat to their chambers. This was it. My attorney had said all he could say. Now it was up to twelve men and women to decide my fate.

"Well, who knows?" Rich said, shrugging. I forced myself not to roll my eyes. He'd have to forgive me if I couldn't be as flippant as he was.

Hours ticked by. The jury still didn't emerge. Everyone said this was a good sign. The longer a jury deliberates, the more likely they are to come out in the defendant's favor. The worst thing that can happen is for them to come out right away with a verdict. At one point, the jury sent out a messenger to ask a question. *This is good*, I thought. *They're really considering all the evidence.*

Six hours came and went. I replayed pieces of testimony in my head, reading into every facial expression and wondering what the jurors might do. I really thought we'd presented a good case. At worst, I thought they'd convict me of second-degree murder and sentence me to fifteen years in prison. It wasn't great, but it was better than life.

Mommy had already left for the day by now. Rich told her the jury would pick up with deliberations Monday morning, since it was already well into the evening. And then, there it was. A messenger gave word that the jury had reached a verdict. *Shoot, here it is*, I thought.

My heart pounded as I stood in the courtroom, waiting for the jury to walk in. As I took a seat, I desperately searched their faces, just like I did all those months ago when Kathy had the result of the transfer hearing. Not one of them looked at me. Suddenly, one of them met my eyes, the black guy whose nephew was in trouble with the law. He shook his head sadly and dropped his gaze, almost as if he was ashamed at what he'd done, or maybe he'd fought the battle but lost. I knew right then and there they'd sentenced me to life.

I stared at the jurors, mean-mugging them, daring them to look me in the eye as the guilty verdict was read. Of course, cameras caught my expression, the perfect moment for tomorrow's "Cyntoia Brown Guilty" headline. I could feel the tension radiating off Wendy and watched Rich's blue eyes boring holes through the jury, as if he sensed the same thing I did. This so-called jury of my peers didn't understand one bit of what I'd been through or the experiences I'd overcome. None of them ran in the same social circles I did. This whole circus was rigged against me from the start. Facts weren't facts, not in the courtroom. It was all about which attorney could weave the best narrative, and whichever one sounds better gets your vote. Rich always said a trial was nothing more than a show. It turned out he was right all along.

The judge looked weary, as if the weight of his duty weighed heavy on his shoulders. "In accordance with Tennessee law, I hereby order you to serve an automatic life sentence with the Tennessee Department of Correction," he said without fanfare. The whole thing, from guilty verdict to life sentence, happened within the space of two minutes. The judge asked us to rise as the jury filed out of the courtroom.

Wendy folded her arms and said what we all were thinking. "I'm not standing up for those people." We all sat there until we were dismissed.

I kept it together until guards brought me back to the holding cell. Wendy and Dan were more upset than I was, both of them crying. Rich walked in and threw his hands in the air.

"Well, I tried," he said. In my eyes, his words were no better than if he'd said, "Oh well!" This man had a bad day, but in the end, he got to go home to his family. I, meanwhile, was never going home again.

"We're gonna fight this," Wendy said, her eyes blazing. She told me she would file a motion for a new trial within the next thirty days. She rattled off her plan of attack, but I could barely listen. I was in a daze, unable to process the fact that life as I knew it was over.

I changed back into my jail uniform and called Mommy. Dan's

camera was rolling as I told her they found me guilty on all counts and sentenced me to life. I could hear her crying on the other end. "Oh, honey," she cried over and over. I took a deep breath. I could count on one hand the number of times Mommy had broken down throughout this whole ordeal. She wanted to stay strong for me. It was the same reason why I refused to cry in that moment. I couldn't make this worse for Mommy than it already was.

"That had to be hard," Dan said as I hung up the phone. "What are you thinking right now? You've been keeping it together really well."

I grabbed the cordless microphone on my shirt and pulled it close to my mouth. "I think I may cry when I get to my cell," I whispered. I wanted to be alone, to lay on my bed with the lights off, just like I always preferred it. After five days of holding everything in, I was ready to just let go.

An officer came to check on me shortly after I got to my room. "I'm fine," I told him, wiping away my tears. "I'm going home."

The guard said nothing but looked at me as if I'd lost my mind. "God is going to get me out of here," I said with a confidence I never knew I had. The guard's eyes filled with sympathy as he patted the door and walked off. I curled my body into a ball, facing the wall and crying out to God. I still wasn't sure what I thought about God, or if he really existed. But lying in that jail cell, facing a life sentence, he was the only hope I had left. I clung to him in that moment, like a life preserver in an ocean.

"Lord, I can't spend the rest of my life in prison," I prayed. "If you get me out of here, I'll tell the whole world about you."

My words were only a bargain at the time. In truth, I wasn't sure if anyone was listening.

13

TWO PATHS

I had two weeks before they transferred me to my new home at the Tennessee Prison for Women. Word about my sentence had spread throughout the jail, and it seemed like I couldn't go an hour without talking about how I was getting ready to do life.

I was eighteen now, and no longer required to be kept away from the adult prisoners. But to be honest, I felt like I was lying when I said I would spend my whole life here. I never pictured myself with gray hair, my skin wrinkled, sitting in a jail cell. It didn't seem real. *I wouldn't let it happen*, I thought. *I wouldn't stop fighting until I was free.*

Rich had already filed a motion for a new trial before I was transferred to the prison. He still visited me frequently to keep me updated and help him prepare for our upcoming court date. I didn't exactly look forward to those visits. Rich and I butted heads pretty frequently. I didn't care much for him telling me what to do, and he didn't appreciate it when I refused to listen to him. But on one particular visit, Rich leaned forward in his chair, looking at me intensely, his blue eyes deep in thought.

"Do you want to get out of prison one day?" he finally asked me.

I looked at him like he was crazy. "Of course I do! Ain't no way I'm spending my whole life locked up. I'm gonna get out one day."

He nodded. "What I'm about to tell you could decide whether you ever go home." I sat up, waiting.

"You don't have a choice about going to prison, but you can choose how you serve your time. You can go in there and get caught up in the mix of drugs, fighting, and running wild, if that's what makes you happy. But I can tell you right now that doing time the easy way will cost you your life."

"What do I do?" We may have butted heads in the past, but he didn't get an argument from me this time. Now that I had nothing to lose, I was fully with him.

"If you ever want to get out of prison, you have to walk a different path," he said. "Take every class you can. Get involved with the volunteers. Many wives of powerful people volunteer in prisons. Make sure you have their ear."

I felt like I should be taking notes. I looked at him, waiting for him to go on, feeling anxious.

"If you have a prayer of getting out one day, you have to play it smart and stay on the right path. There are two paths in front of you. The choice is yours to make."

I left our meeting determined to stay on the right path. Rich's words were burned in my brain and stayed with me for years to come. Fighting didn't interest me anymore. Drugs did nothing for me. All I wanted was to go home. If being a square was what it took, that's what I would do.

"You ready for prison?" a white girl named Brittany asked me. I knew she'd already been to prison, and was waiting to find out if she was going back for another stint.

I shrugged. "I already been in jail two years. It can't be much different."

"Oh no, girl." Brittany shook her head furiously. "You got it way worse in jail. Prison's a whole lot better."

I stared at her, confused. Prison is supposed to be a punishment. How could it possibly be better than jail?

"Their commissary's way better than county," she told me. "It ain't just snack food. You can order food you can actually cook. I'm talking chicken, ramen noodles, you just order it and they bring it to you."

Now she had my attention. I hadn't had my beloved ramen noodles since I got locked up. If prison meant I could have them again then I was here for it.

Brittany wasn't done. "You get to keep your own clothes in your cell."

I raised my eyebrows. Here in jail, all our clothes got thrown in the laundry together, and you were just handed another uniform in your size. I'd learned by now that not every pair of pants fit the same, even in the same size. Having a set of clothes all my own, even if it was just a prison uniform, sounded like a luxury.

"And, girl, they have real blankets. Not like these thin-ass rough blankets we got here."

I imagined myself curling up with a fluffy comforter, closing my eyes, feeling the warmth rush over my body. *Maybe prison won't be so bad after all*, I thought.

Brittany taught me how to walk around the prison with my chest poked out and my head held high, my arms flexed as I moved. She made me practice it for her until she felt I had it right.

"Ain't nobody gonna mess with you if you walk around like that," she said approvingly.

By now, I had a roommate in jail, a forty-year-old lady named Theus who liked to show everyone her tail—the spot on her back where she said doctors separated her from her conjoined twin. She asked me if I knew how to fight, but when I said yes, she shook her head.

"Fighting in prison is different from any fight you've ever had anywhere else," she said. She even made me practice.

My throat went dry as I rehearsed taking swings with my fists. *Staying on the right path might not be easy*, I thought hesitantly.

I was transferred to the Tennessee Prison for Women on September 11, 2006, along with a handful of other girls. Guards loaded us into the van and hauled us to the outskirts of Nashville. A girl named Alisha was on the van with me—she got a life sentence two weeks before I did. I could tell she was nervous by the way she bounced her knees and squeezed her hands together.

"I hear they got real afghans in prison," she said, looking hopefully in my eyes. "One girl told me it was more like a college campus than anything else."

"Yeah?" I could tell she wanted me to reassure her, to help her believe prison wouldn't be so bad. She hadn't heard anything that I wasn't already familiar with. But that wasn't what she needed to hear right now. "That sounds real good," I told her.

One girl in the van had already been to prison and was intent on filling us in on how things were. I kept my eyes fixed on the view outside, beyond the metal grate covering the window, watching the landscape grow bleaker and bleaker. "I already had my prison prep," I told her.

"How long are you in for?" another girl asked.

"Life," I said bluntly. That shut everyone up.

"Well," the girl said shyly a couple minutes later. "Are you nervous?"

I shook my head. "I guess I feel relieved."

They all looked at me like I was crazy. I didn't know how to explain to them that the worst thing I could have imagined had already happened. I'd spent the last two years worrying about my trial, stressing about the possibility of doing life, and trying to figure a way out. Now, all that was over. I had nothing hanging over my head. I knew what I was up against. The way I saw it, life could only get better.

The prison van exited from the highway and I kept my eyes glued to the window, searching for a glimpse of what would be my new home.

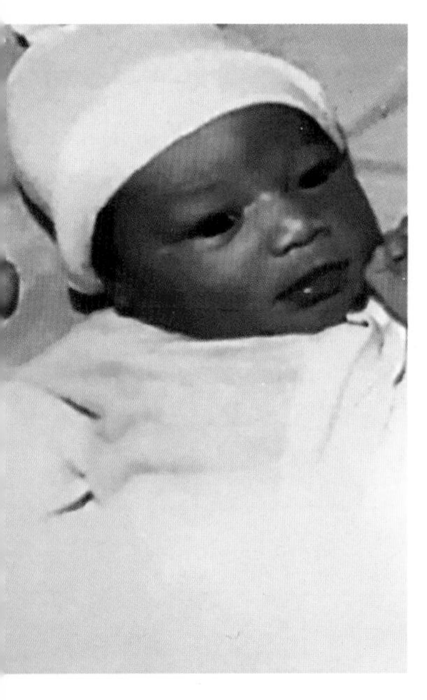

Cyntoia at just two days old (January 31, 1988).

Taking pictures for my fourth birthday (January 1992).

Cheerleading for local peewee football team at ten years old (1998).

At fourteen, with Vanessa Terry, fifteen, and Jessica Kemp, fifteen, listening to speakers brought in by a local entrepreneur while at Woodland Hills Youth Development Center (2002).

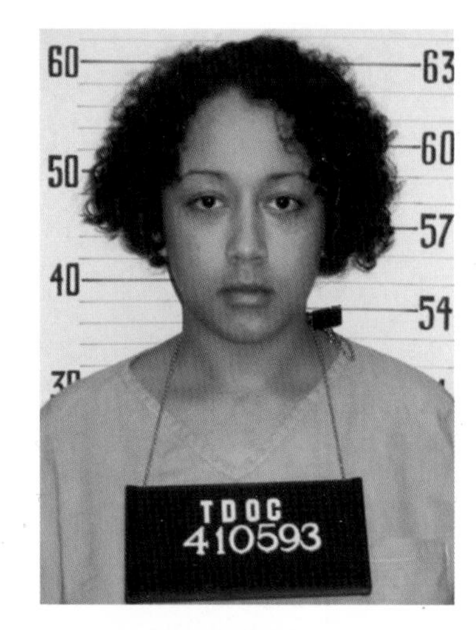

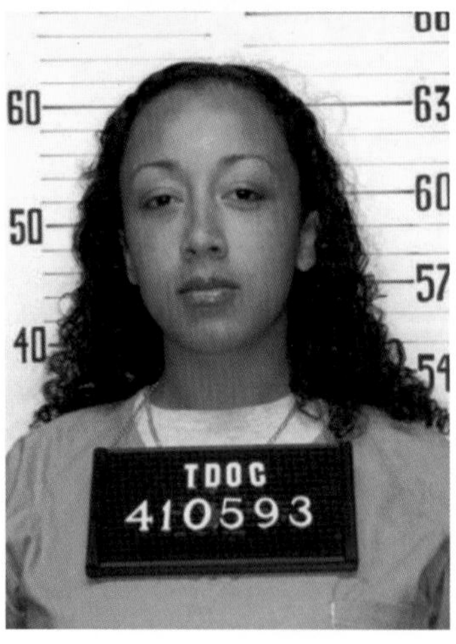

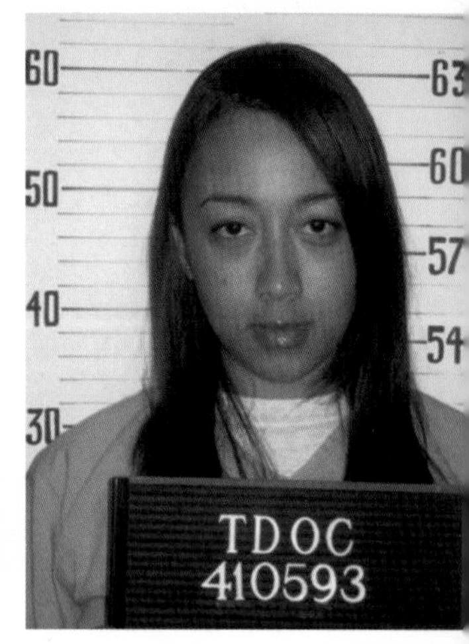

I was just a teenager when I was sent to live behind a razor-wire fence. My entire coming of age was within the walls of the Tennessee Prison for Women. I may have been physically grown in this 2013 mug shot, but I still had a lot to learn (2006, 2008, 2009, 2013).

Visit from Mommy, at the Tennessee Prison for Women, during Thanksgiving, at twenty-one years old (2009).

Visit from my sister, Missy, at the Tennessee Prison for Women, at Thanksgiving when I was twenty-six years old (2014).

Cake decorating with Kanesha and Evette in culinary arts at twenty-seven years old (2015).

Hugging Dr. Kate Watkins after delivering a commencement address at graduation, just before receiving my associate's degree from Lipscomb University in Nashville, Tennessee (December 18, 2015).

The first photos that I received from my now-husband, Jaime Long (2017).

My husband, Jaime, Mommy, and my mother-in-law, Mrs. Jackie, at the Houston Texans vs Dallas Cowboys football game in Houston, Texas (August 2018).

(Left) At my clemency hearing in Nashville, Tennessee (May 23, 2018).

(Below) Ebony Jones, right, and others march from Bicentennial Capitol Mall to Tennessee State Capitol in support of clemency for Cyntoia Brown. Two days later, Cyntoia was granted clemency by Tennessee governor Bill Haslam (January 5, 2019).

Together, and finally free. Ready to start our lives together, outside the walls of the Tennessee Prison for Women. Taken just seconds after I was released (August 7, 2019).

On a visit to Strong Tower Bible Church, Pastor Chris Williamson led Jaime and me in a special prayer with our family and my legal team and Lipscomb friends joining us in the pulpit (August 11, 2019).

My family at my celebratory dinner (left to right): Missy, Mommy, Jaime, me, Aunt Dez, Missy's fiancé Robert, and Poppy (August 10, 2019).

Pastor Tim McGee leads us all in prayer at my celebratory dinner (August 10, 2019).

Mommy, Missy, and me going through pictures on my phone taken on my first three days out (August 10, 2019).

© Flip Holsinger

Poppy getting emotional as he stares at his daughter all grown up and finally free (August 10, 2019).

© Flip Holsinger

Mommy breathing a sigh of relief at the end of a long journey to freedom (August 10, 2019).

We whizzed by a wrecked car lot before pulling up in front of the brick prison. Later, I'd learn a massive landfill sat nearby. I was living in a district for the city's refuse, where things or humans go to be thrown away and forgotten. Would I be forgotten too?

Shackles rubbed my wrists and ankles as we were herded into the prison for our intake. An inmate who introduced herself as Billie was in there like she had the run of the place, taking our sizes and asking us questions. Back at county, everyone was high-strung and on edge, but Billie was noticeably more relaxed. I couldn't stop looking at her hair, which she'd dyed a vibrant chocolate-cherry red.

"I like your hair," I told her.

Billie touched her locks and gave me a half smile. "Oh, thanks. I need to get it done again, my roots are growing out."

"Dang, you can get your hair done in here?" I asked incredulously. I didn't even get to use conditioner in the county jail, much less get a dye job.

"Mm-hmm. We got a beauty school here. You can go get your hair done anytime."

I watched her flit around the small intake room, taking command of the process. When she finished up with us, she told us she needed to take a smoke break and excused herself.

"Y'all can take smoke breaks?" I was stunned. When she told us you could buy cigarettes from the commissary, we were downright flabbergasted. *What is this place?* I thought. *Maybe it'll be all right after all.*

The other new inmates and I took turns being strip-searched and showering. Each of us was handed a medicine cup of delousing shampoo—whether we had lice or not, they weren't taking any chances.

When I was finished, I stared at my reflection in the half-length mirror above the sink. It was the first time I'd seen myself in a real mirror in two years. Back at county, we only had a glorified aluminum serving platter that served as a blurry mirror. They didn't want us breaking glass and using it for shenanigans. I took in my short curly hair, soaking wet around my face, my frame decidedly heavier than it was the day I was first arrested, dressed now in a prison-issued blue scrub shirt and dark blue jeans stamped with "Department of Correction."

I could almost hear Wendy's voice in my head, telling me not to go into my trial looking like a football player. *Wow, I really do look like one*, I thought. But today I was proud of my weight. Unlike the days when I was the scrawniest kid in Woodland Hills, I had some size on me. No one would dare to mess with me now. I saw my size as a badge of honor. I thought of Brittany as I poked my chest out and threw my shoulders back, walking out of the bathroom. I was ready.

When you go to prison, they don't just throw you into your permanent cell and wish you luck. Everyone has to go through orientation first for as many as thirty days. They housed us temporarily in the special needs unit as they handed us a packet and gave us the rundown of all the rules and procedures. We learned their fire safety protocol and emergency precautions. We got a medical checkup and a dentist checked our teeth. The education department tested us for our academic placement and verified that I had my GED—I earned it back at county in March 2005.

I spent most of my time reading through the Lord of the Rings books Kathy had sent me and pounding ramen noodles. Commissary food wasn't as great as other inmates had described it, but they did have my noodles—a delicacy to me now. I gorged myself on cup after cup of noodles, with a side of Snickers bars and Dr Pepper. By the time the prison assigned me to my permanent cell, I had already gained six pounds. I quickly burned through the whole $300 Poppy had sent me to buy comfortable sneakers and a television, blowing it all on food instead. I wasn't concerned about tomorrow. I walked around for three months in heavy state-issued steel-toe boots before I called home and asked Mommy to buy me the package with everything I should have bought in the first place. My legs still bear a dark shadow from the constant rubbing of the hard pleather material.

After two weeks in orientation, guards ordered me to load my stuff into trash bags and led me across the compound to my new cell, unit 1 West D-59. The unit door slammed shut behind me as I took in my new surroundings. The cell seemed smaller than the one I just left, but that might have been because it was so crammed with stuff—a big bookshelf, fan, TV, and even a cooler for ice. One of the beds was even draped with an afghan. *I gotta get me one of those*, I thought. My cell had a wooden door—just like the one I'd had back at Woodland Hills. I could open and shut it myself. I'd spent so much of my life in facilities that another cell didn't faze me. I was too focused on how much better this situation was than the last, even if it was ultimately a punishment. Compared to the sparse surroundings at county, my prison cell seemed downright homey.

I shared my eight-by-ten-foot cell equipped with burgundy metal bunk beds with a roommate, a girl named Tut. The short, heavyset woman with close-cropped hair was at TPW on drug charges and looked like she might cut you if you looked at her wrong, but her appearance couldn't have been further from her personality. Our cell turned out to be five doors down from Alisha, the girl who rode with me in the van. I noticed how pretty she was, with super-long dark hair.

"Hey!" I called out in surprise.

She smiled, clearly happy to see a familiar face.

"You got an afghan yet?" I asked, laughing.

"Not yet," she chuckled back. "But I'm working on it."

As I walked by her cell, I couldn't help but notice a picture of a little girl who couldn't have been more than two years old.

"That your little girl?"

She nodded, her face turning sad. I wondered how old her daughter was when she first got locked up. I could tell she couldn't bring herself to talk about it, so I quickly changed the subject.

"Alisha, this is my roommate, Tut." They shook hands, grinning at one another. I didn't know it at the time, but I'd introduced each of them to their new best friend.

Tut was a sweetheart who showed me the ropes. She taught me how to cook commissary food in the microwave—an essential in prison. She let me smoke in our room, even though she wasn't a smoker. And she made it her personal mission to keep me out of trouble—not an easy feat. I hadn't been around people much for the last two years. County jail kept me in segregation until I turned eighteen. Now that I was in the general population, I felt like I was back at Omni, where daily fights were a fact of life. The determination I'd felt sitting across from Rich disappeared as I looked around at the other ladies, wondering if they were whispering about me. Fighting was what I knew. It was how I knew to survive in a facility. I wanted to prove to the inmates around me that I didn't play.

I walked around that place two seconds from swinging my fists, just waiting for someone to cross me. Anyone who set me off was cussed out up and down. The other inmates looked at me like I was crazy, all of them clearly thinking, *Why does that girl act like that?* I was living on pins and needles while everyone else was relaxed.

"Roommate, you gotta chill," Tut told me. "We gotta figure this out."

She tried to teach me the rules that, in my opinion, were petty and inconsistently enforced. To me, they were an unnecessary form of control that triggered my impulse to rebel. This was especially the case in the kitchen, where I was assigned my first job ever. I had been in and out of facilities since I was twelve, so I didn't exactly have a part-time job on my résumé. I had to get up at three o'clock in the morning to make it on time. I spent the morning stuck in the hot kitchen scrubbing pots and pans next to women who didn't want to be there, rarely even getting a five-minute break to sit down. We slaved away to feed over six hundred people three meals a day, for a whole whopping seventeen cents an hour. My philosophy was that the least the prison could do in return was offer us the perk of extra food.

BLT day was the last straw. I got scolded for giving inmates too many pieces of bacon on their sandwiches—which were slightly larger than a stick of gum, not the thick-cut slices you'd eat at home. When I was told to take my grievance up with the supervisor, that's exactly what I did. I marched right to his office and really did try to be civil with him. But he put his hand to his chest and cried, "Six pieces of bacon? My god, that's plenty!" in a thick southern accent that just set me off. I launched into an hour-long tirade about how he should be ashamed of himself, and that the kitchen was so nasty with cockroaches and mice that he's lucky I don't report him to OSHA. I was so hyped up when I was done that I headed out to the back deck for a smoke break and reprised my rant for my coworkers. I was convinced I was on a crusade for what I believed was justice.

The idea that I might get in trouble didn't cross my mind until that night, when a guard showed up at my door with a write-up for the incident. *Dang*, I thought as I looked at the slip of paper. *I done it again. This ain't exactly the right path*.

Tut shook her head when the guard left. "Roommate, this ain't gonna work," she said. "You can't be snapping out on people like that. Something's going on here."

"What's that supposed to mean?" I shot back.

Tut had a whole list of incidents to draw from, including the time I cussed her out in my sleep and yelled nonsense about Yahweh being on the lamp.

"You gotta get it together," she said. "Those meds you're on are tripping you up."

I realized she was right. As much as my behavior said otherwise, I really did want to walk the right path. The prison had put me on Elavil and Risperidone, which together made me want to do nothing but eat, sleep, and complain. I'd heard from more than a few inmates that those drugs could make people mean. Maybe that's what was happening to me.

I decided to stop taking the drugs cold turkey and would refuse any more psychotropics from here on out. The problem is, when you stop taking something that alters your brain chemistry, you feel worse before you feel better. I felt straight-up crazy.

My brain was still in the process of adjusting to life without psychotropics when another inmate called me a bitch. The timing couldn't have been worse. I was sitting in the lobby eating noodles, when an older lady complained that she was down there cleaning by herself when the girl who was supposed to help her was in her cell putting on makeup.

For some reason, I decided this was unacceptable. I hollered to the girl's open cell, "Why you up there putting on makeup? You ain't even going nowhere. You need to be down here helping this lady clean up."

The girl yelled back a smart response, ending with "bitch." That was it. "Bitch" was a trigger word now. Kut was the last person who would ever call me that. I pushed myself back from the table, away from my noodles—you knew it was serious when I left my noodles behind—and stormed up the steps to the girl's cell. "I don't have four legs and a tail," I hissed before shoving her into a wall. When the girl came at me, I whaled on her. This was no slap fight. I'm talking a fist-flying, choke-holding, flat-out fight. I even tried to shove her through the top-tier walkway bars. At one point, I blacked out, conscious and yet not aware of what I was doing. I snapped back to reality when I heard someone scream.

Multiple officers swarmed the catwalk, trying to pull me off her. I fought right back, as if I could actually escape them. Years later, one of the officers would show me a spot in his wedding ring where one of his diamonds had fallen off while he was fighting me.

They hauled me straight to segregation, or seg, as we called it, to wait for a special hearing. Once again, I didn't think through what I was doing until I was alone, suffering the consequences. *I done messed up again*, I thought.

I thought for sure I'd learned my lesson this time, that I would stay on the right path from here on out. That didn't last through my special panel hearing. When I thought one of the panel members was being smug, I went off. It was "f— you" this and "f— you" that.

"I have a life sentence anyway," I taunted them. "What are you going to do to me? I ain't scared of lockup. I grew up in solitary. I ain't scared of max."

My tirade earned me a year in maximum security. That meant living on lockdown for twenty-three hours a day, with showers only three times a week. My only recreation was spent in a kennel with barbed wire around it. I couldn't leave the cell even to shower without first being cuffed through the pie flap. Then I had to kneel on the bed while the guard shackled my ankles.

I don't care, I thought defiantly. *I don't want to talk to anyone anyway.* My pod was quiet, and for the first time I slept in peace, without the constant noise of inmates yelling to one another. I found comfort in the silence, with my television and commissary to keep me company. I didn't even care about the shackles. I had pretty much come of age in shackles, so it was nothing new. The backs of my ankles are still scarred from the metal that constantly dug into my skin. After a while, you stop feeling it.

When I was due to see Mommy for the first time after being transferred to max, I realized the full weight of what I'd done. Mommy had faithfully visited me every other week, no matter who I'd cussed out or punched that week. She listened to me run my mouth and never complained that she barely got a word in edgewise. She was the only constant in my life. And now that I was on max, our visits were spent with a Plexiglas wall between us. I wasn't allowed to hug her anymore or take her hand. I deserved max security, but Mommy was the one being punished.

I can't keep doing this, I thought when I was back in my cell. *I gotta turn this around*. But I still wasn't committed. Not yet. I thought I had hit rock bottom, but it turned out I had even further to fall.

14

SELF-DESTRUCTION

After a few months on max, the thrill of watching *The Young and the Restless* on a TV in my room and reading in silence had worn off. Endless hours of listening to my radio and chilling now seemed boring. I still wasn't interested in becoming a social butterfly, but I needed some kind of conversation or interaction. Slowly, I finally took an interest in my neighbors.

My cell was in the corner of an L-shaped unit, with my door facing another. If the girl directly across from me stood in front of her window, I could make out part of her face. Otherwise, the only other sign of life I saw was if someone stuck her arm out of her pie flap. It was just like the cell I'd shared with Tut, only I wasn't allowed to leave. My day had no structure, no rhyme or reason other than the meal trays shoved through the pie flap three times a day. I never knew what time the guard would open the door to take me to the shower, or for my one hour I was allowed for recreation. Days dragged on, one after the other, with nothing to break them up.

All day long, the other inmates yelled to one another through their doors. It was the only way we could communicate. I wasn't into all that, but every once in a while, when I couldn't take the silence, I struck up a conversation with Keke, the lady next door. She was the only person I could talk to in a normal voice who could hear me through her door. We weren't exactly best friends, but it was something to do. Years later, I learned she died in prison, when a tooth abscess turned septic and shut down her organs. I can still hear her complaining about a toothache, begging to see medical. I wonder sometimes if that was the tooth that killed her.

When Keke left, a girl named Shana moved in. She'd earned a trip to max after she and four other women had an overnight slumber party—they're the reason women at TPW are still required to stand and be counted at nine o'clock every night. Shana and I bonded instantly and became fast friends. We stood at our windows talking for hours on end, gossiping about other inmates and officers. Both of us were obsessed with the show *Big Brother*, and when I found out Shana watched *General Hospital*, I started watching it too. When no one was looking, I'd pass her pizza wraps I made in my cell through the pie flap. Once, we even shared a batch of hooch I made in my sink. We thought we were drunk, but truth be told, we probably just had food poisoning.

You wouldn't think people on max would have much of an opportunity to get into trouble, but these ladies were creative. One girl on death row was always getting busted with some kind of electronics. They passed notes to one another under their doors, tying the paper to a string attached to a comb and sliding it across the hall. Other girls claimed they had sex with officers through the pie flap. I have no idea if they were telling the truth, and I'm not even sure how it would work. That pie flap has a pretty big ledge on it. But I saw more than a few officers standing at someone's door, trying to size up the possibility.

Personally, I wasn't interested in any kind of attention from men. My two weeks with Kut, not to mention the sexual assaults before that, were enough to make me swear off men altogether. The thought of someone touching me made my skin crawl. Any counseling I had access to in prison wasn't helpful. Their only attempt at rehabilitation was sending a slender lady who looked like a black Olive Oyl to check on us once a week. She asked what day it was and who was the president to make sure we weren't going crazy. If you had a problem, she offered you meds, but I wasn't having that anymore.

Only two officers made the mistake of coming at me inappropriately, but they sure didn't do it twice. There was Boyle, the resident man whore, who grabbed my butt as he escorted me upstairs, handcuffed and shackled. He caught an elbow in the gut for that. After him, there was Joyner, whose wife worked as the recreation assistant. He saw a thong I'd crocheted and had the audacity to ask to see it—on my body. I cursed that man up and down before launching into a half-hour lecture in the rec yard for how ashamed he ought to be for disrespecting his wife like that.

To me, these officers confirmed what I already knew: men were creeps who couldn't be trusted. Married or single, Christian or atheist, it seemed like every last one of them would jump at the first opportunity to get in a woman's pants, whether she was a willing participant or not.

When I wasn't talking to Shana or watching television, I was writing to pen pals. For some reason, people who heard my story wrote me letters out of the blue. They told me they were praying for me, and that they hoped I'd get out one day. I wrote back mostly out of boredom, even to the men. I figured there wasn't any harm, seeing as I wasn't going anywhere and didn't have much of a chance of running into them. I kept a calendar of who had written me and kept track of when I replied. Eventually, I had about twenty pen pals I exchanged letters with on a regular basis.

Most of my pen pals were locked up, too, with nothing but time on their hands. Somehow, I ended up writing back and forth with a forty-seven-year-old inmate named E. J., a notorious gang member. He'd been in max for thirteen years and was smart as a whip. He wrote me about how he used his time on max to keep his brain sharp. "You can't let the isolation get you down," he wrote me. "Guards expect you to break down under the pressure, to become nothing more than a dumb dog who takes orders." E. J. refused to let that happen. He was all about self-education, reading, and exercising, and sticking to a schedule.

E. J.'s letters arrived at exactly the wrong time. I was this close to snapping. In my state of mind, I couldn't put them into practice. Months of sitting in my cell all alone took their toll. I begged and pleaded to get out early, but it was no use. Prison staff said I had to finish out my year on max. The fact that I wasn't even four months into my stint on max became overwhelming. It wasn't long before I just shut down completely. I stopped talking to my neighbors, didn't come out for rec, and didn't eat from the trays shoved through my pie slot. Stuck inside that box, I caved into myself.

I became determined to use my time on max to make myself a better person. *I'm not going to rot and go crazy*, I decided. *I'm going to live my life.* I created a detailed schedule with time carved out for working out, studying textbooks, and even watching *The Young and the Restless*. I thought I was being resourceful and making good use of my time. Instead, I was back to my old obsessive ways, just like the days I spent in segregation back at the county jail.

I got my hands on a self-help book by a popular motivational speaker. I tore through page after page, soaking in each word describing how I could tap into my inner power. I was trapped in a box, feeling utterly powerless and desperate, and I devoured every word. The book said that food affects every part of your life, so I stopped eating everything except lettuce. Between the book and my lack of contact with other human beings, I lost my doggone mind. I looked down at my body and convinced myself I'd lost one hundred pounds in two days. I pressed the call button over and over, crying out for a guard to help me because I'd lost too much weight.

"That's your own fault for starving your damn self," they'd say. "Quit pressing this button."

I even wrote to my attorneys saying the prison was trying to kill me. Wendy called and asked the prison to send a mental health staff worker to check on me, but even that didn't help.

Nothing changed until the weekend, when guards led me to the visitation gallery and I saw Mommy through the glass. It had only been two weeks since I'd seen her—she still showed up faithfully every other week. But when I saw her, I felt like it had been years. I was so tripped out that I didn't even recognize my pod. I couldn't remember which way I was supposed to walk, like I was seeing everything for the first time.

Sergeant Henry, who was with me in the gallery, took pity on me and let me see Mommy without the glass between us. I threw myself into her arms, hugging her as if she were my only lifeline to the real world. Mommy handed me snacks she'd bought from the vending machine and held me as Sergeant Henry filled her in on how I'd secluded myself and gone crazy reading this self-help book.

Mommy's voice reached down to me and pulled me into reality. "Girl, throw that book away," she said bluntly. "The only power you need comes from Jesus."

"I don't know if any of that's real anymore, Mommy."

Mommy smiled sadly. "God is the only thing in this world I can be sure of. Deep down, I think you know that too. God's got you, whether you recognize it or not."

I let the tears roll as I laid my head on her lap, sobbing. Mommy was the only person who had loved me unconditionally my entire life, no matter what hell I put her through. Even when I ran away or got locked up, she never gave up on me. Even now, she trekked out to the prison every other weekend just to talk to me through a pane of glass. For the first time, I put myself in her shoes, imagining how she must feel watching me self-destruct. She had tried everything to save me—strict rules, kindness, extracurriculars, church, heart-to-heart conversations. She even offered counseling, which, of course, I refused. Nothing worked. I wouldn't allow her to help me.

Now, as the walls caved in around me and I felt like the entire world was against me, Mommy was still here. Still praying. Still loving me. Finally, her words found their way into my psyche. She was my refuge, the only person who could talk me down.

"Are you good, Toia?" she asked at the end of our visit. I nodded. Somehow, those brief moments had pulled me out of the sunken place.

I didn't pull out the Bible when I went back to my cell, but I did throw away the self-help book. Mommy was right. That book was bad news.

My visits with Mommy got me through the endless hours of sitting in my cell. I remembered her words as I forced myself to get out of my own head. I talked to my neighbors again, and I learned to cut off obsessive behaviors before they got out of control. As long as I had my visits with her every other week, I was good.

I'll never forget the day I was supposed to visit with Mommy and Missy—October 27, 2007. I bounced down the hall, ignoring the shackles around my feet, anxious for a glimpse of them. *Maybe the guard will let me hug her again*, I thought.

When I only saw Missy on the other side of the glass, I stopped short. Missy's eyes were wet and swollen, her nose red. Something wasn't right. I felt my chest tighten as panic set in.

"Where's Mommy?" I asked, not sure if I wanted to know the answer.

"She's not coming." Missy's voice caught in her throat as she attempted to choke back a sob.

Now I was really freaking out. "What are you talking about? She told me she was coming. Where is she? What happened?" I shot out the questions rapid-fire, not waiting for Missy to answer.

Finally, Missy couldn't hold it in any longer. "Mommy has cancer," she blurted out, erupting into sobs.

I felt the bottom drop out of my stomach. I'd known fear back in the days of sitting in the courtroom waiting to hear my fate. This was worse. I had already lost the biggest battle of my life, and now I faced the very real possibility that I would lose the one person who inspired me to keep fighting each day.

I climbed onto the countertop and pressed myself against the glass, trying to be as close to Missy as possible as we cried together. Missy was inconsolable and I couldn't even put my arm around her to comfort her. I slumped forward, the weight of my actions too heavy to carry. *This is all my fault*, I thought. *I'm the reason Missy can't even be with her sister on a day like this. I'm the reason Mommy is sick.* Mommy was the picture of health. She exercised, she ate right, she was the last person you'd expect to get sick. I fully believed the stress I caused her was the culprit in her cancer.

I didn't know until later that Mommy had been diagnosed with stage zero breast cancer, meaning her condition was very treatable. Thanks to her dedication to her health and her regular self-exams, she got a mammogram just in time and caught her cancer before it spread. Missy didn't fill me in on the details. All I knew was I was only nineteen years old and I needed my mother.

Back in my cell, I fell all the way apart. I heard Shana calling my name, asking if I was okay. I was sobbing too hard to give her much of a reply. It didn't help that PBS aired a documentary on death that very night. I boo-hooed through the whole thing, especially the part when a man made funeral arrangements for his father who had just died of cancer.

I can't keep doing this, I realized through my tears. *I am killing my mother. I have to change.* But it wasn't just my life. Every action had a ripple effect, hurting the people I loved the most.

If I'd ever wondered what rock bottom felt like, this was it. This was my pivot point. *I'm going to turn around*, I thought. *Even if I'm stuck in prison the rest of my life, I can still have a life with meaning right where I am.* I didn't just owe that to myself. I owed it to Mommy.

My commitment paid off. After ten months, I was let off max due to good behavior. I was still living in the segregation unit, but I was allowed to come into the lobby with other inmates, I could shower every day, and I could work. This time, my job was much better than kitchen duty. I got the coveted assignment in the lobby area of the building, where I was responsible for cleaning the unit management offices, the visitation area, and the kitchen. I roamed around looking for tasks to fill my time—as long as I was busy, I wasn't stuck behind a locked door. I'd had enough of that.

Soon, a new policy came out allowing me to be housed in the main compound with a close security designation. Rich's words echoed through my mind as I immediately signed up for every class I could take. I was determined to stay on the right path this time. Maybe I was only accepted into an anger management class, but I still made sure I kept myself too occupied to get into trouble. When I wasn't working or cleaning the pod, I was exercising or reading anything I could get my hands on.

Not everyone had the same mind-set. To many women, being on close security was a rite of passage. It was a badge of honor, proof that they were troublemakers you didn't want to mess with. Getting off max was a ticket back to their old ways. I watched many of them get hauled back to our old unit after running around like an animal released from a cage, going on rampages, slamming doors, hitting their fists into their hands, and screaming every curse word or threat they could think of.

Others, like Shana, quietly went back to their old ways of getting high. We were roommates for a few months now that we were in the main compound, giving me a front-row seat to her backslide. She and a group of friends would pop and snort pills together until they were numb to the world around them. I wasn't having that. I was well aware drugs were a major factor in my own downfall, and I wasn't fixing to play that game again. I knew drugs had already cost Shana her freedom and her child—somebody shot her baby up with Demerol and threw him off the balcony. It frustrated me to see her become caught up in the same trap. She moved out of our room after a while so she could live with a girl named Cincinnati, someone who would help her get drugs. Finally, after avoiding her in the lobby and at rec time, I ran into her at the top-tier railing of the pod. I knew it was time to speak up.

"Why are you doing this to yourself?" I demanded. "Most of the time it's like you're not even here. Why do you want to get high like that?"

Shana looked me dead in the face. "Look around!" she shouted. "Of course I don't want to be here. Who would? I just want my mind to be somewhere else."

"I don't know how we're supposed to be friends when you're tripping like this."

Her eyes narrowed. "Look at you. You acting brand-new."

I shrugged. "I guess we're on different paths now."

I knew Shana was intent on walking the very path Rich had told me to avoid. If I was going to choose the right path, I had to leave Shana behind. I owed it to Mommy to do the right thing for once.

But the right path was starting to feel pretty lonely. I wondered if anyone else felt the way I did, if other inmates wanted a better life too. I didn't know how close I was to meeting the people who would save my life.

15

PROVING MY WORTH

Now that I was back from max, I knew I needed a good influence. From my little group in alternative school to Trina to Kut, I had a long track record of allowing people who didn't deserve my trust to lead me down a path to destruction.

I decided this time it would be different. After stepping back from my friendship with Shana, I sat back, watching for people who lived the kind of life I wanted for myself. That's when two law library clerks caught my eye.

Erika and Tabitha lived a few doors down from me. While everyone else was running around, acting like an idiot, they were always sitting at a table studying or talking about *Masterpiece Theatre* or some other PBS show. They were nothing like me, and everything I wanted to be. *These chicks probably wouldn't want me around*, I thought glumly. We'd never really talked, but I'm sure they'd heard I was the girl always cussing somebody out or getting in fights. Not the kind of girl they'd want to welcome at their study table. And yet, I couldn't get the idea out of my head. I wanted to be around them, but I wasn't sure how.

I also knew they were taking college courses through a private Christian college called Lipscomb University. I'd heard about the Lipscomb Initiative for Education, or LIFE program, about a month after coming to TPW, when I heard Dr. Richard Goode speaking about it in the prison's visitation area. He told us they were offering their high-dollar education to inmates for free. Everybody who was accepted would study side-by-side with students from the outside. I watched him speak, my mind drifting back to that seventh-grade trip to take the ACT. Mommy always thought I would make something of myself. She thought I'd go to college and get a degree. *I'd never had that dream for myself, but as I heard Dr. Goode speak*, I thought Lipscomb was exactly the kind of program my attorney, Rich, would have told me to take. Back then, I didn't care much about earning a degree. I just wanted to do whatever I could to get out of prison. *Maybe a degree would help*, I thought.

I applied right away but wasn't accepted with the first bunch of students. I had to have been at the prison for at least a year before I was eligible. At the time, I just shrugged my shoulders. I was looking at nothing but time ahead of me. There would always be another chance to apply. But I remembered Erika and Tabitha were selected for that first class. You could just tell there was something different about them, the way they went around studying and taking their classes so seriously. It was like they had a new sense of purpose.

One day, when I saw them studying in the library, I made up my mind to approach them. "What are you doing?" I asked.

"Homework," Erika said.

"We're taking criminal procedure at Lipscomb," Tabitha added.

"Oh really?" After my long history with the judicial system, a class that actually impacted my life sounded intriguing. "What kinds of things do you talk about?"

I sat at the table with them as they filled me in on their class. I grew up hating school, but now I found myself hanging on their every word. *This is it*, I thought. *This is my chance to live a better life.* I remembered the look of pride on Mommy's face when I was chosen for the gifted program back in elementary school. She drove me across town to take the ACT when I was only thirteen years old. She loved nothing more than bragging to her friends about how smart I was. I imagined giving her that same feeling again, hearing her say, "Well all right now, look at you!" the way she always used to when she was bursting with pride. I would get into Lipscomb for Mommy, and Erika and Tabitha were the ladies who would get me there.

I kept an eye out for them each time I passed the library, and if they were studying, I sat down with them. I did puzzles as we talked and they flipped through law books, taking notes.

I didn't understand why these ladies were as calm and cool as they were. I'd heard around the pod that both of them were in prison for killing abusive exes.

They didn't ask to be thrown in the situation they were in. But somehow, they weren't angry. They weren't running around cussing out guards and getting in other girls' faces. They still led a fulfilling life, even in the prison halls. *I wonder if I can do that too*, I thought.

Today, Tabitha is out of prison, but Erika is still there, serving as the law clerk. She never once got into trouble, and she was so busy helping other inmates appeal their cases that she didn't appeal her own. Unfortunately, America's prisons are full of women who were arrested in similar circumstances. They're forgotten, left to waste away in prison, with no one interested in showing them mercy.

"I think they're choosing a new class of students for Lipscomb in December," Tabitha told me one day. "You should apply!"

The chances of me getting in weren't looking good. I couldn't be accepted into Lipscomb, or even any vocational classes, until the prison took me off the close security classification. Technically, you only had to stay on close security for six months, but since the prison is only required to reclassify inmates once a year, I was stuck on close until December.

I marched down to the office of Connie Seabrooks, the prison education principal. I had met her back when I was first tested for my education placement. Even though I already had my GED, I had to take the test anyway, and Miss Seabrooks had told me I'd scored extremely high. I felt sure she would give me a chance, knowing I had the brains to handle Lipscomb.

"Miss Seabrooks, how can I get into Lipscomb?" I asked as soon as I burst into her office. "I know I'm still on close. But I gotta get into this program. Please. You gotta help me."

Miss Seabrooks motioned to the upholstered wooden chair in front of her desk. "Why don't you have a seat? Let's take a look here."

She turned to her computer, clicking and typing away. I stared at her flying fingers, imagining what they were doing to the screen in front of her.

"Now, to get into Lipscomb, you have to be discipline-free for six months," Miss Seabrooks said. "You have to get a letter of recommendation from your work site and your unit manager. And you have to pass a test."

I nodded. "And that's all I gotta do?"

Miss Seabrooks smiled gently. "Cyntoia, if you really want to do this, you have to stay out of trouble. This particular program is very limited. They only accept fifteen students, and they usually receive at least forty applications. It's pretty stiff to get in."

"Yes, ma'am," I said. "I can do it. I know I can."

"I believe you," she said, looking me in the eye. "Why don't you come by my office sometime? Maybe we can talk. I'll check in with you, make sure you're staying on the right path."

"Yes, ma'am," I said, nodding eagerly. "I can do that."

It was the first time anyone who wasn't Mommy seemed to care whether I stayed out of trouble or raised Cain all day long. Some of the prison staffers were clearly there to collect a paycheck, but Miss Seabrooks seemed like she cared about helping people get better. In some ways, she reminded me of Mommy. She talked to me with respect, like I was actually a young woman. If Miss Seabrooks believed I could stay out of trouble, then I would prove her right.

I left Miss Seabrooks's office determined to keep my head down and do the right thing. But following through with that commitment was another thing entirely. It seemed like every day brought a smart comment from some chick trying to bring me down. Before I knew it, I was cussing another girl out, launching into another tirade. While I wasn't getting write-ups, I also wasn't turning my life around like I'd promised myself I would.

While I was trying to get into Lipscomb, I'd stop by Miss Seabrooks's office every once in a while and she'd invite me to chat with her.

"I know you've been getting into trouble," she said. "What's going on?"

I shook my head. "I try not to, but you oughta hear what these fools say to me. I gotta defend myself."

Miss Seabrooks nodded, quiet for a moment. "That must be hard. But you don't always have to fire back. You can ignore them. You can talk it out. Using profanity and tearing someone down isn't the right way."

"I'm not sure how to do that," I finally said.

She paused. "Do you ever go to church?"

"Nah," I said, shaking my head. "I don't believe in that stuff anymore. My momma used to bring me to church. I know about the Bible and all that. But God doesn't seem to care much about me, seeing all that's happened to me so far. So, I don't care much about him."

I expected her to argue with me and defend her so-called God. But she was quiet. "I can understand why you might feel that way," she finally said. "But Cyntoia, your life isn't going to get better until you find a relationship with him. We can only do so much to change ourselves. God is the one with the power to transform our lives. And if you let him, he can do that for you too."

I stared at my work boots, the linoleum tile, anything but Miss Seabrooks. Normally this God talk would have sent me running out the door, but she seemed so sincere. I could tell she really believed what she was saying. The least I could do was listen.

"Do you have a Bible?" she asked me. I nodded.

"I want you to read it," she said. "Try reading it every day. See what happens. You just might find that it's easier to ignore the other girls and not get in so many arguments."

"Yes, ma'am," I said. I doubted she was right. I still didn't crack the Bible, but I'd be lying if I said I didn't think about it.

Miss Seabrooks kept up the God talk, but I still found myself flopping in a chair in front of her desk time and time again. She'd hand me another book to read, always about God, or challenge me to read a passage from the Bible.

One day, after yet another profanity-laced tirade, Miss Seabrooks called me to her office to chat.

"I get the feeling you don't think much of yourself, Cyntoia," she said.

I shifted in my seat, suddenly uncomfortable. "I think about myself just fine."

Miss Seabrooks touched my arm. "You are a smart, intelligent, beautiful girl, and it doesn't matter what anybody says to you. When somebody says something you don't like, you don't have to respond. You know why? Because your value comes from the Lord, not what anybody else thinks."

"Yes, ma'am," I said softly. I wasn't sure what else to say. The truth was I wasn't sure I believed her. Besides Mommy, no one seemed to have much use for me except what my body could do for them. No one, it seemed, was looking out for me—not when I was on the run and certainly not in prison. If I didn't stand up for myself, no one else would. All I had going for me in prison was the confidence that most other inmates were too afraid to mess with me.

"Cyntoia, your life isn't going to change until you get into a relationship with God," Miss Seabrooks told me over and over again.

"You're trying to take the right path all on your own and get yourself out of this place. But it's never going to happen without God guiding you."

"I don't need no God," I scoffed. "I got this by myself."

Miss Seabrooks looked deep into my eyes, as if she were speaking words she'd just received from heaven. "I believe God isn't going to let you out of this prison until you come to him," she said. "Once you return to him, he will set you free."

I thought of all the women around me, hollering at me, calling me a bitch, saying I was white. Their words made me feel like I was nothing. But was it possible they were the ones who didn't matter?

Maybe their opinions didn't count. But what about mine? I wasn't ready to accept that I didn't have to prove my value. After all, I was the one who had screwed up every opportunity that was ever handed to me. I'm the one who walked away from Mommy, who let men tell me how much I was worth. I'm the one who killed somebody, who got myself condemned to life. There had to be more, and I had to show myself. I dreamed of getting into Lipscomb, acing my classes, and proving to everyone how smart I was. Once I got that diploma, everyone would see I was worth more than my life sentence let on. I wouldn't let myself be thrown away. I would make something of myself, whether anyone believed I could or not.

In addition to staying out of trouble, Miss Seabrooks told me I needed to take a career management success course and pass an anger management class. I wasn't thrilled about either class—they sounded stupid, and I doubted that their pathetic anger management class could help me, but if that's what it took to get into Lipscomb, I'd do it without complaining. The problem was, these courses didn't require much of me outside of class time. I still had my job as a dorm aide, but I quickly learned there was only so much to clean in my pod. I had more time on my hands than I had activities. And boredom, it turned out, is a dangerous thing.

My first concern was figuring out a way to buy the basic toiletries

I needed to get by. Some people don't realize this, but prisons don't provide you with the basic necessities beyond toilet paper—a brand called Feather Soft, which is anything but—and maxi pads that don't even have wings and are pretty much useless. Everything else, you have to buy from the prison commissary using the wages you earn at your job. I was only making a measly seventeen cents per hour, and half of that was deducted by the state to pay for a handwriting expert they'd used in my prosecution. That left me with about ten dollars a month to pay for soap, shampoo, and deodorant. Those items were already a stretch, and anything else was out of the question.

I didn't want to ask Mommy for help, even though I'm sure she would have gladly given me anything I needed. She was divorced and paying for her cancer treatments, all on a teacher's salary. When I asked Missy, I could practically hear her roll her eyes through the phone.

"Can't you be self-sufficient?" she said.

"How the heck am I supposed to do that?" I demanded. "I'm in prison, in case you forgot."

"Well, you can do something to make extra money."

"No, actually, I really can't."

It was true. A side hustle of any kind was strictly banned in prison. They didn't want you earning money off the books. Even so, most girls did it out of necessity. After one too many nights crying, not knowing where my next bar of soap was coming from, I knew I had to come up with some kind of gig while still flying under the radar. I didn't want to do anything that would put my chances of getting into Lipscomb into jeopardy.

I chose the least risky options I could think of. I braided hair. I arched eyebrows. I cooked for people. I made eye shadow from baby powder mixed with chalk dust from my friend Tasha's arts and crafts supply box. The other inmates paid me by ordering commissary items for me from their accounts. Every scheme I came up with was successful at first, but it never lasted long. You can only buy so many squares of eye shadow or plates of fried chicken. I was always coming up with the next hustle. Frankly, it was exhausting.

Then Peanut showed up. The Tennessee Department of Correction transferred her to Nashville after she became notorious for smuggling tobacco, weed, cologne, and jewelry in the Memphis prison. Without the option to buy tobacco from the commissary, the door was wide open for a black market. The Nashville prison was dry when Peanut arrived, but that would soon change. She sauntered in with a big gold chain around her neck and crystal studs in her ears that everyone whispered were really diamonds. Everyone was intrigued. I'd be lying if I said I wasn't too.

Peanut hadn't been in Nashville for two weeks before I found myself sitting next to her on a metal picnic table in the pod. We both lived on the east side of the prison, and out of nowhere, she struck up a conversation with me, telling me all about what life in the Memphis prison was like. Eventually, she told me she was looking to start selling tobacco in Nashville, but none of the leads she'd followed had been successful so far. "Do you know any cool officers?" she asked me one day.

I should have said no and moved on. Instead, I thought of my friend Officer Perry. I cleaned her office and helped her out here and there, and in return she brought me lip gloss, perfume, and hair accessories.

Instead of connecting Peanut directly with Perry, I became the middleman. Perry brought pouches of tobacco and hid them at the bottom of her trash can. I came in early each morning to clean her office and stuck pouches in the front of my pants. I packed the tobacco in plastic wrap and stuck little portions in torn-off fingers of latex gloves. Then, I brought them to Peanut in exchange for items of my choice from the commissary. I'm talking hundreds of dollars of food, candy, and hygiene every week. I went from struggling to fill one cubbyhole in my cell to filling seven cubbyholes with commissary—I borrowed three of my roommate's.

In the meantime, six months came and went without a single write-up. This fact alone was by the grace of God—I was certainly no angel.

I popped in Miss Seabrooks's office right at six months to the day from the first time I'd stopped in.

"I'm six months discipline-free," I announced.

Miss Seabrooks smiled broadly. "Well okay then," she said. "Sit down. Let's see what you need to do now."

The letters of recommendation were no problem—now that I was trying to stay out of trouble, I wasn't on the officers' blacklist anymore. I completed anger management and received a positive recommendation from the career management success teacher. The only roadblock standing in my way was my close security classification. The unit manager said he wouldn't take me off close until my classification date, which was a year after I was taken off max, and that wasn't until December. I'd be cutting it close.

"I think you can go ahead and take the entrance exam," Miss Seabrooks said. "We'll just trust you'll get off close in time."

I could barely contain my excitement. This was the chance I'd been waiting for. The chance to do something with my life, the chance to make Mommy proud, the chance to prove to everyone I was more than my sentence. Then suddenly, I frowned. "Miss Seabrooks, do you think I'll get in?" I waited, not sure if I wanted to know the answer.

Miss Seabrooks paused. "You are a lifer," she said bluntly. "There are a lot of people here in this prison who think lifers shouldn't be in this program. They think it should be geared toward people who are ready to leave prison, not someone who'll never leave these walls."

My face fell. I felt condemned all over again until Miss Seabrooks reached over and touched my chin, gently pushing it up.

"But I'm not one of them," she said. "Whether you get out of prison one day or not, you should be afforded the opportunity to have a better life."

Peanut signed up to take the entrance exam with me. We sat next to each other the day of the test. I was the first to finish and proudly handed my sheet to the teacher. I knew I'd done well before I ever received a score.

"How do you think you did?" I asked Peanut, not letting on I'd seen her struggling out of the corner of my eye.

She shrugged. "Fine, I guess," she said.

The results confirmed what both of us already knew. I had passed with flying colors. Peanut, unfortunately, did not.

"I don't care," she said defiantly. "I already got a full-time job selling tobacco." But a wedge was driven between us that day, whether either of us wanted to admit it or not.

Weeks later, I received the news I'd waited months to hear—I was classified off close security. Relief flooded my body as I immediately thought of Lipscomb. I hadn't heard anyone say they were chosen for the program yet. It wasn't too late. Maybe, just maybe, there was a spot for me. I'd passed the test, gathered the recommendation letters, even passed an in-person interview. I'd stayed out of trouble. I'd done everything Miss Seabrooks had asked me to do. If that didn't get me in, I didn't know what would.

That same day, a guard showed up at my door. "Miss Seabrooks wants to see you," he said.

My heart pounded as I skipped down to her conference room and found myself seated with a roomful of girls. Quickly I counted—fifteen girls, including me. We looked at one another nervously, wondering if we made it.

Finally, Miss Seabrooks walked in to break the suspense. "Ladies, I am so thrilled to announce that each of you was chosen for the Lipscomb Initiative for Education program," she said proudly, her eyes beaming.

As the room erupted with shouts and squeals, I felt my heart swell with joy. My whole life up to that point had pretty much been one big disappointment. I'd dropped out of school, run away from home, hung out with the wrong crowd, and ended up in a nightmare. Being locked up with a life sentence was the cherry on top of a screwed-up life. I'd tried since the day I came to TPW to walk the right path, but I'd failed over and over again. This was the breakthrough I had longed for.

I thought of the years Mommy had suffered, all the while thinking I was intent on throwing my life away.

I knew how much my education meant to her, and how proud she would be. In the beginning, I'd wanted to get into Lipscomb for her, but now I wanted it for myself too. I knew I was better than the choices I had made and the horror that had happened to me. It wasn't too late for me. I could still live a good life.

There was just one more thing I had to do. I had to walk away from my arrangement with Peanut. With each day that went by, I grew more and more uneasy that my cover would be blown. I could end up on max. If that happened, I could kiss Lipscomb goodbye. My well-stocked toiletry cabinet wasn't worth it anymore. This was another moment where two paths stretched in front of me. This time, I would choose the right one. I told Peanut I was out.

Not long after that, I learned Peanut was caught and put on max. I had ducked out just in time.

16

THE HANDS AND FEET OF CHRIST

Butterflies filled my stomach as I stepped through the prison classroom doorway and into my first Lipscomb course, judicial process. I was twenty-one years old, and I hadn't had a first day of school in years. I felt the same nervous excitement I felt as a kid. At this point, my only goals were to get the heck out of prison and make Mommy proud. My mind was on how Lipscomb could help me accomplish both.

The classroom was filled with plastic chairs connected to metal desks, all set up in one big circle so everyone could see each other. *That's kinda neat*, I thought. Each desk was waiting for a student with a copy of *Changing Lenses*, by Howard Zehr, and a little blue notebook that was stamped with the words "Blue Book."

I'd heard a former prosecutor named Preston Shipp was teaching the class. I wasn't too excited about that part. I figured he was probably an old white dude who would teach us about how we need to lock up all the hardened criminals in prison and throw away the key. *I'm gonna tell him something about that*, I thought.

I sat down and flipped through my book, waiting for the other students to arrive. While I hadn't been in school for a while, there wasn't a doubt in my mind I could ace this class. Heck, I pretty much lived the subject matter. Anyone who wants to know what the judicial process is should just ask me or look up my case.

My only true nervousness came from the fact that Lipscomb was a Christian university. And by now, I was most definitely not a Christian. Quite the opposite. Back in the county jail, I would have told you I believed in God. I didn't think I had much of a choice. He was the only one who could get me out of that mess, as far as I knew. But all that ended with my life sentence. I cried out to God and heard nothing in return. Seeing as Jesus had left me to rot in prison, I wasn't interested in bowing down and praying to him. Still, I was raised to believe in something. Letting go of that completely just felt wrong. So, I looked into it further. I spent hours researching religions and found stories from ancient mythologies about floods and virgin births and God sacrificing himself for people. *Whoever wrote the Bible freaking stole all of this*, I thought. *This is just the American interpretation. It's all lies.* In my mind, there was no God. There wasn't even such a thing as a soul. All I felt inside me was a deep, dark anger. I felt deceived, furious that I had ever believed a god could really save me.

The people in charge of Lipscomb had told me it didn't matter if I was a Christian or not, but I walked into class that day with my defenses up. I just knew the Christians of the class would judge me for not believing what they did. *I'm not gonna let them convert me*, I thought. If anything, I was ready to prove to them that this whole God story they believed wasn't true.

Other students filed in, some wearing the same blue prison uniform as me, others wearing street clothes. One of the coolest parts about the Lipscomb program was that it included both incarcerated students, who they called "inside students," and free students, who they called "outside students." The leaders figured we could all learn from each other. The kids from the outside world didn't know our stories or why we were in prison. All they knew was we were accepted into Lipscomb, just like they were, even though we wore prison-issued blue jeans stamped with the Tennessee Department of Correction logo and blue shirts, while they wore khakis cut in the latest style, polo shirts, dresses. These kids smelled like Pantene and Calvin Klein Eternity, not the bar soap and perfume smuggled in Visine bottles we all sported. Their hair was gelled and neatly parted. Their faces practically glowing. We were all students, but these kids got to load up in their cars and leave when class was over. The rest of us would have to be back in our pods in time for count.

I had to laugh to myself as I looked at these precious little white kids around me. They all looked so earnest as they talked to one another, like they really could fix anything if they put their minds to it.

"You know," I overheard a white boy in khakis say, "if everyone came to a prison and sat down with the men and women there, it would totally change their minds about criminal justice."

Oh bless your heart, I thought. It didn't change my DA's mind. It didn't change Detective Robinson's mind. Some people just don't care. But this kid didn't know that yet. I was the same age as the outside students, but I felt very much like their elder. We came from completely different walks of life. Looking at them, I wondered how my life might have turned out if I had made different choices. Would I have ended up in college too? Try as I might, I couldn't picture myself as one of them. I couldn't even picture myself out of my prison-issued uniform, much less on the grassy quad of Lipscomb University. My self-image as an inmate was too ingrained. *This is who I am*, I thought.

"Can you believe these kids?" another inside student whispered. I turned to find Ashlee Sellars next to me. I'd seen her around my pod but never talked to her much. She was strikingly beautiful, with long brown hair she usually pulled into a ponytail. I'd always wanted to talk to her but didn't have much of a chance. She was the kind of girl who usually kept to herself. The kind of girl who was the positive influence I needed. And now here she was in Lipscomb.

"Mm-hmm, these kids about to find out how it is," I said with a laugh.

"You wanna sit by me?" she asked.

"Sure!"

I took my seat next to her in the circle of desks and looked around the classroom, searching for someone who looked like Uncle Sam to stand up and get us started. Instead, some young guy walked up to the front of the classroom and introduced himself as Preston. I about fell out of my chair. *That's our professor?* I thought, incredulous. He didn't look like any prosecutor who'd ever gone up against me in court. With his reddish-brown hair and goofy grin, he looked like a cheesy youth pastor, not a fierce attorney.

Preston told us we'd spend the next semester discussing indictment, arraignment, and all stages of the judicial process. Every Wednesday night, we'd come to class and examine the roles of victim, offender, attorney, and the other different roles people play in the criminal justice system. Then, we would write a five-hundred-word response in our Blue Book based on our discussion, which we would later share with someone else in the class. If you were incarcerated, Preston had you switch Blue Books with a free student, and vice versa. I didn't mind that part. I could whip out an essay like nobody's business.

I went into the class with my defenses up, ready to strike the second I felt judged. The first time someone brought up God in a discussion, I shot my hand up. I barely waited for Preston to call on me before I blurted out, "Excuse me, not everybody believes that. Some people think that ain't true."

I looked around, waiting for the attack I was sure to come. Instead, I saw a few outside students nodding.

"You have a good point there," one girl said. "We can't forget that not everybody believes in God."

It was all I could do to keep my mouth from hanging open. This had to be a onetime thing. The Christians I knew from my churchgoing days didn't listen to anybody who didn't agree with them. They just knew they were right, and they loved ripping the dreaded unbeliever to shreds. These people were different. It didn't matter how many times I argued with them and insisted God wasn't real. They listened. They responded kindly. And they treated me and the other inmates the same as they did their fellow free students.

They clearly don't know what I did, I thought at first. *If they really knew who I was, that I'm a murderer, a whore, they wouldn't give me the time of day.* I felt like I was hiding in plain sight, and that one day, when the truth came out, they'd see how ugly I really was. But it soon became clear they didn't care about any of that. It's not like my story was a secret. Any one of them could have gone home and done a simple Google search to find out I was really a monster. But if they did, nobody brought it up. Nobody acted different.

"We're all one community," they'd say when anyone tried to make a distinction between us and them. "Not one of us is perfect. We're all sinners. And in God's eyes, all sins are the same, whether they put you in prison or not."

Other than Mommy, I'd never had anyone from the outside world treat me like I wasn't a dangerous threat to society. Once, I tore my ACL within forty-five seconds of joining in a soccer game in the ballyard. Prison guards shackled me up and shuttled me to the nearest hospital for surgery. As they wheeled me in, I saw mothers clutch their children, turning them so they wouldn't even have to look at such an evil person. Patients sitting in the waiting room looked at the tile floor, the fluorescent lights, anywhere but at me. My prison uniform and chains around my waist were like a neon sign screaming, "Hey everyone, stay away from this lady! She's obviously unhinged and dangerous!" These Lipscomb kids were different. Every week, they talked to me and the other inmates about what we'd done that day, our families, normal topics you'd discuss with any other person. When they said our class was like a family, I actually believed them.

Up until now, calling someone a Christian felt like saying a dirty word. I didn't even feel right using that description about my new friends. They weren't like the Sunday Christians I'd known all my life. These people, from the students to the professors, were the closest thing to Jesus I'd ever seen.

The students weren't the only ones I had misjudged. I went into this class fully expecting to hate Preston. In my experience, prosecutors were pretty much the devil incarnate. They didn't bother to get to know you or find out what circumstances led you to commit the crime. They defined you by the worst mistake you ever made and refused to entertain any narrative that might not fit that mold. I was sure Preston was no different—just another attorney who would demonize me if it served his purposes.

But even I had to admit he was an incredible professor. Each Wednesday night, it seemed like he crawled around inside my head, examining every belief and prejudice I had, testing them, and leaving them strengthened, dissolved, or replaced. I thought I could have taught that class since I had the most experience with judicial process, but Preston wouldn't let us stick to the surface. When some of the outside kids said juveniles shouldn't get life sentences, he pressed them. "What about a seventeen-year-old who kills someone?" he asked. "What if two years isn't enough to give them the rehabilitation they need?"

He introduced me to the idea of restorative justice, and the practice of shalom. Instead of condemning and punishing, he taught us about restoring balance and repairing what was damaged. Instead of throwing a criminal away, he taught us about reconciling the person who had done wrong to the person who was wronged.

Yes! I thought excitedly. *This is exactly what we need!* I thought back to the courtroom, seeing the mother of the man I'd killed sitting across the aisle. I wanted more than anything to tell her I was sorry for what I'd done, but my attorney, Kathy, wasn't having it.

"You can't do that," she said. "It could tank your case."

I realized how truly messed up the system was. Don't we want people to feel remorse, to swallow their pride and reach out to the person they hurt? There's no room for reconciliation in the criminal justice system, not the way it's set up today. I never got to apologize to my victim's mother. She would die before I had the chance. Now Preston taught me another way.

Preston was the first person I'd ever heard put my thoughts on the adversarial nature of the criminal justice system into words. "Why is it the state that's against the person being tried?" he asked. "Why is it always the state versus someone? The victim's family doesn't get a say. Even if they wanted to give the perpetrator leniency, they don't have that power anymore."

I listened, thinking back to a kid I knew at Woodland Hills. He got locked up at twelve for killing someone and was tried as an adult, but they kept him in juvenile because he was so young. For years, his victim's family had pushed for leniency, but the state wasn't having it. I'd always thought that part of the system was so messed up. Hearing Preston say the same thing blew my mind.

"The state is put in the position of an adversary," Preston continued. "The district attorney doesn't talk to the person facing charges. They don't know you. All they know is the worst thing someone ever did."

In that moment, I felt seen. All this time spent wondering why the DA hated me so much, why he seemed to have a personal vendetta against me, finally made sense. It was the system.

Our discussions also forced me to look at the DA who prosecuted my case with new eyes. All this time, I'd thought of him as a heartless jerk who would love nothing more than to see me die in prison. I wanted him to look at me as a human being, when I'd refused to do the same for him. Maybe there was more to him than I realized. Maybe he was so focused on keeping the community safe and stopping violent crime that he didn't realize there was another side to the story. Yes, the conclusions he reached were still wrong, but I realized his intentions probably started from a good place. If Preston had been a prosecutor and could be a good person, then maybe other prosecutors could too. For the first time, I let go of the bitterness and anger I'd held on to toward my DA.

Weeks flew by as I settled into life as a Lipscomb student.

In my class, I raised my hand every single time. I wasn't scared to speak up or play devil's advocate. And when I spoke, people listened. I saw even the outside students staring at me intently, nodding as I spoke. They looked at me like I mattered. Like I had something to say.

So when I overheard outside students talking crazy during class breaks, I spoke up. I'd stare them down as they joked about what they did over the weekend and frown. "You were smoking pot, weren't you?" I demanded. "You want me to reserve a cell for you in my pod?"

I grew bolder with each exchange. Like the time a girl who was in Lipscomb on a scholarship told me she wanted clear braces, but they cost $5,000 and she couldn't afford them.

"I'm thinking about being an escort to help pay for them," she said as casually as she'd tell me about applying for a job. "All you have to do is go to dinner with an old guy and he gives you money."

I held up my hand to stop her. I couldn't take another word. "Let me explain something to you," I said bluntly. "You gonna wind up dead somewhere is what's gonna happen. You gonna wind up in Russia. Girl, you're tripping if you think that's gonna work out for you."

The kids would laugh and say, "Cyntoia, you're crazy." But they listened.

My relationships with the inside students grew too. I sat by Ashlee every class and started hanging out with her after class was over. We'd do homework in the computer lab or play volleyball on the rec field.

She had one heck of a serve, but I got to be pretty good myself. Ashlee was sure of herself in a way I'd never been. She knew exactly what she wanted to do when her sentence was up. She was always telling me about how she wanted to be a mom and help people. Man, I stopped dreaming a long time ago, I realized. Even when I signed up for Lipscomb, I wasn't thinking about myself or what I wanted to do. What if I could really do something? What if I could get out of this prison and help people somehow? For the first time in years, I let myself imagine what my life could be like beyond the prison walls. I pictured myself as an advocate somewhere, helping to keep young girls from making stupid mistakes and winding up where I did. If these Lipscomb kids listened to me, maybe other kids would too.

Even being around Preston was a healing experience. Preston wasn't like anyone else I'd ever met. We didn't talk outside of our exchanges in class, but he seemed like he was actually cool. He was the first man I'd met who was faithful to his wife and never looked me up and down. I'd held firm to my belief that all men were pervs, but he and the other Lipscomb boys treated me with nothing but respect.

It was an ordinary class in April 2009. I raised my hand more than a few times—by now, everyone knew I was outspoken, and I never kept my opinions to myself. We laughed together, swapped Blue Books, and wrote down our reading assignment for the week. Every once in a while, I noticed Preston staring at me with a concerned look on his face.

What the heck is his problem? I thought, thinking maybe I had something stuck in my teeth or my tag was hanging out of my shirt.

Preston stopped me on my way out the door. "Are you okay?" he asked.

"Uh, yeah," I said, smiling. "I'm great! See you next week!" I went right back to waving goodbye to my friends as I floated down the hallway.

What was that all about? I wondered. The next morning, I got my answer.

"Brown, you got legal mail," a guard called. My heart leaped. It had to be something about my appeal.

My attorneys had promised we would fight my conviction and they weren't lying. They filed an appeal practically the day after I got my life sentence. You've got to understand, the appeals process is long, slow, and painful. You have to file a brief, then wait for a response, which can take forever because the state has such a big caseload that there's almost always at least one extension. Then you file a response to the response and play the waiting game again. Then you wait to see if they'll grant you an oral argument in appellate court. If you get it, each side gets twenty minutes to argue their case. Then you can wait six months to a year to find out the decision. It's excruciating. The whole thing took nearly three years.

I always believed my appeal would be successful. My attorneys had thrown every argument in the book at the state, hoping at least something would stick. Something had to succeed. There was no way the state would uphold my life sentence. I told myself that every day. When you have a life sentence, you have no choice but to hope. It's all you have. After starting Lipscomb, I had it all figured out. Once I got a good plea bargain out of my appeal, I'd keep taking Lipscomb courses and finish college when I got out. I'd go to law school, become a youth advocate, and reform the justice system. The way those young Lipscomb kids thought was contagious. I now believed I could change the world, too, and I was itching to get out and do just that.

I practically skipped to the visitation gallery to pick up my mail. *This could be my second chance*, I thought

I signed to receive my mail, just like I'd rehearsed in my head a thousand times. I imagined myself screaming and jumping up and down. The mail clerk would wonder what on earth I was so excited about until I showed her the good news, then she'd jump and scream right along with me. *Wait'll I tell everybody at Lipscomb about this*, I thought. *Preston will be so happy for me.*

But when I read the first line, I thought for sure my heart must have stopped beating.

"I am sorry we did not prevail with the Court on any of our appeal issues," my attorney wrote. I stopped reading. My eyes were too clouded with tears to read the other forty-four pages of reasons why I didn't deserve a second chance.*

Maybe Preston can help me fight this, I thought. The LIFE program's literary magazine was having a reading that night. I decided I'd tell him what happened, and beg him to jump into action. I swallowed my emotions and wiped away my tears, pretending to be okay as I frantically searched for Preston. But he didn't show up.

It wasn't until Friday that I read the full opinion. I had an appointment with my friend Erika, the law clerk, to help me figure out where I should go from here. I sat down, tears already forming in my eyes, ready to fall apart until I saw her staring at me, a no-nonsense look on her face.

"Are you done?" she asked impatiently.

"What now?" Didn't she know I just had my hopes and dreams crushed?

"We're not gonna have a pity party for you. We're going to look at this and see what we can do now." I could tell she meant business. That's how Erika was. She didn't waste time on tears. Tears couldn't get you out of prison.

"Well okay," I said, opening the envelope holding the opinion. "Let's see what we got."

We sat there reading along until I flipped to the second page. I felt my stomach drop, the blood rush out of my face. "Oh my god," I gasped.

---

* Cyntoia Brown and Preston Shipp, "Misjudging," in *And the Criminals with Him: Essays in Honor of Will D. Campbell and All the Reconciled*, eds. William D. Campbell and Richard C. Goode (Eugene, OR: Wipf and Stock Publishers, 2012), 225–30.

There it was, where the parties of the case were named. "Preston Shipp, Assistant Attorney General."

"But . . . but how could he do this to me?" I sputtered. This man was supposed to be my friend, my professor. I trusted him, and I knew he wanted to see me succeed. Yet here I find out he used his intelligence and excellent debating skills to convince the court that I should spend the rest of my life in prison. Betrayal crushed me in that moment. I didn't feel angry. All I felt was a devastating hurt.

"You need to think about this." Erika was calm, as always. "He didn't know you then. He argued this case before he ever met you. You hadn't even been accepted to Lipscomb then. He was just doing his job."

"But he knew all about me this whole time and never said nothing?" Suddenly his behavior Wednesday night made perfect sense.

"Maybe he never connected your name with your face," Erika said. "It was a long time ago. I'm sure he didn't realize you were the same person."

I nodded, looking down at my sneakers. "Yeah, maybe."

I spent the weekend wrestling with my feelings. Erika's words rang in my head as I tried to decide what to do. If I had talked to anyone else, my feelings might have been different.

But sitting in my cell, I realized Erika was right. There was no point in being angry. It didn't make sense to feel betrayed, I reasoned. The whole thing was an unbelievable coincidence. I needed to forgive him, if for no other reason than to let go of the hurt I felt, to let myself off the hook. By the time I went back to class the following Wednesday, I was ready to do just that.

As I sat down, though, I felt so exposed I thought I might as well have been naked.

As much as I knew in my heart it wasn't his fault, thoughts kept popping back in my head. *He sits here and talks this game of restorative justice, but he just fought like hell to keep me in prison. What kind of fraud would do something like that?* For a moment, I would have loved nothing more than to stand up and cuss him out, to make a scene and expose him for the horrible person he must be. But then, there was Erika's voice in my head again. *It doesn't make sense to be angry*, I reminded myself. *He didn't know. Do what you came to do and let it go.*

When Preston announced we'd take a ten-minute break, I asked if I could talk to him outside. I wouldn't let my thoughts sway me. I'd already decided what I'd say.

I could barely look at him as I told him I forgave him.

Preston looked genuinely sad and conflicted. "I feel really bad," he said.

"You don't have a reason to. You were just doing your job."

I didn't know what else to say. How are you supposed to summarize something like that in a ten-minute break? I just wanted to get it out of the way or I knew I could never concentrate in his class again. I had no desire to bring it up again.

But on the last night of class, when we had a party to celebrate, Preston approached me. "Can we talk?" he asked. I nodded. I figured he wouldn't want to leave it with that short conversation.

We sat in silence for a moment before Preston sighed. "I looked through the court documents again," he said slowly. "I just don't know how to reconcile the person I know from those court records with the person I know you to be."

"That's because I'm not that girl." I told him about Kut, about the men who had assaulted me in the weeks leading up to my arrest. I told him about Gina, and the constant feeling that I didn't belong. I told him about the anger, and the uncontrollable urge to lash out, only to regret it later.

He listened to me intently. "None of this was in the trial transcript," he said when I was finished.

"Nope. It wouldn't have been. No one was too interested in finding out why I did what I did."

He nodded slowly. "I can honestly say I don't know what I would have done if I were in your shoes. I might be wearing a prison uniform right now too."

In that moment, Preston and I experienced true shalom. True restorative justice. Both of us had misjudged each other, but we also realized we didn't have to stay there. There's beauty in reconciliation. I had never seen that more clearly than that night.

Whether I needed to face another test or not, I got one anyway. Since I was first locked up, Dan Birman had interviewed me and followed me. He was there, rolling his camera, when I was interviewed by a court psychologist as a newly arrested sixteen-year-old. He was there when the jury announced my guilty verdict. Now, he told me, his documentary, called *Me Facing Life*, was about to air on PBS. Not only that, but Lipscomb would host a screening as part of the *Independent Lens* PBS cinema program.

I felt my stomach flip-flop. If I felt exposed before, this was another level. Every personal, private, horrible thing I'd done or said would be laid bare for all to see. It wasn't that I didn't want the documentary to air. While I had some serious second thoughts about people seeing such personal moments, I wanted my story to make a difference and keep other girls from ending up in the same spot I did. But having people I know watch it and whisper about me behind my back was a whole other issue. I'd seen it happen too many times. Somebody ends up on *Snapped* or on the news and the next thing you know her name is on everybody's lips.

Hiding was the wrong approach. I couldn't just sit on the information and hope nobody saw the documentary. There were too many loyal PBS watchers up in here for that to happen. *Maybe if I get out in front of it, I can control the narrative,* I thought. It's like when somebody tries to use gossip against you. If you claim it as truth for yourself in front of them, you take the power from their words. *If I tell them to watch it, they can't say nothing about me.*

So that's what I did. I told everybody when it would be on. "Make sure you watch it!" I said. The day after it first aired, when it was on TV again, I joined a GED class that had planned a viewing and watched it right along with them.

I have to admit, it was weird. I remembered how I would have sworn I was grown back then. Now, when I looked at my sixteen-year-old self, practically drowning in an orange jumpsuit, I thought I looked like a baby. There were moments I didn't want in the film, like the list of every man I'd ever slept with. I cringed with embarrassment, wondering if everyone was thinking about what a whore I was. But I forced myself to keep watching. I forced myself not to hide my face or sink in my chair. *Maybe my story isn't all for nothing*, I thought. *Maybe this documentary can help people. Maybe kids who see it will realize what can happen to them if they make the wrong choices.*

When the documentary was over, nobody said a single negative word.

"I can't believe they did that to you," one girl said, wiping tears from her eyes.

"I'm gonna pray for you," another woman told me. "That's messed up."

Instead of people gossiping about me, I discussed the documentary right along with them. I let them ask me if I still talked to my birth mother, or if different self-defense laws would have helped me. I answered every question, no matter how much I would rather have gone back to my cell. "I hear from her every now and then," I said. "And no, Tennessee has a self-defense law. But I'm still here."

I looked around the cell, taking in the emotion on each lady's face. In that moment, I thought back to my dream of being an advocate. In a way, I realized, that's already happening. I can make a difference right where I am. This documentary can help me do that. I don't have to be embarrassed by my story. My past is past. What matters now is what I do with it.

17

"THE CHICK IN THE BOX"

After a few years in Lipscomb, I was fully committed to walking the right path. Even if I never got out of prison, I knew I wanted to have a meaningful life. I couldn't do that if I kept cussing out everybody who looked at me wrong.

Yet over and over again, I kept finding myself back in segregation. Sometimes it was over a guard enforcing a rule that I thought was ridiculous. Other times I argued with officers over something tiny, just for the sake of being right. I couldn't keep my mouth shut. I wouldn't think twice about it until the inevitable write-up was brought to my cell. *Dang*, I thought each time. *I done did it again*.

I'd end up on probation at Lipscomb, which would motivate me to get it together just long enough to get off probation. But it was never long before I ran my mouth again and was right back where I started.

"I tell you what," Miss Seabrooks said one day, when I was painting her office. "The girls who work in my office aren't just prison employees. They're representatives of the entire education department. I take that very seriously. So, I'm going to give you a challenge."

"I know I can do it!" I cried before continuing, "I mean, what is it?"

"If you can stay out of trouble, no write-ups, no trips to segregation, you can come work for me. You can tutor GED students and be an assistant. And I'll hire you."

"All right now," I said, grinning. I could already picture myself sitting in her calm, serene office, away from the constant noise of inmates yelling at one another. I wasn't particularly interested in tutoring, and I certainly didn't have any experience with it, but if that's what she wanted me to do, I'd figure out a way to be the best tutor she'd ever seen.

I was back in her office a few months later to announce I'd made it without a write-up. Now, I did not magically figure out how to shut my mouth. While I worked hard at staying out of trouble, I also became an expert debater when I was accused of an offense. I looked for loopholes and got more than a few write-ups thrown out for technicalities, like the officer forgot to write down my name at the time of the incident, or if details in the report were wrong. A few times, I swallowed my pride and begged the officer to tear up the report. "That was just a bad day," I'd say. "Can we just forget about it?" Somehow, it worked.

I'm sure Miss Seabrooks was well aware that I hadn't been a perfect angel, but she still made good on her word. I quit the paint crew when she hired me as one of her four aides.

On my first day, Miss Seabrooks ushered me into her conference room set up with a giant L-shaped mahogany desk, a rolling chair, and a whiteboard. "This is all yours," she said with a smile. "I want you to make this your own little space. Set it up however you'd like. I want you to be comfortable."

I felt a surge of pride as I looked around my new little kingdom. No one had trusted me with any kind of space to call my own since my childhood bedroom. I knew the other aides all shared the office complex with Miss Seabrooks. I was the only one with an office all to myself, and I was determined to make the most of it. I didn't care what kind of work Miss Seabrooks might have for me. I could tell this was going to be my dream job.

Within days, I'd outfitted my new office with a bookcase and plant. I put my crocheting skills to work and made my own brown-and-gold rug in a diamond pattern, and added a picture frame to pull together a homey look. My desk was now adorned with a shiny new stapler and Post-it dispenser, and a black organizer kept my schedule neat and orderly. I even had my own pink tote bag to carry any supplies I needed to and from my cell. But the best part was the window. This was my own glimpse into the outside world, a view only for me. I spent a few minutes every day leaning back in my chair, gazing out the window at the highway beyond the parking lot and the administration building, and dreaming of the freedom that lay just over the fence. *Someday*, I thought, *I'll be out there. I'll be free.* Until then, this office gig was pretty dang good. I had a deeper sense of peace than I'd ever experienced behind bars.

With my own computer, and a color printer Miss Seabrooks found in storage, my office felt complete. Thanks to downloads from Miss Seabrooks, I spent my downtime playing *Angry Birds* and *Cake Shop*, listening to D'Angelo and Xscape, while drinking coffee with French vanilla creamer. By prison standards, this was the dream. *Life ain't gonna get much better than this as long as I'm in here*.

In the background of my life, lawyers were still fighting for my freedom. By now, I was working with a prestigious attorney named Charles W. Bone, who out of nowhere took on my case pro bono. After my first appeal was denied, he took over the case and went right to work on a second appeal to have my sentence overturned.

Where my last appeal threw every argument in the book at the courts, this one centered on new evidence pointing toward me having a cognitive impairment. My birth mother, Gina, admitted to Dan Birman during the filming of his documentary that she drank a fifth of vodka a day while she was pregnant with me. As smart as I was, and as well as

I was doing at Lipscomb, even I couldn't deny that my ability to control my impulses was shaky at best. So my team brought doctors to the prison to do an electroencephalogram, or EEG, to record my brain wave patterns and determine if I had a diagnosable disorder. They put me through a physical exam and a neuropsychological exam, they took my medical history, they put me through the whole process. One of my attorneys had said the EEG would basically back up what the experts said, but that was it. So I assumed we were still waiting for them to come in.

A few months later, when I was back in court for a hearing, I didn't know what was coming. I most certainly wasn't warned that three experts would spend the next few hours describing in great detail how mentally impaired I was.

I sat right there in open court, cameras flashing, Dan Birman filming, as one doctor said I had a fetal alcohol spectrum disorder. That wasn't just based off the EEG. He seemed to take great pleasure in describing how you could tell I had the disorder just by looking at me.

"Oh yes, she has the physical features typical for someone with an alcohol-related neurological disorder. You can see how her mid-face is somewhat flat," he said, gesturing toward my apparently deformed face. "The area between the bottom of her nose and the top of her upper lip is also significantly flattened."

Everybody in the courtroom practically strained their neck to stare at me. You could actually hear "mmms" and "aahs" and "oh, I sees." My cheeks burned as I leaned my forehead into my fingertips. I had sworn before that I would never cry in court again. Now I was struggling to hold to that promise. The pictures snapped of that moment would be used in newspaper articles about me for years to come.

"She has a remarkable IQ of 134, but she does not function like a typical person of such high intelligence," the doctor said. "Her functional abilities are terrible, and they are so terrible they are equivalent to a person with mild mental retardation."

Those words were a punch in the gut. They're so horrific they aren't used anymore. Yet multiple doctors used that word to describe me that day. And that wasn't even the worst of it. The worst came when a doctor used an analogy of two chicks to explain my apparently impaired behavior. He told the court to imagine two baby chicks in a box, and that box has a window where they can see a bowl of food. Behind those chicks is a door, where they can walk right out and eat the food. At first, both chicks jump at the window and smack their faces into the glass. The first chick doesn't make the same mistake twice, but instead finds the door to go outside and get the food. But the other chick—that poor, impaired little chick—keeps running up to the window, smacking its face in the glass, never figuring it out.

"Cyntoia is like that chick in the box," he said. He and pretty much everyone in the courtroom had themselves a good laugh over the analogy.

I looked around, my throat constricting, tears clouding my vision. *This isn't freaking funny*, I thought. *This is my life.*

One doctor went on and on about how I was incapable of controlling my actions, and that there was a huge discrepancy between my IQ and my behavior. This was the only part of the hearing that sounded an alarm bell for me. I thought back to the stealing, the sexual behavior with random guys, the screaming rages that bubbled out of me when I was a teenager. Maybe it wasn't my fault. Maybe this was an explanation. The doctor said people with a fetal alcohol spectrum disorder don't reach their full cognitive potential until their early thirties. *Great*, I thought. *I'm seven years off from that happening.*

All through the hearing, doctors kept projecting an image of my brain onto a screen. The image from the EEG showed neurons on both sides all lit up, sending messages to my body. Then there was a section in the middle that was just dark, like there was no activity there. That image haunted me for days. I thought of every skill I hadn't mastered, every reaction I ever had, every thought that had crossed my mind. Suddenly I was seeing my life from a completely different perspective, one where something was horribly wrong with me, and there was nothing I could do but wait it out. It wasn't a reality I was ready to accept.

I sat at the front of the room for all to see my humiliation, on display for their enjoyment. This whole freaking hearing was supposed to help my case. It wasn't supposed to crush me. My self-esteem, my confidence, my hope in the future—all of it was built on my intelligence. My brains were what gave me value, what made me a worthwhile person. I take initiative, I'm tenacious, I'm capable. Now these doctors were saying it was all a lie. *If I'm just stupid and impaired, what am I even doing here? What hope could I possibly have?*

When the hearing was over, Mr. Bone marched furiously to the attorney in charge of setting it up. "You didn't tell her ahead of time?" he asked, shocked. "How could you not let her know what to expect?"

"I wanted a genuine reaction. And I got it." This smug little attorney was clearly so proud of himself he was practically smirking. It was all I could do to stop myself from clapping back at him.

"You sure did," I said simply.

I flashed back to the days of rehearsing for my trial with Rich McGee. "A trial is all one big show," he told me. Once again, he was right. I sat under the holding cell's fluorescent lights and wondered when my life would stop being displayed for others' entertainment. I never had privacy, no space to process the facts in front of me. Everything was thrust under the spotlight, whether I wanted it there or not. I felt like a cadaver donated to a medical school. My whole life had been donated to science. Nothing was mine.

As my self-esteem plummeted through the floor, I found myself searching for a Band-Aid. I needed something to boost me up, to show me I wasn't worthless or stupid. This should have been the moment I realized my desperate need for God, the moment I turned to him. But it wasn't. Instead, I found myself chatting with a flirtatious officer.

This dude was going on and on to me and my friend, Leann, about how he loved working for the prison's tactical team because he got to travel around the state. "Y'all wouldn't believe it, but there are so many Tennessees."

Leann and I exchanged glances. "You mean, there are so many *cities* in Tennessee?" I offered, trying to help the brother out.

"Nah, man, they're all Tennessee," he insisted. "There's like sixty-seven of them. Like, Nashville, Tennessee. Springfield, Tennessee. All kinds of Tennessees."

As Leann and I busted a gut laughing, I knew exactly what I wanted. *This dude is my Band-Aid*, I thought. This is exactly the confidence-boost I need. I lost all perspective on what really mattered in that moment. I felt like crap, and I wanted someone to make me feel better about myself. All this time, I thought I was okay, that I'd healed from my issues with men, and here I was, right back where I started, finding my validation in what a man thought of me.

After years of avoiding officers like the plague, I was suddenly in a secret relationship. It was mostly passing each other letters and saying hi to one another when he was on a post near me. But then, I let down my guard even further. Out of the sightline of cameras, I had sex with that officer twice. It was the first time since I was sixteen years old, back at the InTown Suites with Kut. A man's touch didn't feel as traumatic as I thought it would. I didn't have flashbacks. But as I crossed that line, the line everyone in prison knew we weren't supposed to cross, I was overwhelmed with guilt. It was a new sensation. When I was a teenager, I never felt a thing. I was numb, on autopilot, going through the motions. Now, as a grown woman, still in the process of healing, I felt everything. *I'm better than this*, I realized. This mistake wasn't worth it. I was worth more than this.

To make matters even worse, my Band-Aid boyfriend went around the prison telling everybody our business.

Before long, he told inmates and other officers, even having one of his fellow officers bring me a letter he'd written. I felt like my intestines had just fallen on the floor. I couldn't believe I'd put myself at risk of losing everything I worked for—Lipscomb, my job at Miss Seabrooks's office, my self-respect—all for this dude who didn't even know the difference between a city and a state. He wasn't worth going to max. He wasn't worth my time. I knew I had to end it, and fast. My only hope was I could pull the plug before anyone higher up found out.

But it was too late. Out of nowhere, I got a write-up for being out of place. One officer wrote me up because she insisted I wasn't wearing panties. I knew what they were really doing. They were trying to catch me red-handed with my officer boyfriend.

And when they searched my office, that's just what they did. They found all the letters he'd written me hidden in a filing cabinet, along with a little Visine bottle of perfume. Everyone was up in arms, taping off the cabinet like it was a violent crime scene and bringing in a whole tactical team.

The cherry on top was when I was "randomly" selected for a drug test. It was obvious to everyone that they were using my urine for a pregnancy test, since there was a rumor going around I was knocked up. The test was negative.

I ended up back in segregation while I awaited a disciplinary hearing. *Oh, lord, this is it*, I thought. *I'm about to lose everything*. All because of this stupid fling.

By the grace of God, I was able to hang on by a thread. I was shy just one point of the six points that would get you kicked out of Lipscomb, and Miss Seabrooks let me keep my job simply because she believed in me. However, the vibe was different now. I was kept on a short leash. I heard the other aides whisper about me as I walked past them. And the officers who used to leave me alone took my past relationship as an open invitation for their most inappropriate comments.

Everything in my life had come crashing down in a matter of months, I thought. I had single-handedly dismantled my respect, my peace of mind, my comfort. Everything I most valued was tainted, even if it wasn't taken from me.

18

MEMPHIS

For five months, I waited for the other shoe to drop. After the drama about the officer came out in the open and I served my short stint in seg, I knew more was coming. You don't have a relationship with an officer and get away with it. I'd seen plenty of women taken down for lesser mistakes than I had made. But nothing happened.

Then, at five thirty one morning, someone knocked on my door. The door opened to reveal two search team officers standing there. "Get up," I heard a deep voice bark out. "You gotta come with us."

This is it, I thought. *They body snatching again.*

Every so often, the prison makes a so-called population management move. They call it a routine procedure and claim it ensures no prison is strained with too many people. Occasionally, they'll move dozens of people all at once, sometimes because of a new program that opened up at another prison or new beds that became available. It's a phenomenon we liked to call "body snatching." The only warning you get is a five o'clock in the morning knock telling you to pack your stuff. Prison staff will tell you they pick inmates at random for body snatching, but that's not the case. Everyone knew they used it as a form of punishment. So when I got the 5:30 a.m. wake-up call, I knew I was being punished for my little fling.

"Get your shoes on," the officer ordered as I slowly sat up in bed, my eyes still adjusting to the darkness.

"Well do I have time to brush my teeth or what?" This man was crazy if he thought I was fixing to go anywhere without my teeth brushed.

"Just get your clothes on."

"Okay, okay, I'll be right there." I rushed to the sink, where I brushed my teeth and washed my face. I threw on my uniform and let the officers walk me down the hall.

We stopped at the multipurpose room already crowded with ten other women from my unit, along with a guard scoping us out for gang tattoos. My heart sank. *This is it. I'm leaving Nashville*.

"Wait here," one of the guards said as I sat down. The lights were dim, and I could see the sun slowly making its way up from the horizon through the big glass window.

"What's going on?" I demanded. All they could tell me was that the warden of security was coming to speak with us personally. I knew that couldn't be good.

Once we were alone, the other ladies and I theorized about where we were going.

"Maybe it's a drug test," one girl said.

I shook my head. "This ain't a drug test. I ain't never been tested in the multipurpose room."

Finally, we got our answer when the warden of security himself, Bill Chris, strutted through the door with a grin on his face. This short, round, white dude sported glasses and a crew cut to match his good ole boy vibe, but he never missed an opportunity to mention that he was dating a black captain from Jamaica. I couldn't figure him out. But one thing everybody knew for certain was he wasn't on the side of inmates. I swear his smile that morning was aimed at me, and it wasn't friendly. The moment I saw his face, I knew I was screwed.

The inmates around me moaned and held their heads in their

hands as Bill Chris announced they were transferring us to Memphis. Warden Chris, meanwhile, could hardly contain his glee and was less than subtle when he looked at me for a reaction. *This dude came down here just to see the look on my face.*

I forced my mouth into a smug smile, even as I fell apart inside. Sure, the last few months hadn't been great, but I had made a life for myself here in Nashville. I was acing my Lipscomb classes and was on my way to earning an associate's degree. Mommy came to visit me every other weekend, and I could call my family as much as I wanted. Once they shipped me to Memphis, I could kiss college goodbye. There was no way Mommy could make the three-hour drive to visit me twice a month. And phone calls would be way more expensive, which would mean they'd be harder to come by. *What is Mommy going to think?* I wondered. I dreaded telling her the bad news.

On top of everything else, these jerks were body snatching us on what was supposed to be Inmate Appreciation Day. I had already paid six dollars for my two pints of rainbow sherbet and now I wouldn't get a single bite.

I shot the warden a look. "Don't worry, I'll be back." He just smiled and walked out, but I wasn't joking. *I'm gonna make it back to Nashville just to spite that man. I don't care what I have to do to get here.*

We had an hour to head back to our cells and pack our belongings. Bill Chris was there holding the door for us as we carried our bags to the bus in the sally port. We had waited so long in the lobby that we got our hot dog and Coke we were promised, but I sure didn't get my rainbow sherbet.

"One hell of an Inmate Appreciation Day," I said, looking Bill Chris in the eye. He just chuckled.

That three-hour drive on the bus was a trip in itself. All twenty-five of us were handcuffed with our wrists secured to a black box chained around our waist. Then, our ankles were shackled to another person. I was relieved when the guards shackled me to a girl I'd chatted with in the lobby.

My jaw dropped when we pulled up in front of a building straight out of a 1950s prison movie. The women's prison was directly across from the men's federal prison, and two guard towers were still in place. I half expected to see guards up there surveying the inmates during rec time, a rifle in hand.

Right off the bat, we were hauled into an old tile bathroom and strip-searched by not one but two officers. By now, I had been strip-searched so many times I barely batted an eye, but having two officers was downright weird.

I walked into the medical unit in a haze. I still hadn't had time to process that life as I knew it was over. I could feel officers staring at me, looking for some sign of emotion. But I was still resolved to remain as stoic as possible. *They won't get the satisfaction from me.*

I sat on the cold tile floor waiting to be taken back, the dim fluorescent lights flickering above me. The fixtures looked like they hadn't been replaced in decades. Exposed pipes and duct work rusted above our heads, and I looked up, wondering if they might leak on us at any moment. The cells were just as ghetto, complete with an actual padlock and key on every cell instead of the magnetized automatic locks we had back in Nashville.

"Um, is this safe?" I called as the guard walked away from me. "Is this a fire hazard?" No one answered.

The guards who patrolled the halls were a whole new ballgame here in Memphis. I was used to the practically all-white staff at Nashville who walked around like Dudley Do-Right, just looking for a reason to write you up. We called it badge-itude. These Memphis guards were different. They'd laugh and cut up with you all day long, but if you came at them wrong, instead of writing you up, they just cussed you up and down and told you what was what. If you made the mistake of fighting them, they'd fight you right back. They didn't care.

I found myself in the middle of a straight-up culture shock. I was used to guards controlling when we were in and out of our cells. They let us out for certain periods, but for the most part, we were locked up all day. I learned to get by just by looking like I was supposed to do whatever I was doing, whether or not that was true. Once, when a new commissioner instituted "controlled movement," where you couldn't leave a unit without a pass, I still walked wherever I wanted. If a yard officer asked me where I was going, I looked right back like he had seven heads and asked rhetorically, "Where are *you* going?"—and kept on walking. Corporal Watson, a frequent guard on the yard, nicknamed me Cruise Control.

In Memphis, everybody was out all the time. There was no need for a pass. I imagine if you asked for one, the officers would look at you and laugh. I'd walk around the corner and find one inmate cutting another inmate's hair with clippers, or someone chewing out another inmate for stealing her Coke. It was a free-for-all and I was ready for it. I felt like I had moved to a halfway house instead of a prison.

This is great, I thought. *I'm never going back. I'll trade less structure for Lipscomb any day.*

I had no idea how stressed I was until I was completely removed from the situation. In Nashville, the pressure to be a model inmate was relentless. I constantly worried I'd say or do the wrong thing and screw up all the progress I'd made. Guards there held up everything I cared about like a carrot on a stick—visiting with my mom, my job in Miss Seabrooks's office, Lipscomb. Even the people on my side put me up on a pedestal. I couldn't make one wrong move without letting someone down.

I knew Kathy was mad at me for letting everyone down. The truth was, I was angry right back at her. Angry for forcing me up on that pedestal when I didn't ask to be there. Angry for making me feel like the ultimate failure just because I was a twenty-five-year-old woman who let my hormones get the best of me. There was no way a white, middle-aged, upper-middle-class court administrator could begin to understand what it was like to be a minority prisoner, surviving on twenty-five dollars a month, piecing together life from scraps that the justice system left behind when I was just sixteen years old. I never wanted to be a role model. I never claimed to be one. I was already imprisoned. All I wanted was to get by and live my life as best I could.

Rich McGee had made taking the right path seem so easy all those years ago. I tried, I really did. I didn't do drugs, I hadn't fought in years, I stopped getting constant write-ups. Yet here I was anyway. Once again, I had let the attention of a man lead to my downfall.

Now that I had lost everything, I felt the same strange relief I'd felt years before, when I first stepped into my prison cell. There's a freedom that comes with having nothing left to cling to, nothing left to worry about losing. Memphis was exactly the break I needed. I had heard from Preston within my first month in Memphis that he'd already met with Tennessee Department of Correction bigwigs and a Nashville legislator to discuss my transfer. He told me they'd promised I would return to Nashville after I served six months in Memphis. I made up my mind to spend those six months wisely and relax as much as I could.

My first order of business was to get the heck off kitchen duty. I reported every roach I saw. I made an official request for bug spray. I spilled a pan of grease in the middle of a walkway and smeared it around with a mop, just as a tour came through the kitchen for an inspection. I claimed to have a fungal infection on my hand. I told my supervisor I had explosive diarrhea. In one of my more extreme moves, I purposely burned my hand using salt and ice, later claiming I burned it on a hot pipe.

"This pipe is not safe!" I cried out dramatically. "I told you last week this thing is a work hazard!"

The joke was on me, though. After wrapping up my hand at work, I unwrapped it that night to find my hand bubbled and gray. "How long was I supposed to leave that salt on my hand?" I asked the girl who had taught me the trick.

"Five minutes, why?" she replied innocently.

"Oh my god. I left it on for thirty minutes!" Now I was in full freak-out mode, screaming, "Am I gonna lose my hand?" I had to go to the freaking burn unit. I looked around at patients with true injuries and real problems and thought, *I am an idiot.* And I still didn't get fired.

The final straw for my supervisors came when I refused to sign my training manual. I told them I hadn't been properly trained and wouldn't sign anything claiming otherwise. "Sir, I will not compromise my integrity for you," I said in an Oscar-worthy performance. "I am not going to lie."

Finally, my supervisor threw out his arm and pointed to the door. "Take her to seg!" he shouted to the officer on duty.

The officer just scrunched up her face, looking at him like the fool he was. "I can't do that," she said. Embarrassed, he sent me back to my cell instead. He tried to write me up, but another officer thought it was stupid and refused to serve it to me.

Memphis was so laid-back that no one seemed to care I was unemployed, and I wasn't about to mention it to anyone. For the next five months, I was jobless and free to relax. At first, I worried what I would do without the income, but suddenly, strangers started sending me money. The documentary had aired again, and my story picked up a new wind of popularity. Men and women across the country donated so much money that the fees that had weighed me down for nearly five years were paid in full within a few months. The blessings from these strangers allowed me to float around the prison comfortably without the need for a job.

At the time, I chalked it up to luck. But it would turn out to be the first sign of God pursuing me.

With nothing but time on my hands, I found my thoughts drifting back to my ongoing wrestling match with God. By now, I told myself there was no chance of any divine being like God actually being real. Those people I'd met in Lipscomb were so convinced that God was their source of life. They all got together and swore up and down that they felt the spirit moving among them. But the way I saw it, what they were really experiencing was community. Religion seemed to cause nothing but problems in our world, but true community really was beautiful, even without a spiritual element attached. *The real solution to our problems is learning to live in community with one another*, I thought—*and realizing our actions affect other people*. Everything else has a logical explanation, I believed. And anyone who says God talks to them is either lying or straight-up crazy.

Then came the dreams.

From the day I first came to Memphis, everyone talked about how they used to have a puppy training program. A local shelter brought in dogs that the women helped socialize and train for their future owners. Everybody loved being around the dogs and told me how therapeutic it was just to sit and pet a dog who gave you unconditional love. But then some idiot drugged up a dog with Benadryl to make him sleep, and the whole program got shut down. We brought it up every now and then, but the officers made it clear those dogs were not coming back.

I was laying in my cell one day trying to nap when I heard my roommate, Deanna, out in the hall talking to another girl. "Deanna, go get your roommate!" I heard someone say to her. "We're getting puppies!"

My eyes snapped open. There was no way I could sleep when this was going on.

"Get Cyntoia," the person told her. "We're going to get the dogs."

I was still laying in my bed when Deanna walked into our cell. She didn't say a word but headed to the sink to rinse out her bowl. Finally I sat up, annoyed.

"Ain't you gonna tell me to wake up?" I asked accusingly.

She looked around, confused. "What?"

I popped my hand on my hip. "I heard them tell you to wake me up because they're getting puppies."

Deanna looked at me like I was crazy. "They didn't say that."

"Yes, they did!" Now I was pissed. "I was sitting right here and heard the whole thing."

"Honey, you're tripping," Deanna said, laughing. "You need to go back to sleep."

"No, I'm not. All you had to do was tell me and you wanted to keep it to yourself."

I decided to find out for myself what was going on. I stomped out of our cell and into the pod. Sure enough, two girls, Alissa and Karen, were sitting at the table.

"Did y'all tell Deanna to wake me up because we're getting puppies?"

"Uh, no," Karen laughed.

Alissa shook her head. "We told you, the dog program is over. Go to sleep."

I threw up my hands. "Man, I am not crazy."

All day, I wondered what the heck I had heard that morning. I've had my share of tripped-out dreams, but I knew what I'd heard was real. *Am I losing it, or are they lying to me?* I wondered.

But that evening, after count, Alissa and Karen burst into my cell, out of breath from running. "Oh my god, we're getting puppies!" Alissa shouted. "They're calling us right now. They said we can go get them."

I was not having it. "Whatever. Make fun of me. Real nice."

"I ain't lying!" Alissa said. The two of them turned and walked away, and I thought that was that. But fifteen minutes later, they were back. My hands flew to my mouth when I realized Alissa was cradling a little bitty puppy.

"Oh my god, can I hold him?" Without waiting for an answer, I snatched up the pit bull and beagle mix, nuzzling his soft, fuzzy fur to my cheek. He couldn't have been more than four weeks old. I inhaled deeply, taking in that sweet puppy smell. His innocent eyes were set off by those puppy wrinkles they get from walking around in skin too big for their bodies. He was so cute that I didn't even mind when I could hear whining puppies carrying on at all hours of the night.

"How did you know about the puppies?" Karen finally asked me. "You literally just said they were coming and now they're here."

"Yeah, I'm not gonna lie, that's kind of freaky," Alissa said.

I shrugged and shook my head. "I'm sure there's gotta be a rational explanation," I said. "It's probably just a coincidence. Maybe I overheard someone else talking about the puppies and thought it was you."

Karen nodded, not convinced. "Yeah, maybe."

I didn't let on that my entire belief system was spinning into a frenzy. Where the heck did that come from? I wondered. I knew I'd heard something. I tried not to dwell on it, instead spending every second I could in the puppy training room, feeding them from the palm of my hand. Their perfect wet noses and wagging tails were the balm I didn't know I needed.

About a month after the first dream, the woman in charge of the puppy program told us we probably wouldn't get any more dogs. They were just overflow from a local puppy mill, and it wasn't likely to happen again. I was disappointed, but I understood.

My dream that night told me otherwise. It was so vivid I couldn't keep it to myself.

"Karen," I said the next morning, "I swear I saw your next dog in my dream."

"What was it?" she asked curiously.

"I'm not sure what kind of dog he was, but he was white with black spots, and for some reason he had a knot on his head and a pink tip on his tail. I saw you handing him to me in my dream."

Karen stared at me. She obviously wasn't expecting a description that specific. "Well, I guess we'll see what happens," she said.

We didn't have to wait long. A couple days later, Karen walked into my cell with her jaw practically on the floor. "This is Luke," she said, her voice quavering, as she led a white bird dog mix with black spots into the cell. He had a hound's knot on his head, and on his tail was a pink spot where he'd worn the hair off by repeatedly beating his tail into the shelter's concrete wall.

My eyes grew ten times larger as they locked in on Karen's. Neither of us moved. We were frozen in amazement.

What the heck is happening? I thought constantly. This couldn't be a coincidence. What rational explanation was there for seeing a dog in my dream and then meeting him a few days later? Something supernatural was going on here. *Could this possibly be God? What purpose could he possibly have in showing me puppies in my dreams?*

I wrote the dreams off as a weird coincidence. But then I had a third. I saw Luke outside off the breezeway, running alongside another big black dog. Luke was the biggest dog I'd ever seen aside from a Great Dane, but this dog in my dream towered over him. *There's no way this one will come true*, I thought, but I told the girls about it anyway.

"I don't think it's possible," I told them.

"You don't know that!" Karen insisted. "Let's wait and see!" They were all bigger believers in my own dreams than I was.

Within a few days, we welcomed Zeus into the pod, a solid black Irish Wolfhound who hulked over Luke.

When I had a fourth dream, none of us could wait to see if a black-and-brown dog with some kind of nationality attached to it would show up. Sure enough, in came Lucky, a black-and-brown German shepherd. I couldn't deny it anymore. Some kind of higher being was behind this. It was the only answer that made sense. I thought of the story of Joseph in the Bible, when he dreams about his brothers bowing down to him. Those dreams came true, just like he saw them in his head. I felt like the same thing was happening to me. Maybe God was trying to reach me in a way I couldn't ignore. I couldn't chalk my dreams coming true up to a coincidence. Not when there were four of them. There was no other way I could see something happen before it actually happened. When the supernatural reveals itself like that, you can't ignore it.

Okay, God, I know it's you, I thought. *I think you're real. I don't understand you, but I know you're here. I still don't get why you left me to rot in prison. I'm still hurt. But I see you.*

I'd been angry at God for so long. I pictured myself as a sixteen-year-old, practically a little girl, pouring out my heart to him on my county jail bed. I begged God to stop me from being transferred, from getting a life sentence. He didn't do any of those things. Why? Why would a good God let a teenager be thrown in prison?

In an instant, I looked back on the last eight years with new eyes. What if there was another part of Joseph's story that applied to me? Joseph was in jail, just like me. Joseph was treated unjustly, just like me. I remembered Joseph's words to his brothers, just after they bowed down to him, and he revealed himself as their brother. "What man intended for evil, God intended for good." Could anything that happened in the last eight years possibly be good? I thought of the moment I learned Kut had been shot. If I hadn't been in jail, I might be dead too.

I thought of the documentary sharing my story. Letters had poured in ever since, letters from kids asking me for advice. One girl even told me she struggled with thoughts of suicide. I tried to find other ways to get them help and connected them with Kathy—if their parents didn't know they were writing to an inmate, they might freak. But something about my story resonated with them. What if my story had a purpose? Maybe man intended to lock me up and throw away the key, but God had something better in mind.

For the first time, I didn't feel alone. I sensed God's presence in those dreams. I knew he was here, even if I didn't know why. And if God was real, and he was with me, then he could help me figure out how to stay on the right path. I didn't have to do it alone anymore. A God powerful enough to show me something before it even happened was the kind of God I could trust. He was a God who could give me the peace I so desired. I was tired of the convict rat race. I just wanted to live right.

It wasn't a moment with flashing lights and harps playing in the background. I certainly can't look back on that day as the day I fully committed to God.

19

FINDING MY WAY HOME

Six months into my stay in Memphis, I had settled into the idea that I might not get back to Nashville for quite some time. I was comfortable with my laid-back surroundings. I liked living far from the pressure to be a model inmate, study daily, or even work at a job. The prison staff still hadn't said a word about me being unemployed since I got fired from the kitchen, and I intended to keep it that way. The truth was, I had gone soft. I was simply existing, happy to stay out of trouble and fly under the radar, instead of fighting to live my best life. I never lost sight of my goal to get out of prison one day, but I wasn't actively pursuing it either.

I figured I'd leave Memphis eventually—Preston had pretty much promised that was coming. In the meantime, I decided I'd keep my mouth shut and wait for them to come get me. Deep down, I knew this wasn't a good plan. I'd been in prison long enough to know that nothing you want will ever just come to you. Everything in your favor always comes with a fight. I just didn't have any fight in me anymore.

Mommy had only visited me once since I was shipped off to Memphis. I chalked that up to the distance. The phone calls alone cost almost five dollars a call—twice as much as they did in Nashville, and even though Mommy never complained about money, I never pressured her to make an expensive trip to visit. Especially since I was the one who got myself sent to Memphis in the first place.

Everything seemed normal when I called my brother one afternoon in March. He and my sister had gotten in an argument, and I wanted to help diffuse the situation. He was going off about Missy, ranting about how he was mad at her, which wasn't unusual. They butted heads all the time. I said "mm-hmm" absently, partially tuning out his tirade, until one little sentence grabbed my attention.

"You know Mommy's cancer's back?" he said angrily.

In that moment my whole world froze. I sat motionless, the phone in my hand. Other girls milled around me in the housing unit, shouting to one another and laughing. I barely noticed any of them. I was too focused on the fact that my world was crashing around me.

"What?" I finally managed to say. "What are you talking about?"

"Yep. All the way back in December." My brother's tone was harsh, short, unconscious of my pain. "Nobody told me either. Mommy said I talk too much, and everybody would find out if they told me."

I leaned into my knees, my head in my hands. "I don't understand. The doctor said if she went five years cancer-free then it probably wouldn't come back. It's been five years. So what the heck happened?"

"I don't know. I guess it's a different kind of breast cancer."

"Well how bad is it?" Chico was not giving me the details I needed.

"Toia, she was in the hospital. She almost died. They're giving her chemo treatments now. She done shaved her hair off and everything."

"Oh my god," I moaned. I thought for a moment I might be sick. Here I'd been floating around Memphis, twiddling my thumbs, doing nothing, with no idea I was that close to losing my mother. What if she'd died and I never got to say goodbye? Mommy was my rock. My anchor. I thought back to the long list of messes I'd gotten myself in throughout my short life. Each time, Mommy was the only one there for me. I relied on her strength to pull me through when she probably needed a shoulder to lean on just as badly as I did. *I can't lose her*, I thought.

My shock and denial quickly gave way to anger. *How could they keep something like that from me?* I wondered. Didn't I deserve to know my own mother was sick? After calling Missy and thoroughly chewing her out for not telling me, I called Mommy.

"How could you not tell me you had cancer?" I demanded. I figured she'd feel guilty, but Mommy wasn't having it.

"It's not your business," she said firmly. "You were all the way in Memphis. There's nothing you could have done. I wanted to get through it and tell you after I was cancer-free."

"But what if you didn't make it?" I cried. I could barely choke out the words. "What if all of the sudden you were just gone? Do you know what that would've done to me?"

"Toia, I wasn't trying to hurt you." Mommy's voice was gentle now. "All I wanted was to protect you. That's all I've ever wanted."

I hung up the phone that day with a new resolve. I didn't care how easy life was in Memphis. The idea that I wanted to stay here just to keep on doing nothing seemed laughable to me now. Somehow, I would get back to Nashville. I would finish my degree, make Mommy proud, and fight with everything in me to get back home to her. I had come too close to living without her too many times. There was no way I could let that happen without trying everything in my power to be free and reunited with her. I couldn't spend the rest of my life clinging to moments with her in the visitation gallery. I didn't want my mother to leave this earth thinking she had failed me. More than anything, I wanted to look her in the eyes and see that she knew, for once, that I was going to be okay.

WHEN YOU'RE AN INMATE, YOU DON'T JUST GET TO DEMAND A transfer to another facility. You can try, but you should prepare yourself to be laughed out of the room. I was far from the only person to swear I would return to Nashville after being moved to Memphis. For most people, that wasn't even a remote possibility. But I was confident I wasn't most people.

Within days of learning about Mommy's cancer, one of the assistant commissioners just happened to visit the Memphis prison. He was also one of the men who'd met with Preston months earlier. He could have toured any unit at the prison, but somehow, he ended up performing a cell inspection on every room in my unit.

I about jumped out of my skin when he stuck his head in my cell. This was my opportunity. I was not about to let it slip away.

"Excuse me, sir," I began. "A few months ago, you were in a meeting with a man named Preston Shipp. He talked to you about how they sent me to Memphis even though I was a student at Lipscomb University."

The man nodded. I could tell my words were ringing a bell. I kept going in the most professional voice I could muster. "It's very important for me to finish school and earn my degree. Could you please send me back to Nashville so I can finish college?"

He took out a notebook and pen from his pocket. "I'll look into it," he said after scribbling away at the book.

I wasn't too confident. I'd seen too many wardens and administrators write down my questions and concerns. Nothing ever happened. I had no reason to believe this time would be any different. Yet something inside me wouldn't let go of the idea. *This can't be just a coincidence*, I thought. *What are the odds this guy would end up in my unit after he was in that meeting? This is how I get out of here.*

One week later, my suspicions were confirmed when my counselor called me up to his office. It wasn't long before this that he'd told me I had no chance of being transferred. "It doesn't work that way," he said at the time. This day, however, was different.

"Okay," he said without fanfare, "we're sending you back to Nashville."

I crossed my arms like a cocky teenager and nodded. "Mm-hmm," I said smugly, my eyebrows raised. "That's what I thought."

Even after my new revelation, I was too blind at the time to see God's favor in the impossible suddenly becoming possible. I thought I'd done it all, that I'd found a way to work around the system. I was used to giving myself the credit. I didn't stop to think that God was the one pulling the strings.

Within a week, I boarded a van and was shuttled back to Nashville. I knew it was a victory, and I really was happy to be back. But as guards led me off the van and into the prison, my chains clanking against the ground, I felt it. The oppressive, restrictive atmosphere hung in the air so thick it was downright stifling. I knew as soon as I walked through those doors, I would be expected to follow stupid rules, sit in my cell all day long, and ask for permission for every little thing. There would be no going five months without a job. Nobody was fixing to let me sit around doing nothing. This was a place where guards sat around waiting for you to make the wrong move or say the wrong thing so they could write you up.

I'd survived this world before. I knew I could again. But after six months of more freedom than I'd had in years, going back felt that much harder. I could handle Nashville when it was all I knew. Now that I'd experienced the carefree life of Memphis, I felt like an animal moving from a wildlife refuge to a zoo.

While I knew most of the guards from six months before, it wasn't exactly a happy homecoming. I could tell from the way they barked orders at me that they hadn't expected me to come back, and they weren't exactly thrilled that I'd managed it. Everyone looked at me like I had a scarlet letter stamped on my blue uniform. Women officers sneered at me. Men sauntered up to me with their inappropriate comments, telling me my former boyfriend told them it was the best sex ever, as if one relationship with an officer meant I was now open for business. Their words cut me deep. Guilt weighed on my shoulders over crossing that clear line, and having sex with an officer who wasn't even worth the trouble. I just wanted to move on from it, and now these officers wouldn't stop throwing it in my face. It was pretty clear everyone expected me to fail, just like I had before. *Here we go again*, I thought.

Sitting in my cell one night after one too many rude comments, I knew what I had to do. It didn't matter what anyone thought of me. I sat on my bed, my back leaned against the cinder-block wall, my knees hugged to my chest, and closed my eyes. *This is my moment*, I thought. I might have messed up before, but this was my second chance. I refused to blow it again. Anyone who thought I couldn't do it was fixing to be wrong. I would show them. I would show everyone.

In that moment I realized just how far I'd come. I remembered a time not so long ago, when comments and looks like I got these days would have thrown me into a fistfight or a cuss-out session. Now I didn't have to force myself not to respond like that because it no longer occurred to me to do it. I still dished out my share of verbal tirades, and sometimes I still had to clench my fists to keep me from coming at someone pushing me to my limit. But for the most part, I never acted on those impulses. *Wow*, I thought, looking back. *I really have changed.*

In the past, I had taunted officers, saying I wasn't scared, that the worst thing they could do to me had already happened. Now I knew that wasn't true. Whether I was thrown in max or shipped out to Memphis, the people who loved me ultimately paid the price. I had a new motivation driving me forward this time. I wanted to make Mommy and everybody who loved me proud. I wanted to prove I wasn't just a screwup. Before, I was angry. Now, I was determined.

So I started slowly. I was back at Lipscomb within a week of being in Nashville. I played it cool for about a year. Then I decided to venture out and join a class other than at Lipscomb. I returned to the prison's culinary arts program, the one I'd been kicked out of within months of coming to prison when I was thrown into max.

I got a job in the laundry room, surrounded by the scent of detergent and freshly dried sheets, where I met a group of ladies from Mexico who didn't speak much English. One lady, Maria, helped me learn Spanish so I could talk to them. I stuck to that small circle of friends, spending my time with them instead of on the ball field or in the gym. These ladies also opened my eyes to the injustices they faced on a daily basis. They basically had nothing to do, since no prison classes were offered in Spanish, and of the library's five thousand books, only a handful were in the Spanish section. I worked with prison staff to help right those wrongs, and eventually the prison started its first English as a second language course.

Being with these ladies made me realize I had the heart of a crusader. *When something isn't right, you shouldn't have to just sit there and take it*, I thought. If somebody stands up, maybe we can make a real change.

So when Kathy, my old attorney, came to visit me, and we got to talking about how wrong it was for juveniles with life sentences to not even get a chance at parole for fifty years, it hit me.

"Why don't we change it?" I said. "We don't have to just sit here and complain. Let's do something about it."

Kathy sat back and looked at me, her mind racing. "Well, we'd have to find a sponsor," she said thoughtfully. "Someone to introduce the bill for us in the legislature. And we have a Republican majority, so it might be a tough sell."

I didn't care about any of that. "We'll figure out the details. Let's just get started."

Kathy and I got to work drafting a bill. Our idea was for the court to review cases of juveniles with life sentences after a minimum of fifteen years served. They'd look at several different factors, including any associated trauma, how old the person was when they committed the crime, and whether the person obeyed prison rules and took classes since they were locked up.

My attorney Mr. Bone's daughter, Baylor, was a lobbyist and helped us find sponsors in the state House and Senate—Representative Jeremy Faison and Senator Doug Overbey. You could have knocked me on the ground when I found out they were introducing the legislation for us in the Tennessee 109th Assembly. I learned the names of committee chairmen and who we needed to get on board in order to have a chance. As much as I'd always heard everyone rag on politicians, I was amazed at how some of them refused to let politics trump their faith. People like Representative Faison, who were up for reelection, didn't care if standing up for mercy and second chances cost them a few votes. It blew me away.

The bill didn't end up making it to the governor's desk. Everyone disagreed on how much time someone should have to serve before their case could be reconsidered. Some people thought it should be thirty years, while others flat-out refused to vote for a bill that required more than fifteen years. I was frustrated to see that people who had never served a day of their lives behind bars got to keep people like me locked up because they wouldn't compromise. I was disappointed, but I still don't believe it's over. There are still legislators who are determined to get this bill passed eventually. I'm hopeful that Tennessee laws will change, and I'm still involved in making sure that happens.

Kathy kept on visiting me just about every week. She worked for the juvenile court now, after her friend was elected judge. She wanted my ideas on how the juvenile court could be better. Naturally, I had a ton. I wrote her a whole proposal on moving the juvenile court to a holistic approach that doesn't judge young people by one incident. The court needs to send someone in to talk to their families. Maybe a kid is stealing, but her family is poor, so she's stealing just so they can get by. I'd run into too many kids in the juvenile system who came from families racked by poverty and drug use. No one in the court ever bothered to find out how that might have impacted them. That's what needs to change.

Kathy took my ideas back to her boss, where they turned them into a plan to start a juvenile court risk assessment team. I even drew up blueprints for a new juvenile facility with rooms that looked like dorms and where kids wore khakis and polos, not prison jumpsuits. Kathy brought in a consultant to go over my drawings and even let me call in to a meeting to discuss them. I felt like I was a real consultant. I felt important, like I mattered.

I've got a seat at the table, I thought. *These people really care what I think.*

It took two years. Two years of keeping my head down, playing by the rules, staying out of trouble. Two years of Wednesday nights in front of a book, scribbling notes from a professor's lecture. Two years of choosing homework and study sessions over cutting up in the lounge and watching *Big Brother*. I was exhausted, burned out, anxious. But every moment was worth it when I learned I had enough credits to receive my associate's degree in liberal arts.

Back home, when I was walking free, I didn't have many moments worth celebrating. I went out of my way to make sure of that. But now, when I learned we'd have our own ceremony just for the seven graduates that December, it was on. Finally, everything in my life had fallen into place. Graduation was proof that I had really changed and was making the most of my life.

I went all-out for this ceremony. Lipscomb officials told me I could invite four people to watch me receive my diploma that day. "Yeah, that ain't gonna be enough," I told them.

I invited my whole family, then got Lipscomb to invite Mr. Bone, his daughter Baylor, his assistant Carmelina, Dan Birman, Preston Shipp, Kathy, and a woman from Representative Faison's staff as special guests of the university. I had more guests than anybody else. It was a far cry from the days when I felt like nobody but Mommy was in my corner.

The prison's culinary arts class usually caters the ceremony, and since I was still in the class, that meant I got to be part of it. Our instructor let each of us pick which dish we wanted to make. She gave us a few options, like pasta salad and finger sandwiches, but I think cold pasta is disgusting, and I wanted to make something more exciting than a pitiful little sandwich.

"No," I said. "I wanna make the cake."

I knew the cake was the one thing everybody ate at graduation. I was confident that as long as I used a recipe from *America's Test Kitchen*, I'd be good to go. I found myself a recipe for a yellow cake with chocolate icing and knew that was the one.

I practiced making that cake for weeks. I experimented with flavors, testing out browned butter and almond flavoring. This cake had to be perfect.

When graduation came, I wasn't nervous. I knew my cake was light and buttery and delicious. I made two giant sheet cakes, enough to feed over a hundred people. Then I made icing in seven different colors and had each graduate sign her name on the cake with icing from a piping bag.

I got myself all dolled up for the big day. I treated myself to a day in the prison's beauty school. These ladies colored my hair, flat-ironed my curls stick straight, and painted my nails the Lipscomb colors, purple and gold.

I couldn't stop smiling as I heard "Pomp and Circumstance" blaring from the loudspeakers. I hardly recognized the prison gym as the six other ladies and I marched in. Lipscomb event staff had completely transformed it, with silky black drapes hanging from the walls and the university's banner in a glass podium sitting center stage. I could see Mommy sitting next to Chico and Missy, her eyes fixed on me. She already had her tissues out. *Oh, lord, how am I gonna get through this without crying if she boo-hoos through the whole thing?* I was grateful she was sitting behind me and the other graduates. It was the only way I'd make it.

Since we were only seven, we were allowed to say a few words when we walked across the stage to receive our diploma. They said we had about a minute. But when I grabbed the microphone, I told them they could forget that time limit. The teacher onstage with me went to hug me and almost knocked my little hat off my head, but I didn't let that throw me off. This was my moment.

I stood on the stage and grabbed my diploma, that little slip of paper I'd worked seven long years to earn. I looked down at my name stamped, the university seal next to it, and thought of the scared teenager who first walked into this prison. Back then, I thought I was nothing, and I was angry at the world for the injustices it had put me through. This diploma was my way of proving my naysayers wrong. I had clawed my way up from the lowest rungs of society to grab hold of my future. Now I stood onstage in my cap and gown a graduate, with my whole future ahead of me. I would live, regardless of whether I would ever make it out of prison.

I looked out at the other Lipscomb girls, the ones who still had a few classes to finish. "I look forward to seeing each one of you up here," I told them. "You can do this."

I had never seen Mommy so proud as the moment she stood to be recognized as the mother of the graduate. My eyes locked on her, tears streaming down her face as she grinned at me. She didn't even bother to wipe them away.

After all the times I'd single-handedly thrown my life in the trash, Mommy never gave up on me. She stayed with me through the bad, encouraging me that I was still somebody, and that I could still have a meaningful life. Finally, I had something positive to show for myself. I wanted that degree for her more than I ever wanted it for myself. My resolve gave out right then and there. "This is for you," I said, my voice breaking as I pointed at Mommy. "Everything good that I've done is for you."

I grinned as the audience erupted with applause. In my lifetime of disappointments and mistakes, this was easily the greatest triumph I had ever experienced. And I wasn't done. I would get my bachelor's degree next, I decided. Nothing could drag me down now.

Man, I turned this around, I thought, looking around the gym that day. *I can do this.*

20

BURNED LETTERS FROM TEXAS

"Girl, you got another letter!"

My friend and roommate Crystal was already laughing as she held out the envelope. For more than a year, she and I had worked together in a call center they opened up at the prison. One of our favorite things to do together was to read the crazy letters I got on an almost daily basis.

Since the documentary came out, people started to write to me. At first, most would say simply they were praying for me, which I deeply appreciated. These days, however, most of the letters I received were straight-up dating profiles from random men. Every one of them would claim to be two hundred and thirty pounds of solid muscle. Of course, they were all business managers who worked out twenty-four hours a day. I read the letters out loud in funny voices to Crystal, and she would nearly cry she laughed so hard. Every mail call was funnier than the one before.

On a cold day in January 2017, I expected more of the same. But when I opened one of the envelopes, two pictures fell out. That wasn't unusual—like I said, every letter was like a dating profile. But the man in these pictures was one of the finest images I'd ever laid eyes on. His big, dark eyes and smooth brown skin stretched over a muscular frame I might have pinned on my wall as a teenager.

"Oh my god, he's actually cute!" I squealed, shoving the pictures in front of Crystal's face. "Like, really cute."

Crystal grabbed the pictures from me and whistled. "This man has the most perfect eyebrows I have ever seen. You think he waxes?"

I laughed. "I don't know, let's see what he says."

I opened the letter, expecting the same kind of nonsense I usually got. Right away I noticed the edges of the yellow legal paper were burned and jagged, giving the paper an old, rustic feel.

"Look at this," I said, showing the paper to Crystal. "You think he bought the paper like that?"

She folded her arms impatiently. "Are you gonna read this or what?"

"Okay, okay." I turned my eyes back to the letter.

"Cyntoia," the author wrote in neat cursive. "My name is Jaime Long, but most people call me J.Long. It's 5:52 in the morning. I couldn't sleep and somehow I came across your story. I hope this letter reaches you. I just reached out to let you know that you have my support and my prayers. I applaud you for your strength. Your boldness, your honesty, your beauty shines more than your situation."

Normally, when a letter mentioned God, I rolled my eyes.

At this point, I knew there was some kind of higher power. I told a Lipscomb professor that I was ready to believe in God, but I just couldn't bring myself to do it yet. I still argued with anyone who brought up God to me. But for some reason, the man who wrote this letter seemed genuine. The way he talked about God felt natural, like he almost couldn't help himself. I kept reading.

"Keep your head up, your story will have a happy ending. God is bigger than any sentence and He alone has the power to overturn it! You have given me motivation to do better in my life SO thank you for that!! Please respond if you can."

He signed the letter "J.Long," with the words "Free Cyntoia #2017" scrawled next to it. I stared at the word "free" for a moment, a lump in my throat. By now, I'd lost my last state appeal. Unless I was somehow miraculously granted clemency by the Tennessee governor, there wasn't much hope that I would ever get out.

The letter really didn't say much. Back in my regular letter-writing days, this man might have received a standard response. But something about him intrigued me. Maybe it was the burned edges. (Most likely it was the fact that he looked like he'd stepped right off the cover of *GQ*.)

"So are you writing him back or what?" Crystal demanded as soon as I put the letter down.

"Oh, I don't know," I sighed. "Maybe?"

"Didn't he say he wants you to write him?" Crystal had her hand on her hip, like she was scolding me. "Men who look like him don't write every day."

"Well, okay," I said. "I'll think about it."

That night I sat down at my desk with a pen and paper.

I wrote that it was my birthday month, I had an associate's degree, and I was working on a bachelor's degree in organizational leadership. I told him about my recent work consulting for the juvenile court and detention center. And, of course, I couldn't help but ask about the pictures.

"Are you a model or something? Or do you just randomly take really great pictures???"

No way this guy is writing me back, I thought as I dropped my letter in the mail. Whoever this Jaime was, he wasn't like the crazy dudes who wrote me on the regular. This man seemed like somebody who had his stuff together. *He doesn't want nothing to do with somebody in prison*.

But it wasn't long before Crystal was back with another envelope in her hand. "Ooh, girl, it's Eyebrows!" I felt my heart pound as I snatched the envelope from her. Never in a million years did I think he would write back this quickly, if at all.

"Give me that!"

This letter was longer, with more details about his life. He told me he had just lost his father, and he was a father to a little boy. He was a devout man of God, that much was clear. But the way he talked about it didn't make me feel like he was beating me upside the head with it. He was also a businessman who had bought his dream car—a Bentley—and was on his way to sign a deal in Memphis to make him even richer when God stopped him in his tracks. He heard God clear as day tell him to turn the car around, pack up his bags, and go home to Houston. He walked away from everything, even when the entourage around him thought he had lost his mind. Now, he lived in Houston, leading a simpler, Christ-centered life.

Dang, I thought. *I had a supernatural experience in Memphis too. Looks like we have something in common.*

I could feel the corners of my mouth creeping up as I read. This man wasn't just preaching to me like I thought he would after his first letter. I was getting an inside look at his life. Crystal laughed at me.

"Y'all are gonna catch feelings for each other," she said. "I can just feel it."

"I cannot catch feelings for somebody through a letter," I scoffed.

"Mm-hmm," she said, a knowing smile on her face. "We'll see."

THERE'S SOMETHING ABOUT WRITING LETTERS THAT MAKES YOU bolder than you've ever been. I sat there in my cell, a paper and pen in front of me, writing words I'd never have the guts to say if Jaime was sitting right in front of me. I'd seal up my envelope and think, *This is it, he'll really think I'm nuts this time and never talk to me again*. But it was never long before Crystal called out, "Ooh, girl, you got eyebrow mail!"

Jaime wrote about how he'd talked to God his whole life. He was so good and devoted that at first I thought he was some kind of square. Just some good little southern church boy who'd never broken a rule in his life. He quickly squashed that idea. While he'd never stopped believing in God, he did his share of straying. It wasn't until God spoke to him in a Memphis hotel room that he realized his wild life of money and women was coming between him and God.

When Jaime wrote about God, he sounded like he was talking about a close friend, not the faraway being I'd learned about in church all those years before. He never preached at me—that would have sent me running for the hills. I couldn't explain why but I felt drawn to his descriptions of intimate encounters with God, and the divine appointments that changed his life, like the man he met at CVS late at night who ended up investing in Jaime's career and helping him become successful.

Something about his letters sparked a curiosity in me, not just about the man writing them, but about the God he described. As I read about his life-shaping encounters, I thought back to my own experiences I'd chalked up to luck, or karma. The Memphis dreams, making it back to Nashville, even being imprisoned while Kut was shot in the parking lot all those years before—were all of these examples of God watching out for me? I found myself reevaluating everything.

"Are y'all in love yet?" Crystal would ask after yet another letter.

"Nah, it ain't like that," I said. "We're just gonna be Jesus friends."

"Mm-hmm," Crystal said, giving me the side-eye.

"I'm serious! We ain't even talked on the phone! We just writing letters."

It was true. Jaime had given me his phone number, but every time I called, the phone rang and rang before going to voice mail. I'd be lying if I said I wasn't interested in him, but I figured if he didn't answer the phone, he must not be interested. Not that I could blame him. I was sitting in prison with a life sentence hanging over my head. What kind of man would ever want to get involved with that mess? That didn't stop me from talking about him constantly. His character, his heart, everything about him was so pure. All my life I'd been drawn to men with giant egos who treated me like garbage. For the first time ever, I couldn't stop thinking about a man with the light of Jesus shining through him. My prison sentence felt a little bit lighter with him on my mind. Reading his letters took me away from my cell, away from the crappy job and stupid rules that filled my days. Being friends was enough, I decided. I'd have to be stupid to expect anything more from someone like him.

But my entire theory went haywire when I got Jaime's next letter. "Could I come visit you sometime?" he asked.

Immediately my mind spiraled. Why would he want to come all the way from Texas and visit someone in prison if we were really just friends? I pored over his letters again, combing through every word and searching for any indication that something more was going on here. I couldn't find even the tiniest trace of flirting. He was nothing but a gentleman. Even when he called me beautiful, he made sure to clarify that he was talking about my inner beauty. Which was nice, but not what I wanted to hear.

Maybe he won't actually come, I thought. Jaime wasn't the first person to say he'd come visit me. Every time, I'd send a visitation form only for the person to never send it in.

When I mailed Jaime one, I figured I'd never hear back from him again. But within days, I was told his form was approved.

Now I was really tripping. I showed his letters to Crystal and read them out loud to Missy on the phone. Neither of them could find any evidence that we were more than friends.

"This is how you'll know," Missy told me. "When he comes to visit, see if he kisses you. If he does, you'll know he likes you. If not, then maybe you're just friends."

When Jaime told me he'd bought a plane ticket and would visit me

April 22, 2017, I flipped out. If I wanted this man to kiss me, I had to make sure I looked dang good. This was an emergency situation.

Normally, it takes you a month to get an appointment with the prison cosmetology program. I didn't have that long. I marched right down to the school and pulled the teacher aside to plead my case and ask her to make an exception for me.

I handed her the pictures Jaime had sent me. "*This man* is coming to see me, Miss K," I said. Enough said. She squeezed me in to get my hair flat-ironed.

The big day came and I pulled out every piece of makeup I kept in my little bag—eye shadow, eyeliner, mascara, lip gloss, and a little shimmer powder. We don't have a whole lot of options in prison. A few drops of perfume I kept in a Visine bottle and I was good to go. As I waited for the officer to call me, I prayed my deodorant didn't fail me.

After pacing around anxiously in my cell, the officer called me around ten o'clock. I practically skipped down to the visitation gallery.

When I walked in, the tables were empty except for one, where an old white man was seated. I stared at that man with a horrible sinking feeling. I'd never actually seen Jaime. He didn't answer his phone. And what were the chances that someone as fine and successful as him would write me letters and then just jump on a plane to visit me? I thought about the TV specials I'd seen about catfishing and shot the old man a death stare. *If this is the one who was writing me, he is getting cussed out today*, I thought. I was in the middle of rehearsing my verbal takedown when the real Jaime walked in, looking every bit as cute as he did in his pictures.

My anger and fear melted away as joy lit up inside me, a joy I'd never felt before. I couldn't believe he was actually here, smiling at me with his whole face. My heart pounded as he crossed the room and leaned in to hug me, like we'd done it a thousand times before. In the visitation gallery, you're only allowed to hug and kiss when you greet someone and when they leave. If he was going to kiss me, this was one of two opportunities. But when he hugged me without a kiss, I tried to brush it off. *He probably wouldn't do that right off the bat*, I thought. *Maybe he'll kiss me when he leaves.*

"You're not supposed to be in here," he said, shaking his head, his eyes wide, as if he were genuinely stunned. All I could do was smile at him like a teenager.

"I'm serious. You're supposed to be out jogging in the neighborhood or sitting in the park or something." He leaned in and whispered intensely, "You not supposed to be here."

I just chuckled. I spent most of the four-hour visit looking deep into his eyes, smiling, taking it all in. Truth be told, I couldn't tell you what we talked about that day. I was in a daze, realizing that I felt some kind of way about him. That feeling, whatever it was, grew with each word he spoke in his calm, confident voice.

Jaime, however, had no problem talking, telling me story after story. Every once in a while I interrupted him.

"You have the most beautiful eyes," I'd say, between comments about how soft his skin was and how good he smelled.

Jaime just laughed. "You ain't even listening," he said.

I was, but I wasn't. Inside my head, a whole other conversation was going on as I tried to process what the heck was happening here. Where on earth did he come from? How did he find me? And why would the universe tease me like this? I could feel myself falling in love with him, even as I told myself he would surely never be mine. There was no way he'd want to be with someone in prison.

He looked at me like he'd look at a sister, keeping everything on the up-and-up. Meanwhile, I felt like I literally had hearts for eyes. The room seemed to freeze around us, like there was no one in the world but the two of us.

Suddenly, Jaime's words caught my attention. "I don't know whoever told me that I could do all things through Christ who strengthens me," he told me. "But I really can."

All this time, it felt like God had been speaking to me through

Jaime's letters. Now he was speaking to me in the flesh, like the words glowed as they left his mouth. I knew in that moment that God had sent him to me. I knew that I loved him. I didn't know what that meant, or if I would ever tell him. Four hours passed like four minutes, and before I knew it Jaime had to leave to catch his flight. My joy almost instantly turned to sadness as he stood to go.

"I'll write you on the plane," he told me.

I walked him to the door, taking my time, turning my face up toward his. *If you're going to kiss me, now would be the time*, I thought. But Jaime only hugged me.

"I'll call you," I said.

Jaime scrunched up his face. "Yeah, I'm not really a phone person."

Dang, I thought. *This man don't like me like that.* This was his way of letting me down easy. I tried to hide the disappointment I was sure was obvious on my face.

I watched him walk away, wondering what the heck just happened. Part of me was floating, savoring those moments we had together. The other part was in turmoil, wondering how he felt about me and why he would come all the way here if he didn't like me.

I had no idea he was feeling the same turmoil behind his calm, cool exterior.

Two weeks went by without a word from Jaime. I refused to call or even write him a letter. He had promised he would write a letter on the plane. The way I saw it, the ball was in his court.

I couldn't stop thinking about those four hours in the visitation gallery. My stomach did a little flip-flop every time I pictured that cool half smile and imagined the music of his laugh. He'd seemed like he was having a good time that day, so I couldn't figure out why I hadn't heard from him. *I must have scared him off*, I thought. He really seemed to struggle with me being in here. Maybe it was too much for him.

But on my next phone call with Mommy, she barely let me say two words before she started in on me.

"Why haven't you called Jaime?" she demanded.

I was too stunned to speak for a moment. "What do you mean? Did you talk to him or something?"

"He called me. He wanted to know if everything was all right, seeing as you never wrote him or anything."

"It was his turn to write!" I said indignantly. "He said he'd write me on the plane and he never did."

"I don't know," Mommy said. "But you better call him and straighten this out."

Blood rushed to my ears, pulsing so loudly I could hardly hear, as I hung up with Mommy and dialed Jaime's number. This time, he answered.

"Was you just not gonna call me?" he asked, sounding like he seriously didn't know.

"You told me you weren't a phone person!" I sputtered. "How was I supposed to take that?"

"Well, I'm not. But I would do that for you."

I felt my cheeks flush at his words. I still didn't know how he felt about me. But at least he wasn't going anywhere.

From then on, we talked every day, multiple times a day. These calls were costing me a fortune, eating up nearly every dime I made from my job, but I didn't care.

One day, I casually mentioned that I needed to hang up and put more money on my phone account, when he cut me off.

"Hold up. You've been paying for these calls?"

"Well, yeah," I said. "Ain't nothing free in prison."

"No. You gotta let me pay for them."

"No no no." I shook my head, even though he couldn't see me. "I don't want that. I got it. Don't worry about it." What Jaime and I had, whatever it was, was good. It was pure. I knew from experience that any time you involve money in a relationship, it's bad news. Nothing comes for free, I'd learned.

"I don't want anything from you but your conversation," he said, reading between the lines. "I don't want you paying nothing to talk to me. Just show me how to put money on your account. Let me do this for you."

Jaime made good on his word. Nothing changed in our relationship except the fact that I didn't need to carefully watch the minutes on our calls. We kept on writing letters even as we talked on the phone about everything from my day at work to his latest martial arts class. But most of all, we talked about God. Jaime always told me faith was a process.

"God told us that if you seek him, you're gonna find him," he said. "God isn't this imaginary person in the sky like our parents taught us. God is real."

"Look at the ocean," he told me on another call. "If you go to the beach, and you look at all that water, it never goes farther than the water's edge before God tells it to turn around, and it obeys him. If you just open your eyes, the whole world is screaming of God's glory."

With each conversation, I found myself drawn further and further into a relationship with God. Jaime had me praying on the phone with him, first listening to him pray but later praying on my own too. And he had this gentle way of drawing me into more Christ-like behavior. I'd tell him about a comment some girl had made that pissed me off, and how I was fixing to go tell her about herself.

"Don't do that," Jaime would always warn me. "Just pray about it."

His words caught me off guard at first. I was used to chewing somebody out first and asking questions later. Jaime gently showed me how to stop and think before I said something I couldn't take back. Somehow, I never got mad at him for talking me down. I liked to call Jaime the heathen whisperer. He knew just what to say to get me to listen.

But he still didn't tell me how he felt about me. Every once in a while he'd drop me a little nugget, saying things like "You would make somebody really happy," or "You would make a good mom." His words drove me crazy. I wanted to scream, *What are you trying to say?*

"Girl, you know he wants you," Crystal kept telling me. "He obviously has feelings for you."

But I couldn't let myself think that way. Not until the letter arrived.

I had mentioned to him that I loved the song "Either Way," by Chris Stapleton. "When we get off the phone, you need to listen to it," I'd told him.

A few days later, I opened the letter he'd apparently written after listening to the song, letting the lyrics sink in:

We can just go on like this

Or say the word, we'll call it quits

"Who am I kidding?" Jaime wrote that night. "I want it to be you. I want you to be sitting here in this house with me. I know God brought you to me for a reason, and I don't know what it will look like with you being in prison all the way in Tennessee. But I love you. I know the Lord has called me to you."

I screamed out loud when I read his letter. I must have read it five times in a row, eating up every word like it was food for my soul. My feet didn't touch the ground as I floated to the phones, dialing his number as fast as I could.

"So you love me, huh?" I asked as soon as he answered.

"Yeah. I really do."

I wished with all my heart I could hug him through the phone. For the first time, I was ready to surrender my vulnerability as a grown woman, with no deception, no illusions. I was ready to take the plunge with a man who had overwhelmed me with his goodness. I knew there was a possibility I would never get out of prison. I also knew God was the reason we were together. God was the glue that bonded us together. He was our foundation. And he was the reason I could let my guard down enough to tell him the words I'd held in my heart for weeks.

"I love you too."

21

LAST RESORT

By the early summer of 2017, I walked around the prison halls with a permanent smile plastered on my face. I was a woman in love, and I didn't care who knew. I didn't know how long it would last or where it would go—a life sentence kind of puts your personal life in jeopardy. But I was fixing to enjoy it for as long as I could.

It turned out Mommy had fallen in love with Jaime right along with me. Jaime called to check on her regularly. I'd tell you what they talked about, but every time I asked either of them, they both said, "None of your business." Jaime and Mommy texted one another back and forth, talking smack about their rival football teams, the Dallas Cowboys and the Houston Texans. I'd never seen my mother act this way about anyone Missy or Chico brought home. Seeing my man have his own relationship with the other most important person in my life felt great.

That June, I knew Jaime's birthday was coming up. He'd told me he was traveling to L.A. on business with his cousin Justin but he was mailing me a surprise, even though it was his birthday and not mine.

"Well what is it?" I asked.

"I ain't gonna tell you," he said playfully.

I have been nosy my entire life and now was no exception. I had to know what he was sending me. "Can you at least tell me what color it is?"

"It's blue," he said. "But I ain't telling you anything else."

This went on for days. We'd be in the middle of a serious conversation and all of the sudden I'd break in with "Is it a poster?" I couldn't let it go.

On June 10, the day of his birthday, Mommy told me she was coming to visit. "Wear your hair down and curly," she said. "I think you're so pretty with your curls."

"Um, okay." It was a pretty weird request, seeing as I was just going to visit with my mom. I'd never gotten dressed up for her before. I just said "Whatever" and moved on.

I called Jaime to wish him a happy birthday and sat in my cell, waiting for the guard to tell me my visitor was here. I looked at the clock, watching the minutes tick to nine forty-five. Mommy was never later than nine forty in the morning when she visited, even when there was a delay. *Something must be wrong*, I thought. When she still hadn't showed up by ten, I was downright worried. I picked up the phone and called her.

"Toia, hang up and call Jaime," she said as soon as she answered.

I felt my pulse quicken as panic rose in my body. "Why? What happened? What's wrong? Where is he?" It doesn't take much to get me worked up. I can go from zero to sixty in a second. My mind raced to the worst-case scenario. *He's been in a car accident. He's dead somewhere.* I had to force myself to think logically—if he can talk on the phone, he must be okay.

Jaime picked up the phone as calm as ever. I, however, was freaking out.

"Why did Mommy say to call you?" I shrieked. "What happened?"

"Nothing," he said "You all right?"

"Mommy didn't show up. She said to call you. What's going on?"

"So," he said slowly, "your surprise was that I came up here to visit you."

I frowned and looked at the clock. This didn't make any sense. "Well, where are you? Are you coming?"

"Well, they were searching cars when we got here," he said. Every once in a while the prison put a checkpoint at the parking lot entry, searching every car before they let it through. Jaime filled me in on the rest. Guards tore through Justin's truck and discovered a bottle of Crown Royal locked in the glove compartment. It was unopened, and Jaime had no intention of bringing it into the prison. The guards didn't care.

They pulled Jaime out of the car, patting him down so aggressively they tore his blue linen suit—that was the blue that was supposed to be my surprise. They brought him into the building, stuck him inside a cage, where they ran a dog around him, and declared they'd found weed in the truck.

"No, you didn't," Jaime said, just as calm and confident as ever. "I don't smoke, and neither does my cousin."

My hand shook as I listened to Jaime describe how the guards sneered at him, yelling that he looked like he did heroin. *How can they treat the man I love like that?* I thought, my stomach churning with anger. To treat me like that was one thing. I already knew they did everything in their power to strip anyone in prison of their humanity. But to treat someone's family like that? I wanted to scream.

"What did they say?" I finally asked.

"I asked to speak to the warden," Jaime said slowly. "She said I could maybe come back in a year. Maybe. But she said I can't see you today."

I wanted to stomp out to that parking lot and whoop everybody. I wanted their jobs on a platter. I wanted to call the news. I was pissed. But Jaime didn't even raise his voice.

"The whole time, I felt God telling me to humble myself," he said. "So that's what I did."

"What do you mean?" I stuttered. How could he not get angry when he was treated so horribly? He had every right to be livid. "What did you do?"

"I told them all to have a blessed day, and God bless you. Then I shook their hands."

I sat in stunned silence. I could not compute what he was saying. How could he just let them off the hook like that? "And they just shook your hand right back?"

"Well, the warden gave me maybe two fingers," he scoffed. "She treated me like I was dirty or something."

"And you just walked away?"

"I got back in the truck and we got back on the road."

The fact that I had come so close to seeing him, only to miss him by a hair, caused actual, physical pain. My heart ached as I pictured him outside in the Tennessee heat, sweltering in his suit, while prison dogs barked at him like he was some kind of criminal. I held the phone in my hand, sobbing into the receiver.

"It's all right," he said. "It's gonna be all right. Because here's the deal. You don't mess with God's children."

"You sho right," I cried.

"I'm dead serious," he said. "God spoke to me when I left. I heard him clear as day. He told me, because you humbled yourself, they're gonna have to let her up out of there."

I listened, letting his words sink in. I could tell he meant what he said. "I don't get it. You just turned around after driving thirteen hours, and you don't want me to go down there and raise some hell?" Lord knew that was all I wanted to do.

"You can't do that," he reassured me. "God's gonna make a way. He told me that. Now, you can believe what God says, or you can believe what man says. But if you believe what God says, you've got to humble yourself too."

I sat in the chair, my mind racing, my shoulders heaving up and down as I tried to slow my breath.

This was the moment. Once again, I had two paths in front of me. I could choose to walk down to the office and cuss everybody out for disrespecting my man, and risk getting thrown in seg. Or, I could do what Jaime said. I could humble myself, and believe that God would take care of it. I could see so clearly how I'd chosen the wrong path time and time again. I didn't even think about it back then, I just acted and then reaped the consequences. If I was honest, I wasn't sure how to take the right path now.

"What do I do?" I whispered.

"You pray. You wanna pray now?"

"Yes."

Everyone likes to think there's a moment where you drop to your knees and pray the sinner's prayer and are changed forever. It wasn't like that for me. Like Jaime always said, finding my way to faith was a process. But this was the start. This was the moment I saw what faith had done for Jaime, and how God allowed him to humble himself. I knew for a fact that didn't come naturally. Growing up in La Marque, a small black town near Houston, he used his fists more than he ever used his words. If he'd been treated this way just a year or two prior, I'd probably be writing a different chapter. But in the months just before he lost his father, Jaime heard the call of the Lord. Through spending time with God, the Lord delivered him from his anger and rage. I knew right then I wanted that kind of deliverance for myself.

When I wasn't talking to Jaime, I was busy strategizing my way to freedom. My last federal appeal had failed, and the judge had ruled I couldn't appeal his ruling. By all accounts, that was the end of our case. Our only other option, our Hail Mary, was clemency. Our plan was to ask the governor to commute my sentence to second-degree murder. With my time already served, that would allow me to walk out of that prison a free woman. I would still be a convicted murderer, but at least I would be home.

I knew the governor at the time, Bill Haslam, hadn't used his power of executive clemency yet to pardon anyone or commute someone's sentence to a lesser charge. My attorneys told me most governors wait to do that until the end of their terms. Since Governor Haslam still had two years left, they said we had plenty of time to make our case. Everybody warned me that my chances weren't good. Less than 1 percent of clemency applications had been granted in the state of Tennessee in the recent decade. And before that, I'd have to be granted a hearing before the parole board. Even the chances of getting that opportunity were slim at best.

But in my mind, there was still a chance. And now that I had this fine man who wanted nothing more than to be by my side, I had extra motivation working in my favor. I wanted to prepare now and make the most of my last shot. This wasn't something I was willing to leave in the hands of lawyers. Whatever I had to do, I wanted to be at home with Jaime.

Every lunch break and day off work was spent on the resource computer, making a spreadsheet of influential people I planned to ask for help. Kathy laughed when she saw my list of DAs, state legislators, and victims' rights groups.

"You've lost your mind," she said. "This is aspirational at best."

"Well, you never know until you ask," I said slyly. I didn't tell her Jaime believed he'd heard from God that I was getting out of there. I doubt she would have taken that well.

My approach to clemency centered around the fact that I'd worked hard to rehabilitate myself since that horrible day. I went to school, I mentored kids, and I became a different person. But the idea that I could possibly be considered a trafficking victim honestly hadn't entered my mind. When I thought of trafficking, I thought of girls being stuffed into suitcases, or kidnapped by Russian mobsters. It never occurred to me that you could be trafficked by someone you thought was your boyfriend.

The first time I ever heard the word used in the same sentence as my name, I was strolling around a resource fair not long before my associate's degree graduation. Everyone involved with the prison education program had to go, so I figured I'd make my appearance and then split. The whole gym was filled with Tennessee nonprofits offering reentry resources, like Project Return, Tennessee Prison Outreach Ministries, and Nashville Cares, places these ladies could turn to when they got released.

Ain't it kinda sad no one gets the word out about these places before we get locked up? I thought. That's when we really could use a fair like this.

As I walked by a booth for something called the Magdalene House, I noticed a woman looking at me like she knew me. Before I could say a word, she was already sticking out her hand, jumping right into it.

"I'm Sheila, and I just want you to know I signed a petition for you," she said, her eyes locked on mine as she held on to my hand. "I think you deserve a second chance because you were trafficked. You never should have been sentenced as long as you were."

What? This lady is crazy, I thought. "What now?"

Sheila raised her eyebrows, a knowing look in her eye. "You were. I work with girls like you every day. There is no such thing as a teenaged prostitute. You were too young to consent to something like that. That's trafficking."

"You'll have to excuse me," I said, turning away. *This lady is tripping*, I thought. I knew what I was doing when I picked up those men. No one held a gun to my head or stuffed me in a trunk. I did what I did because I thought I was in love. Nothing more, nothing less. I was happy she supported me, but part of me felt like a fraud knowing that's why she signed the petition pushing for my freedom. I felt uneasy, like I'd tricked her or something.

Over the next couple of years, the word "trafficking" popped up every now and then on my radar. I remember watching *Grey's Anatomy* and *Scandal* and seeing commercials for a campaign called "What Is Thirteen."

I couldn't just hop online and look it up, so I asked Kathy to google it. She said it was about trafficking, since thirteen was the average age girls were recruited.

I still wasn't using the word in the fall of 2017, when I walked into the first day of my senior capstone class at Lipscomb. It was one of the last required courses before I could get my bachelor's degree in organizational leadership. With just six of us in the class, it was the smallest Lipscomb class I'd ever taken.

On my first day, our professor walked around the room with giant sticky notes, handing one to each of us and instructing us to stick them to a wall. We stood around the room, wondering what the heck she wanted us to do with these things.

"I want each of you to draw a map of your learning journey," she said. "I don't want you to limit this to your education. Think about what you've learned in your careers, your early life, your years in prison, your real-world experience."

I stared at my blank sticky note, wondering where to start. I sure hadn't had a career that I could pull from.

What have I learned? I thought, racking my brain. As I looked back on my life before prison, it wasn't too difficult to find a pattern. From the time I was just twelve years old, I got myself into one unhealthy relationship with a man after another.

But how did I learn that? I thought, drawing a line on my sticky note. What made me think this was okay? Mommy sure never told me that, so where did I get that idea?

I started scribbling at the blank white space in front of me as my mind flashed to Big John's comments all those years ago, how his words made me burn with anger but didn't draw the same outrage from anyone else. I thought of Trina, and her whole theory of transactional sex, that I can use my body to get anything I want, and that every relationship is formed on the basis of a quid pro quo. By the time I got to OmniCenter, I was so screwed up that when a guy helped me run away, I felt like I had to have sex with him in exchange. For years, I thought of Kut as this bad dude who put all these terrible ideas in my head, when the truth was, I was already groomed and ready long before I met him.

My thinking was so twisted that even now, I would rather starve than let Jaime put money in my commissary account. Nothing is free, I always told myself.

But I also knew I wasn't the only girl experiencing these same issues. Where I came from, our community referred to girls like me as "fast" or "hot in the ass." What they really meant was the girls were to blame for what happened. *Where was this message coming from?* I wondered. With each capstone class, I dove further into the issue, asking prison staff to look up studies for me. When someone handed me a survey of mandated abuse reporters, though, I was blown away. The majority of these people, who come into contact with children every day and are required by law to report any signs of abuse they witness, responded in the survey that they believed some underage girls willingly sell themselves in exchange for sex.

These people are supposed to be on the front lines, I thought. *If they don't get it, this is a problem.*

I was elbow-deep in this research when I asked a prison staff member to look up the federal definition of trafficking and print it out for me. The federal law I was handed flat-out stated that anyone under eighteen who was engaged in commercial sex was being trafficked, period. My body froze as I read the words. *Huh*, I thought. *That kind of sounds like me.*

It was like I'd pulled a string in a knitted sweater and the whole thing came unraveled. Once I started, I had to keep going. I dove into studies explaining that someone under age eighteen doesn't have the full mental capacity to sell sex, even if they think that's what they've done. Trafficking doesn't have to involve a big underground operation with mobsters and girls being gagged and bound and thrown into car trunks. Trafficking can be just one guy tricking one girl into selling her body.

A light bulb went off in my head. I thought of the man pacing around the hotel in the do-rag, the way Kut walked in to smooth things over. *Take care of my boy*, he had said, like he was asking me to buy groceries. I wasn't out there just hustling because I wanted to. That means Kut wasn't my boyfriend. He never was. Kut was my pimp.

My heart pounded as my body coursed with anger. But I wasn't angry for myself. I felt a righteous anger for the girls still out there, the girls no one pays attention to. *Everybody needs to know about this*, I thought. *These messages we're sending young girls are priming them for sex trafficking and violence.* I flew into activist mode.

We've got to do something, I thought. If this problem was ever going to change, people needed to be educated. And I was fixing to do it.

Kathy got me in touch with a woman named Stacia Freeman, who founded a group called Epic Girl. Every day she works with the juvenile court system to find girls in trouble and set them up with identity classes to help them understand their vulnerabilities, learn more about potential risks, and connect them with resources. We even arranged for Stacia to visit me in prison to help me research my project. I sat in the visitation gallery with a pen and paper, scribbling furiously as Stacia told me about girls facing life sentences, girls with no clue what lay ahead of them, girls who refused to listen to a word Stacia or Kathy told them.

As I listened, I thought about the kids Kathy had me talk to on the phone to help set them straight. They listened to me when they wouldn't listen to anyone else. I'd been in their shoes. I knew what it was like to be in state custody, feelings coursing through you that you didn't understand.

When the interview was over, I put down my pen and looked at Stacia shyly. "What if we started a group?" I asked her. "Maybe you could get some girls together and I'd talk to them over the phone. Maybe I could help."

Stacia's face lit up with a grin. "I think I can make that happen," she said. She looked at me like she believed I could make a difference. *If Stacia believes in me, there's no telling what I can do.*

Right as I dug into this subject, bam!—the #MeToo movement began. *This is God*, I thought. *This is his perfect timing, his way of bringing everything together all at once.*

I knew right then my capstone project would be GLITTER—the Grassroots Learning Initiative on Teen Trafficking, Exploitation, and Rape. The thing about glitter is it reflects light. I saw my project shining a light on trafficking and preventing other girls from falling into the same mess I did. This didn't need to wait until I got out of prison. I could help start something like this right now. People were already listening to my voice. I had the ear of state lawmakers as they worked on our bill on juvenile life sentences. The local juvenile court had tapped me as a consultant. I wasn't getting paid, but they paid attention to what I had to say. I could do this.

I envisioned a social media campaign like the ice bucket challenge I saw all over the news back in 2012 raising money for ALS. People could throw glitter bombs or paint their bodies with body glitter, some kind of gimmick to attract attention. But the real goal would be to get people talking about trafficking and what it really looks like. Real change had to come from a grassroots effort. I'd seen on *The Today Show* and *Good Morning America* when social media campaigns caught like wildfire. Mine could do the same thing. This wasn't just a capstone project to me anymore. This felt like my calling.

Since I couldn't exactly post on social media myself, I needed help. I called Kathy and asked her to get me a TV interview. That turned out to be easy—it wasn't long before Kathy told me I had an interview with a local Fox affiliate news anchor, Stacy Case, to talk about the GLITTER Project.

On the day of the interview, I called Kathy's office phone and she put me on speaker. Stacy Case was already in her office waiting for me.

Words spilled out of my mouth without effort for an hour as Stacy listened intently. I told her about my own experiences, and how easy it was for young girls to get sucked into these scenarios.

We'd reached the end of the interview when Stacy asked if I thought I'd ever see freedom.

"That's my hope," I said.

"And are you planning to pursue clemency?"

I sat silently, not sure what to say. Should I tell her I had five attorneys, a lobbyist, a court administrator, a public relations strategist, and a prelaw Lipscomb student intern all working around the clock to put my clemency file together? Should I tell her they met regularly with other government strategists, lobbyists, lawyers, and judges for advice? Out of all our strategic conversations, not once had we considered what to do if a reporter randomly asked about clemency in an interview. I had no idea if I was supposed to keep it a secret.

I just stayed quiet. *Kathy should decide how to respond*, I thought.

Then, suddenly, Kathy went for it. "Yes, we're working on clemency," she said confidently.

Okay, we're doing this, I thought. *I might as well chime in.*

"Yeah, we're hoping the governor will grant it," I said. "It's not something that happens often. No one has been granted clemency in six or seven years. But we're hopeful."

Stacy paused for a moment. "Do you think you'll get it?"

"Well, do you think I'll get it?" I said, caught off guard.

"I hope so," she said.

"You think that was okay?" I asked Kathy afterward.

"I think one mention in a news story is fine," she reassured me. "It's not like that was what the whole story was about. But let's keep it quiet from here on out."

Two weeks later, there it was. I turned on the news as a reporter teased a big investigative report coming up on "the push to free Cyntoia." "Child sex slave in Nashville prison for killing man who used her," the headline behind him read.

Oh god oh god oh god, I thought. *This is it. It's over. My clemency bid is over.*

I felt acid rising in my throat as I watched the report featuring footage from Dan's documentary—me in my pigtails and orange jumpsuit, looking every bit the child I was. The GLITTER Project, the whole reason for the interview, was now a footnote. Instead, Kathy's comments about my clemency bid were front and center.

"It's a very dedicated group of people working on a clemency campaign for Cyntoia," Kathy said on camera, sitting in her office, dressed in her suit jacket. She went on to describe my "unique factors" that might make the governor consider my case, like my associate's degree and my work with the courts.

I am in trouble, I thought, my mind racing. *I am done*.

Up until now, everything about my clemency was hush-hush. I knew from my months working on the life sentence bill that the more attention you got, the more you heard from protesters. Yes, this news story might get more people to support me, but it might also piss off a lot of people who wanted me locked up the rest of my life.

My hands shook as I dialed Jaime's number.

"Oh god, Jaime, what did I do?" I cried, breaking down right there on the phone. "This is my last shot. If clemency doesn't work, that's it. I ain't ever getting out of here."

"That ain't gonna happen." Jaime was as calm as ever, his voice soothing. "This is God's plan. Just trust him."

"But you don't understand. This kind of attention ain't good. They're gonna rip me apart."

"Are you gonna trust what man says, or are you gonna trust what God says?" Jaime paused before he continued. "Maybe you can't see it now, but God can use this for your good."

I sighed. "I just hope this whole thing blows over soon."

22

GOING VIRAL

rown!"

I was on my way into the old school building for my job as a teacher's aide when I heard someone yell my name. I whipped around and saw a guard named Lavelle standing there, her mouth wide open in a huge grin.

"Have your people been on Instagram?"

I stared at her, not understanding what she was asking. "Maybe? I guess? I don't know."

"Girl!" Lavelle put her hand on my shoulder like she was shaking me out of a deep sleep. "T. I. said something about you on there yesterday!"

"T. I. the rapper?" I struggled to make sense of what she was saying. Why would T. I. even know my name?

"Yes, girl! He posted about you!"

I shook my head and laughed. "Naw, they got all kinds of fake accounts set up. That ain't really him." My sister had told me all about a fake account someone had set up pretending to be me.

But Lavelle wasn't letting up. "No, I'm telling you, this was real."

"Well did it have a blue check mark by his name?" I asked hesitantly. Jaime had told me that's how you knew if an account was fake or if it really belonged to a celebrity.

"Yes! It was really him!"

I frowned, feeling confused. Something about this just didn't make sense. Sure, people in Tennessee knew who I was, but my case had never received celebrity attention. *This can't be right*, I thought. *She got it wrong somehow.*

I went on to work, trying to put what Lavelle had said out of my mind. But something nagged at me. What if it was real? What if a rapper is really out there posting about me? How could that even happen?

When I finally got a break, I walked straight to the phone and dialed Mr. Bone's office. What I really wanted was an update on my clemency packet. Even though Kathy had thought I was crazy, we'd gotten our letters of support. I could feel the Lord moving in my favor.

But we never got to discuss clemency that day. "Our phones have been ringing off the hook all day," the receptionist told me. "Everybody wants to know about Rihanna."

"Rihanna?" *What the heck is going on?* I wondered. I'd sung along to "Umbrella" and "We Found Love" like everybody else. I'd watched her on the BET Awards. Now suddenly this singer was posting about me on Instagram? No way that was real.

"Everybody wants an interview," the receptionist said. "We're about to do one with ABC News."

I shook my head as I hung up. I felt like the whole world had gone crazy, like everybody but me believed the same crazy lie. Finally I called the one person I knew was sane—Jaime. He had just returned from a fishing trip with his cousin Justin.

But Jaime confirmed everything. "Yep," he said. "Rihanna posted about you. And LeBron James. And Snoop Dogg. It's blowing up." He was the first person all day who hadn't seemed even the slightest bit excited about what was happening. He knew fame was fleeting. He wasn't about to get caught up in it now.

For a moment my mouth couldn't form words. Nothing about this made any sense. I was nobody. I wasn't some kind of icon. How did these people even hear about my case? The only news coverage I'd had was that local Fox News story. Why would Rihanna or T. I. have heard about it?

"Well what does it say?" I finally asked.

"It's a picture of you in your pigtails," Jaime said. "And above that it says, 'Imagine at the age of sixteen being sex-trafficked by a pimp named Kutthroat. After days of being repeatedly drugged and raped by different men, you were purchased by a forty-three-year-old child predator who took you to his home to use you for sex. You end up finding enough courage to fight back and shoot and kill him. You're arrested as a result, tried and convicted as an adult and sentenced to life in prison. This is the story of Cyntoia Brown. She will be eligible for parole when she is sixty-nine years old.' And it ends with the hashtag, #FreeCyntoiaBrown."

I took a deep breath and closed my eyes. "How many likes does it have?"

"Almost two million."

Suddenly my legs didn't want to support my body. I flopped into a chair as the phone room spun around me. My mind swirled as I tried to process what he was saying. Somehow my story had spread through the whole world, all because a handful of men and women with millions of followers took a moment to type my name.

When I first thought of the GLITTER Project, I knew the trafficking issue had the potential to spread like wildfire. But I never wanted it to be about me. I never thought it would happen like this. I imagined everyday people throwing glitter in the air or doing some kind of stunt to raise awareness for trafficking. I never imagined my picture or my story being part of it.

For a moment I thought I would be sick. I thought back to my conversation with Kathy after the Fox interview. *Let's keep it quiet*, she'd told me. Now my story was a genuine viral post.

"Oh god, Jaime, my clemency," I cried. "They're gonna think we planted this. The governor is never gonna listen to me now." Celebrity support don't play in Tennessee. The last thing people want in this bright-red state is a bunch of Hollywood people telling them what to do. Unless your celebrity support comes from Dolly Parton, no one wants to hear it.

"Just be still," Jaime said as he heard me start to panic. "That's all you can do. Just be still."

"Jaime, you don't understand, the parole board will—"

"God said they're gonna let you up out of there, didn't he?" He waited for a response.

"Yeah."

"Then maybe this is part of his plan. Let's just watch him work."

Being still was easier said than done, especially when the news just wouldn't quit. That evening, I flipped on the four o'clock news just like I always do. There it was all over again. "Celebrities rally to free Cyntoia Brown," news anchors proclaimed.

My routine every day was to watch *Inside Edition* after the news. This show had updated their story to say Kim Kardashian West had also posted about me.

"What?" I shouted out loud. How in the world was this lady from *Keeping Up with the Kardashians*, this lady who regularly blew up the internet with her photos, now posting about me like I was something? The reporter said she'd even written that she'd asked her legal team to reach out to mine. I may have been in prison, but I most certainly hadn't lost touch with the outside world. I watched *Good Morning America* and *The Today Show*. I knew what kind of impact Twitter and social media had on the world. I'd seen countless stories about something going viral and seen tweets get quoted on the news. In my mind, these celebrities were just people with platforms. They had a voice, but Jaime had told me enough to know that fame was here today and gone tomorrow. I didn't get caught up in that world. Now that world was directly colliding with mine.

I switched off the TV and sat staring into space, stunned. Meanwhile, all the girls around me practically exploded with excitement.

"You think Kim will come visit?" my roommate asked.

I laughed. "Naw. That ain't gonna happen."

"Girl, I'ma be watching your mail," my neighbor said. "If I see a letter from T. I. I'm keeping it."

What the heck is this mess? I thought. *Are these people really talking about snatching my mail?*

Jaime was my calming force. "Don't get caught up in the distraction," he said. "Celebrity ain't nothing. Fame don't last. You gotta focus on what God is doing."

Weeks went by as the story built to a fever pitch. Every day, someone told me about another celebrity posting about me, another story in the news. New petitions popped up on MoveOn.org and Change.org., drawing hundreds of thousands of signatures.

Through it all, I forced myself to keep my feet on the ground. Jaime and I prayed together on the phone and listened to Tony Evans's sermons. I read my *Jesus Calling* devotional every day and asked God to keep my eyes on him. All of this was under his control anyway. I couldn't make anything happen just by worrying. I knew I had to rely on him.

It was bizarre to hear these updates secondhand, without any ability to check them out for myself. I couldn't respond to anything—not that I would have. My attorneys advised me that staying quiet was our best course of action. They reached out to the governor's office to make sure he knew we had nothing to do with my story going viral.

Letters poured into the prison, each mail call bringing me stacks of envelopes. "I signed your petition," they told me. "I can't believe they did this to you, I really hope you get clemency."

I couldn't answer any of them. As much as I appreciated them, I knew I couldn't respond. I didn't want anyone to get ahold of a letter and claim I either condemned or encouraged the movement. I may have had a voice, but in that moment, that wasn't my role. So much about my clemency was already out in the public. My job now was to sit back and let God do his thing.

For weeks, we waited. My attorneys filed my clemency application and told me it could be months before the governor's office responded.

While I waited, I figured it was the perfect time to start my group with Epic Girl. There was no structure, title, or curriculum. Stacia and Kathy just gathered a group of girls from the Juvenile Detention Center in a conference room. The craziest part was, Ashlee Sellars was there too. Ashlee, my old friend from Lipscomb, was out now after seventeen years in prison, and she wanted to make a difference in the juvenile court, so I hooked her up with Kathy. She got to come be part of the group too.

I couldn't actually be at the group in person, but Kathy put me on speakerphone so I could talk to the girls. The first time I called, I heard the room whisper excitedly as I spoke.

"What is Rihanna like?" one girl asked timidly.

"Yeah, what's Kim Kardashian like?" another girl chimed in.

These girls are only listening to me because they think I'm famous, I laughed to myself. *But hey, whatever gets me through to them has to be a good thing.* I took it upon myself to be real with them. I told them what they needed to understand about their cases, and what they should discuss with their lawyers. And I listened to anything and everything they wanted to tell me.

Most of the time, they told me their deepest fears.

"Miss Cyntoia, I'm scared I'm gonna die in prison," they'd say. "I'm scared they're gonna find me guilty."

All I wanted was to tell them everything was going to be okay. But I couldn't do it. Not in good conscience. The sad fact was, they might die in prison one day, even though they committed their crimes as juveniles. I still faced that very real possibility too. So I took a different approach.

"Your sentence doesn't define you," I told them. "They can't tell you what kind of life to live. You can still have dreams. You can still live a good life. Prison doesn't have to be the end."

These girls were heartbreakingly young. Everybody was gossiping about one girl who wrote to a boy on the boy's side of juvenile and apparently named a Beanie Baby after him. "Honey, if you're young enough to have a Beanie Baby, you're too young for any boyfriend," I said to her, wishing someone might have said something similar to me, not that I would have listened.

The charges these girls faced were all too real. A lot of them were facing transfers to adult court for murder charges. Yet somehow they were just clueless to how serious their situation was. One girl asked Stacia to take her to get her hair done, like she could just walk out of there, even though she was facing murder charges. Another girl was locked up for killing a member of the MS-13 gang. That gang actually sent people into the facility to have her killed, and she just didn't get it.

"Miss Cyntoia, I got so mad, because they sent me down to intake," she told me on the phone. "I had to sit there all by myself in that cell, and I didn't do nothing."

I sighed. Nobody had told her it was for her own protection. "Baby, you may not always understand what's happening, but sometimes God puts us in a different place for our own good."

A girl named Tamika especially took a liking to me. She used to call me "cousin," since her last name was Brown too. Kathy told me Tamika liked to pick up the phone and walk to a corner of the room so she could have me all to herself. "I gotta talk to my friend," she'd say.

Tamika was having all kinds of problems fighting and getting into trouble in jail. I knew all too well what she was going through. But since she was facing a transfer to adult court, I also understood how she needed to act to keep herself in the juvenile system. "You gotta try to stay out of trouble," I told her. "When they have that transfer hearing, the judge will take into account everything you do when you're in juvenile. You be acting up like that, she might throw you in adult court."

And she tried. She really did. She'd go through periods where she stayed out of trouble. At one point, she even asked for a picture of me to keep in her cell. Kathy gave her one to put on her wall, so whenever she felt like acting up, she could look at my picture and think of what I would say.

But eventually, the group dissolved. The Juvenile Detention Center management company said it was a conflict of interest to have Kathy and Ashlee talking to the girls like that. Without them, I had no way to keep mentoring them. I felt helpless, sitting in prison, with no way to communicate with these girls who needed me. What would they do without someone to talk to? I laid awake at night, wondering what they were doing, if they were staying out of trouble.

I heard Tamika eventually got transferred to adult court. Sometimes, I still wonder if I could have done something about it if our group had kept going.

I knew clemency applications take time. Everyone told me that going in. But still, some part of me had imagined getting a letter right away telling me I got a hearing. So when that didn't happen, it was hard not to be worried.

"We gotta just prepare ourselves," Jaime told me. "God might be making us wait until we learn a lesson. We gotta make sure we're ready for the calling he has for us."

We prayed on the phone for the Holy Spirit to show us anything that wasn't right in our hearts, anything we needed to work on. Over and over, night after night, we prayed the same prayer.

One night, we had just prayed, asking God what we needed to work on, when I told Jaime I needed to call him right back. "I'm going to fix me something in the microwave real quick and then I'll be back," I said.

I headed downstairs to the microwave and waited on my food to cook. My neighbor Vanessa was sitting at the table with another girl from the pod.

"Anything good on tonight?" Vanessa asked. She and I always talked about movies, and she liked for me to let her know when new movies would be on.

"You know what, there's a movie called *Dear White People* coming on Bounce tonight," I said.

The girl next to Vanessa scrunched up her face like she'd smelled something rotten. "Why you talking about white people?" she sneered. "You're white yourself."

Suddenly I was that little girl on the stage again, standing in front of the little boy pointing and laughing. I felt my fists clench, my heart pound, and blood rush to my ears and cheeks. Rage coursed through my body out of nowhere.

I whirled around to face this chick. "First of all, I didn't say anything about white people," I said through clenched teeth. "I told her the name of a movie that's on right now. And second of all, I wasn't even talking to you."

This girl wasn't hearing it. "Whatever. You know what you said."

I could feel my face turning beet red as I stormed back to the phones. My whole life, nothing set me off like somebody calling me white. Back when I was a kid, when someone called me white, they were calling me an outsider, someone who didn't belong.

But I've worked through all that, I thought. *I know community is what you make of it. I know it doesn't matter what anybody else thinks of me, and it only matters what God thinks of me. So why am I still so mad?*

"Well that was the fastest answer to prayer I've ever had," I said when I called Jaime back.

"What do you think God is trying to show you?" he asked after I told him the story.

"I guess it's my anger."

"Look, I didn't want to bring this up," he said slowly. "But I think God wants you to forgive Gina."

I could feel my shoulders tense up at the very mention of her name. This woman was the reason I struggled every day to control my impulses, all because she couldn't stop herself from chugging vodka when she was pregnant. She gave me up, abandoned me, promised to come visit and never did. Since the day I met her before my transfer hearing, this woman had been nothing but a disappointment. She'd promise she was in it for the long haul, only to skip out the first time some man paid attention to her. She wrote me letters only when she was in jail and had nothing better to do. Now, she was out there posing as a devoted mom on social media, even asking for money on GoFundMe to visit me, when she had no intention of coming up here. She didn't care about me. All she wanted was attention.

In my eyes, Gina was a train wreck, somebody who refused to get her life together even now that she knew better. I could get over what she did when she was a kid. Lord knows I made plenty of mistakes when I was young too. I was all for second chances. It was the third, fourth, fifth, and sixth chances that I wasn't so sure of.

"Any time I bring up Gina, you shut it down," Jaime said. "You don't want to hear nothing about her."

"What? What does that have to do with anything?"

"You're gonna be angry until you forgive Gina," Jaime said. "And God's not gonna let you out of there until you do."

I shrugged. "Okay, then, I forgive her."

Jaime laughed. "It ain't like that. You know, I had to forgive my dad too."

"Yeah?"

"Yeah." I knew Jaime and his dad didn't have the best relationship.

"When I found out he had cancer and had six months to live, I packed up and moved back to Texas to be with him," Jaime continued.

"I kept thinking about what would have happened if I had forgiven him sooner. I thought about all that time I missed for no reason. The whole time I was angry, it didn't affect my dad. The only person I was hurting was me."

I held the phone quietly, my head in my hands. I knew he was right. But I also didn't know how to just stop feeling angry at someone who didn't deserve forgiveness.

"How am I supposed to do that?"

"You gotta pray. Ask God to help you forgive. And he'll do it."

Jaime made it all sound so simple when just the thought of Gina sitting in my transfer hearing with her hair in braids made my blood boil.

"You know how you'll know you really forgave her?" Jaime asked.

"How?"

"You know you've forgiven someone when you can run into them in the street and say, 'Hey, how you doing?' and really mean it."

I laughed. "Yeah, I can't do that with Gina. I would turn and walk the other way."

"Well, you got time to work on that."

After Jaime and I hung up, I sat cross-legged on my bed, a journal in my lap. There was no way I was calling Gina to talk this out. I'd end up saying something that would make things even worse.

Every day, I went back to that journal. I filled page after page. I wrote about every moment she verbally trashed Mommy, the only person who'd ever been there for me from day one. I wrote about the visits she'd promised and blown off. I wrote about the pictures Missy had told me she'd posted on Facebook, where she'd cropped out the rest of my family. She'd lied to me over and over to the point where I didn't believe a word that came out of her mouth. Not even when she told me her mother—my biological grandmother—was sick and dying, and she wanted to talk to me before she died. I never called. I didn't believe Gina. I had no reason to. And then, that lady died. I knew it wasn't my fault, and that I had every reason not to believe Gina, but I couldn't push away the guilt that crept into my mind. It was just another reason to be mad.

I got to the end of the journal, every last page covered with my long list of grievances. I chewed her out with my pen, saying every last word I imagined myself saying if I ever saw her. As I closed the book, it hit me. This could have been my life. If I had never gone to prison, never hit rock bottom, never been forced to look myself in the mirror and decide to change, I might be just like her. I might be letting people down right and left, just like I did when I was a teenager.

God, I don't want this anger no more, I prayed. *I'm no better than her. Every good thing in me now, every good thing in my life, is all because of you. You forgave me when I didn't deserve it. Please help me to forgive Gina when she doesn't deserve it either.*

I kept praying. I kept deciding to let go, deciding she wasn't going to control me anymore. I kept praying until one day, I pictured Gina's face. I pictured her sitting on the witness stand in a sleeveless top, the word "Suicide" tattooed on her arm for all to see. I pictured her braids, her white skin, her vacant eyes. For the first time, I felt nothing. The anger her image always conjured for me just wasn't there.

"I think I really do forgive her," I told Jaime that night. "I think if I saw her now, I would be fine."

The Lord has a funny way of holding you to your word. Months later, on one of the most important days of my life, the day of my clemency hearing, I'd get that opportunity.

I'd walk in, escorted between two guards, past the vending machines and the blue plastic chairs filling the gallery. Gina would be the last thing on my mind. I'd be too busy praying for God to work in the hearts of the committee members about to hear my case. Then suddenly, there she'd be, sitting next to Mommy under the fluorescent lights, wearing a T-shirt that said "Good Vibes Only." I'd swallow, close my eyes, and take a deep breath before turning to her.

And sure enough, I'd find the courage to say the very words Jaime had told me.

"Hey Gina," I'd say, looking her in the eyes. "How you doing?"

This time, I really meant it.

In the months that followed, I'd learn that forgiveness doesn't mean someone needs to be part of your life. Forgiveness doesn't mean welcoming someone in with open arms, regardless of the fact that they continue to hurt you. I'll never have that picture-perfect relationship with my birth mother. But now I'm no longer defined by anger. Her actions don't control me. I choose to walk in God's grace and let go.

23

ASKING FOR MERCY

After weeks of nonstop frenzy, there was silence.

Every morning, when my alarm rang at five thirty, my eyes snapped open, thoughts swirling in my head. *What if Governor Haslam thinks we asked Kim Kardashian to tweet about me? What if he was so mad about my story going viral that he threw out my application? What if I get denied without ever getting a chance to plead my case?*

I told myself I shouldn't be nervous. I shouldn't let those thoughts take root. But every quiet moment, every time I was alone, there they were.

Those were the moments I closed the wooden door to my cell. I sat on my metal bed, leaning my back against the cinder-block walls, hugging my knees to my chest, my Bible on the tray next to me. I closed my eyes, trying not to listen to the ladies hollering and carrying on in the pod. And I prayed. Every day, every moment when the nerves became too much, I prayed.

Funny how my prayers had changed since the day I was handed a life sentence. Back then, my only prayer was for God to bail me out.

Those prayers eventually turned to silence. Silence in return for the silence I thought I heard from God. By the time I was shipped off to Memphis, my prayers were a plea in the dark, wondering if he could possibly be real. And now here I was, asking God to show Governor Haslam what he needed to know. I wasn't begging for my freedom anymore. God's plan was better than mine. All I asked was that God take away my nerves and clear my head. That he would speak to the people who needed to hear from him. That justice would ultimately prevail. What would my prayers be like in five years? I wondered.

Calling Jaime helped calm my fears too. As we talked, I constantly heard Jaime bring up his pastor and mentor, Tim McGee. Tim was a prayer warrior and a true man of God, and I knew how influential he was in Jaime's faith journey. So when Jaime asked what I'd think of having Tim counsel us and pray with us over the phone, I jumped at the chance. I was still learning how to walk by faith and lean on God, and I wanted all the help I could get.

Talking to Jaime and Tim kept me grounded when we got to February—two months after filing—and still hadn't heard a thing. I knew Governor Haslam still had nearly a year left in his term, and there was plenty of time for me to get a hearing. But every day I had to spend in prison without someone telling me I was fixing to get out was like torture.

When I called Jaime one day in February, I knew something was different. His voice sounded lighter, like he'd heard good news.

"I talked to Tim," he said. "And he said the Lord was telling him that something is going to happen for us in March. He doesn't know what it is, but there's some kind of date coming that's important for you to get out."

A year earlier, I would have said someone was straight-up nuts if they tried to tell me something like that. But I knew better by now than to question something Jaime or Tim had heard from God. Those two seemed like they had a direct line from the Lord's mouth to their ears. So I listened.

"Okay," I said. "I receive that."

By the time March rolled around, I woke up every day wondering if this was the date Tim was talking about. Would Mr. Bone call Jaime today? Was this the day we got a hearing? But Mr. Bone didn't call.

I called Jaime on March 10, hoping he'd have some good news for me. When he picked up the phone, he was crying. Now this man does not cry. Nothing gets him upset or excited. He's so calm and cool it's almost annoying. So when I heard him boo-hooing on the other end, I thought somebody must have died.

"Jaime, what's wrong?" I demanded. "What happened?"

"Baby, you're coming home." His voice was thick with emotion as he spoke through his sobs.

"Well what happened? Did you get an email from somebody?"

"No." He cleared his throat, trying to stem the tide of sobs that wouldn't stop pouring out. "I was just in the car and I heard it clear as day. I heard it just as clear as the first day I met you. God told me then that you were my wife."

I closed my eyes, soaking in the love I could hear pouring through that phone. My whole life, I had dreamed that someone would love me. That someone would want me as his wife. When I got that life sentence, I thought that was it. No one would want to be with a girl in prison. Even when Jaime told me he loved me, I thought for sure it wouldn't last. I figured he'd be out of there eventually, especially after the warden suspended him from visiting me. And now here he was, loving me, honoring me, obeying the call he knew God had on him.

"God told me my wife is coming home," he said.

I could feel my whole body smiling in that moment. If God said it, then I believed it. "Okay," I said. "I receive it."

"When you pray tonight, just thank God," Jaime said. "Thank him because he's already said it. It's done."

That night I went through my cubbies and drawers in my cell, throwing away junk I didn't need. In my mind, I was going home. If God said it, I was going to get ready now.

For almost fifteen years, I'd been an inmate. A student. A low-wage worker at jobs I hated. I'd learned to accept those roles without putting up a fight. Yet as I threw papers into a garbage bag, I knew I wanted more. I never stopped dreaming. I wanted to make a difference. I wanted God to use me to change the world.

I sat down at my desk, my sanctuary since the day I came to the Tennessee Prison for Women. This was where I wrote essays, replied to letters, even drew blueprints for a new Juvenile Detention Center. The woman sitting at the desk today was a different person from the girl who sat there years ago. Who would I be as a free woman, with no rigid structure, no guards barking at me?

Would I be sitting on a soft bed in my own house, a baby in my lap, maybe even another kid running down the hall? I imagined myself leaning back on my pillow, sun streaming through the windows, freshly brewed coffee wafting up the stairs. Jaime would already be up getting breakfast for me. No need for my five-thirty alarm clocks anymore. There would be no guards waiting to write me up for being out of place.

Not that I was lazy in my dreams. I pictured myself changing the criminal justice system, dressed in J.Lo style, my hair flat-ironed, my nails polished, my makeup fresh. Sometimes, I even fantasized about storming back into this prison, firing everyone who shouldn't be here, and changing all the rules.

I wouldn't sit much at home either. I saw myself in my kitchen, pans sizzling, the air thick with olive oil and garlic. When my first Thanksgiving as a free woman rolled around, I'd host. I'd spend three days in the kitchen, rolling out pie dough and brining the turkey.

No more prison laundry for me. I'd wash my own clothes, choosing a water temperature that wouldn't make everything shrink. My house would smell of Pine-Sol and bleach, I'd have that place so spick and span.

I'd never stopped dreaming of life outside of prison, no matter how many appeals were denied. Clemency was a last resort, a long shot. But it was something. If I couldn't hope, then what did I have?

I didn't know what would happen in March, but Jaime and I decided we'd cover that month in prayers. We prayed for our family and friends, the teachers and leaders, the influencers and people in power, the sick and the elderly, for the heart of man, for my influence on society, for our priorities and schedules. We prayed for the parole board members, that God would guard their hearts and protect them from the Enemy's influence. Jaime made a whole list and we prayed through it each and every day.

But still, nothing happened. By the end of the month, I started to worry.

"Do you think the date Tim was talking about was that encounter you had with the Holy Spirit?" I finally asked Jaime.

"I mean, maybe?" Jaime sounded doubtful. "We gonna pray that God confirms if that's the date Tim was talking about."

But God had something even better in store for us. I could hear it in Jaime's voice when I called him on March 30.

"So, I got a call from Mr. Bone," he said, all chill, as if this wasn't the moment we'd been waiting for. "You have a clemency hearing in May."

I screamed into the phone. I didn't care who heard me. No one but Jaime and Tim thought I'd get a hearing. Everyone else, even Mommy, was too scared to hope anymore. I knew the chances weren't good. But I also knew what God said. Seeing God pull through for me like that straight up gave me chills. I was tripping out.

"Jaime, do you understand that less than two percent of applications actually get hearings before the parole board on clemency?" I wanted him to get excited with me, to realize how crazy this was. "Like, period. Less than two percent. They're almost all rejected. The institution's parole officer told me I shouldn't even bother. And now I have a hearing."

"Are you surprised?" Jaime didn't even raise his voice. "God don't surprise me."

I laughed. "Boy, whatever. This is a miracle!"

Twelve years earlier, I spent the weeks leading up to my trial flipping out, strategizing with my attorneys, staying up all night reading law books. I was bound and determined to find a way out of this mess. I prayed, but really it was all about me, and what I could do for myself.

In the weeks prior to the clemency hearing, I let my attorneys handle the worrying. The only strategy I needed was my prayer strategy. I read Psalm 71 seven times a day after Tim told me the Lord put it on his heart for me to meditate on that scripture.

In you, Lord, I have taken refuge;
let me never be put to shame.
In your righteousness, rescue me and deliver me;
turn your ear to me and save me.
Be my rock of refuge,
to which I can always go;
give the command to save me,
for you are my rock and my fortress.

The words were my refuge among the noise of news coverage and publicity. I refused to let myself get caught up in backroom meetings and who said what. I knew by now that legal strategies couldn't save me. I'd had the best lawyers in the world working on my case for over a decade, and every time I went before any court, I lost. Jaime and I knew this was in the Lord's hands, whether anyone understood that but us or not.

Mr. Bone and his team visited me a few times to help me prepare for my statement. They wanted to know what I was going to say and how I would say it. I told them not to worry about that. I wasn't interested in writing out a speech. I knew the Holy Spirit would tell me what to say when the time came. Obviously, this wasn't what they wanted to hear. They're attorneys—they like to prepare. I gave them a few vague answers, but I knew I would speak from my heart when the day came. Luke 12:11–12 was my constant refrain: "When you are brought before synagogues, rulers and authorities, do not worry about how you will defend yourselves or what you will say, for the Holy Spirit will teach you at that time what you should say."

ON THE MORNING OF MAY 23, 2018, I LAY IN MY BED, MY EYES CLOSED, breathing in and out slowly. For weeks, everyone had asked me if I was nervous. That wasn't a question I allowed myself to entertain. It was a question that could get in my head, trigger my anxiety, bring me back to my old fix-it mode. On this day, the most important day of my life, that wasn't an option. I took deep inhales, willing my heart to stop pounding, to beat normally. One mantra was in my head, one mantra that would carry me through this hearing. *God's got this. It's in his hands.*

I repeated that mantra to myself as I splashed my face with water and brushed my teeth, pulling my straightened hair into a smooth ponytail. Standing at the sink-toilet combo in my cell, I stared at my reflection in the blurry tin. The woman who looked back at me was serene, peaceful, joyful. I thought back to the girl I once saw in my reflection, the girl in the pigtails and orange jumpsuit—thin, gaunt, terrified. That girl thought a life sentence would effectively mean life was over. That girl thought there was no chance of a meaningful life within the walls of a prison. She had no idea that those very walls might also save her life.

Those twelve years in prison hadn't just turned me into a woman. They'd transformed me. The girl who desperately wanted to belong, who felt powerless, who clawed and scratched her way out of every corner she was backed into, was gone. No matter what happened that day before the parole board, that girl would never be back. Slowly, without me even understanding how it happened, I had become a new person. I didn't need anybody else to tell me I was valuable. I knew my value came from the Lord. I didn't need to be free to live a meaningful life. I could help young girls right where I was, use my voice to push for change. I could stand up for other ladies in prison, help them file their appeals, and shine a light on the fact that so many great women are locked up long after they're completely rehabilitated. I could keep on working with legislators, help them pass bills that get deserving men and women out of prison faster, that keep juveniles from being thrown away for life.

The prison tactical team showed up at my door to escort me to the hearing. Normally they were dressed in their black gear, but today they were wearing their best suits. Today, it seemed, was different. So I was surprised when one of them pulled out a pair of handcuffs.

I walked slowly and deliberately down the hall, between members of the tactical team. I kept my hands laced behind my back. I was more focused on this tactical team lady looking like she was about to slam me than the hearing. No way was this girl going to embarrass me with cameras from just about every news outlet in America recording my every move.

The whole prison was on high alert for the hearing. Since my name had gone viral, my hearing attracted major news coverage—much more than my original trial. They closed down the parking lot for staff, only letting in people there for the hearing. They actually shuttled staff back and forth from the lot where they made them park.

The tactical team led me down to the intake room, which is the first stop for anyone new to the prison. They stuck me in a holding cell, where I had to wait on a metal bench, surrounded by cinder blocks, for what seemed like forever. Then, before I could come out, the tactical team lady was back again, telling me I couldn't talk to anybody, looking at me like they were fixing to slam me. It was like they didn't want me to forget who I was. Don't get a big head now, they seemed to say. You're still locked up. You're still nothing but an inmate.

I still couldn't go into the hearing. They had to search me first, which I thought was ridiculous. *I'm coming from my cell*, I thought. *What could I possibly have on me?*

I was on my way to the big foyer area where they had chairs set up for the hearing when my attorneys came out to see me.

"Mr. Bone!" I held out my arms to hug him. Once again, tactical team lady was in my face.

"You can't hug him," she said gruffly. I forced myself not to roll my eyes as I shook Mr. Bone's hand instead.

Don't let her get to you, I thought. *This ain't about her.*

I never looked at the cameras as the team led me past a line of vending machines and around the blue plastic chairs to the table where I would sit. Back when Dan was filming his documentary, he told me never to look at the camera. But I knew they were there. I could hear the shutters clicking and see the flashes from the corner of my eye.

I looked for my family through my peripheral vision—I didn't want to turn my head and make this lady freaking slam me in front of the cameras.

All the stupid, self-conscious thoughts I'd ever had came flooding back to me as I walked to my seat. *Oh God, don't let me trip. Aw crap, I forgot to suck in my stomach. I should have looked in the mirror before I let them take me out here*.

I sat at a table in between Mr. Bone and J. Houston Gordon. I could see Mommy, Missy, and Chico sitting to my right. Gina was with them, wearing that "Good Vibes Only" T-shirt. It was a strange contrast—the woman who'd been there for me consistently for fourteen years, no matter how low I sank, and the woman who had only shown up when it was convenient for her. This was the true test of my forgiveness, the moment where I'd find out if all my talk was just that, or something more. But to my relief, none of the old anger crept back in. I smiled at my family—well, as much as I could, without that tactical lady slamming me. She was sitting right behind me the whole time, and I could feel her eyes boring into the back of my head.

Jaime wasn't there. He was still suspended and wasn't allowed to come. I knew he was sitting in his Texas house, praying the whole time.

I swallowed hard, taking deep breaths as I looked at the parole board seated in front of me—two white women, four white men. For a moment, I could have sworn one of them winked at me. *That's gotta be a good sign,* I thought. I took a deep breath, relishing the moment. Everyone told me I wouldn't see the parole board for fifty-one years. And now here I was.

God, let these men and women hear your voice today, I prayed, closing my eyes. *Just fill this room with your Spirit. Let everybody feel it.*

Twelve years earlier, I spent my whole trial studying the jury's faces, wondering how each word was landing with them. Now I knew better. It was in God's hands. No raised eyebrow or frown could change that.

"We're gonna go ahead and start," the board chairman announced, quieting the room.

I could feel my chest heaving, my heart pounding, as the chairman explained my request to have my sentence commuted to second-degree murder. I sat there as he read to the crowd a whole summary of what I'd done when I was sixteen. The person he described in his report didn't sound like me. It was a person I didn't recognize anymore.

"While you've been incarcerated, you've been quite busy," the chairman said with a smile. I listened as he listed my Lipscomb degree, every job I'd ever had and every class I'd ever taken since I came to the prison. Then, it was Mr. Bone's turn to speak.

"I want to introduce to you what I think will be a remarkable story for you today," he said.

I closed my eyes as Mr. Bone spoke. *God, just let your will be done,* I prayed. *Let the board members hear what you want them to hear.*

Mr. Bone told the board he took on my case after seeing my documentary. "This is not about the criminal law today. We're not here to argue about the facts of the original crime. We are here with a story of transformation."

I looked out at Mommy and smiled. *You got this*, her face seemed to say.

We'd spend that hearing listening to people who knew me testify about my character, Mr. Bone said. "I want you to hear the conviction in their voices and their stories about Cyntoia," he said. "This is a story, a record story of transformation in the life of a wasted child who has become a beautiful, intelligent, caring, educated woman who can make things better in this world."

I swallowed hard as he spoke, forcing back tears. I thought back to my trial twelve years before, when the DA told the courtroom I was a danger to society. I felt the condemnation of a roomful of eyes as he described me as a murderous whore not worth saving, an evil person who must be thrown away forever. Now Mr. Bone was describing me as someone who could make the world a better place. It was almost too much for me to take.

He turned the microphone toward me and I took a deep breath. I remembered the cold resolve of my trial, my refusal to show any emotion. *Don't let them see you cry*, I thought. Now I laid everything on the table. I couldn't fight back these tears even if I wanted to.

"I have prayed for a very long time to be able to meet with you," I said softly, my voice shaking. "I know it's purely an act of mercy that you'd even give me a hearing, and that means everything to me."

The words flowed from my lips as if they were always there. It was just like I prayed—the Spirit spoke for me.

"When I was sixteen, I did a very horrible thing," I said, my voice thick with emotion. "I have carried that with me this whole time. And that is why we are here today. I understand the things that I've done, that it was so necessary for me to change. It wasn't a choice. I had to."

I told the board that if it weren't for the people they were about to hear from, I would not be there that day. It was their love that brought me to this point.

"They loved me despite the worst thing I had ever done, and I can't tell you what that did for me. It made me feel that I could better myself. That I could still live a life that was meaningful. I could still be a better person. They've given me an education. I was locked up at sixteen. That was it. But I have a college degree now. I have a whole new family. A whole new community of people who love me, who support me. There isn't a dream that I could have that they wouldn't support. They've given me so many opportunities, and I'm so grateful for that. It's because of what they did that is the true reason why I am rehabilitated."

I closed my eyes as I remembered my victim's family, who weren't there that day. I remembered the grief on their faces as they sat at my trial. Back then, I thought about how they hated me, how they were mugging me. It was all about how I was affected. Now I knew the depth of pain they must have felt, and I wished more than anything that I could take it away.

"There are people who I've hurt. They've been hurting for fourteen years, and I did that," I said. "I can't fix it. I can't go back. The only option I have is to change. I could not live with myself being the same person who did that."

I looked up at the ceiling and took a deep breath. This was my final plea. All I could do was pray that they listened.

"I do pray that you show me mercy and you give me a second chance. That is my prayer. I can assure each and every one of you that if you do, I won't disappoint you. I won't let you down."

The whole room was a blur as the people who had loved and cared for me over the past fourteen years one by one took the seat next to me. Miss Seabrooks was there, telling the board that I blossomed in the Lipscomb program and that I was a bright self-motivator. My eyes were blurry with tears as she compared Lipscomb to a cocoon transforming me into a butterfly.

I felt my eyes grow red and tears stung at my eyelids as she spoke. I looked up and took a deep breath. *Keep it together, keep it together*, I thought. One of my attorneys handed me a tissue.

Dr. Richard Goode from Lipscomb told the board about the GLITTER Project, and that I was a wise, mentoring presence among my peers. Preston Shipp described our story as two former adversaries who became friends.

"Here I am ten years later, not arguing against her, but arguing in favor of her release," he said passionately. "I have borne witness to the kind of person Cyntoia is, to her compassion, to her commitment to do good, to her desire to serve and help others."

The speakers kept coming like an endless cast of characters. Kathy. My friend Ashlee. Stacia Freeman. By the time they were finished, my eyes were red-rimmed from bawling.

Man, I thought. *These people really love me.* I'd spent the last two hours listening to the most amazing people say positive thing after positive thing about me. It was such a contrast to my trial, where I'd felt judged and condemned at every turn.

When it came time for the victim's side to present their case, two people spoke, including someone I recognized all too well. It was Detective Robinson, his arms crossed, his reading glasses perched on his forehead above his eyebrows. I listened politely as he told the board that in his opinion, I knew exactly what I was doing that day when I was sixteen. *Don't let him get to you*, I thought. *He doesn't know you today. He doesn't know how you've changed.*

A woman who said she was close friends with my victim also spoke. His voice was lost in all this, she said. She was there to make sure he wasn't forgotten, and to say that his life mattered. I saw the pain on her face and felt a stabbing pain in my heart. *They gotta know I care*, I thought. I fidgeted in my seat, waiting for a chance to respond.

"His life mattered," I whispered when it was my turn to speak again. "It did. I don't want anyone else to go through what his family has gone through. They've grieved for fourteen years. I think about that every day. Nothing will change that. Whether I'm in here or out there, I will think about that, and I will live differently."

I held my breath as the board took a short break to consider their votes. I knew whatever they said that day wasn't binding. The governor would ultimately have the final say. But I'd be lying if I said their votes didn't matter to me. *Just pray*, I thought. *It's in God's hands.*

Finally, the board members read their votes—two recommendations to grant my request, two to deny, and two to move my parole eligibility date to twenty-five years served.

Each vote against me was a punch in the gut. There was a time when I would have been furious that they dared to vote against me. But that day, I understood.

It's a complicated case. They don't know me.

God, what does any of this mean? I prayed. *It's not a win, but it's not a loss either.* I had no idea what the governor would do with their recommendation, or when he would make a decision.

The board ended the hearing with no indication of when I could expect news.

"I guess we'll see what happens," I told Jaime afterward.

"Hey, if God said it, he's gonna do it," Jaime said confidently.

"He sure will."

24

FINDING HOME

Those days after the hearing were what I like to call the wilderness. Time seemed to stand still, the hours stretching out endlessly. I was back in the unknown, and as hard as I tried to keep myself grounded, it didn't feel good. I fought every day to keep my mind from slipping into an anxiety spiral.

Governor Haslam had no deadline for making his decision other than the final day of his term the following January. That meant we could potentially be looking at months before he made up his mind.

When we got to July with no word, I started to worry. *What the heck is taking him so long?* I thought. Mr. Bone found out the governor's counsel was still waiting on the report from the parole board, but he expected it in the next few weeks.

"They told me there might be another clemency announced before yours," Mr. Bone told me. "But they said for you not to take that as a bad sign or to feel left out."

"Okay," I said, not sure what to think. "I guess it's a good sign that they're considering my feelings."

"So we're looking at this summer," I told Jaime after my latest update from Mr. Bone.

He sighed. "Man. All I want to hear is them saying you're getting out."

I couldn't help but smile. I don't think he wanted me to get out more than I did, but he was a close second. "They already heard everything," I told him. "We just gotta pray that they're obedient to what God said."

The first round of clemencies was announced without my name on the list. I knew what the governor's office had said. I knew that didn't mean I couldn't get clemency too. But you've got to be some kind of strong to have been in prison for fourteen years and not feel jealous when someone else gets out. One person in that first round was someone in Lipscomb with me, somebody who I knew did drugs in prison and hadn't stayed as straight as I had. *Why do I have to be the one who's gotta wait?* I wondered. I could feel myself getting choked up when I told Jaime the news that night.

"You can't act like that," he said firmly. "God hasn't run out of blessings. He don't run out. He still has a blessing for you."

I hung on to his words as I watched yet another press conference, where Governor Haslam announced that he would give more clemencies before the end of his term.

"Governor, what about Cyntoia Brown's application?" a reporter asked him. My heart pounded as I waited for his response.

"We're still reviewing her file," he said. My heart sank. What did he need to know that he didn't already know? I looked around my cell, now crowded with my Bible and devotional books, pictures of Jaime and my family. I'd gotten used to life here. You have to. But somehow the cell seemed even smaller, the walls more stifling, as I waited to learn if I'd ever be free.

That night I dreamed I was wearing a yellow dress. I was on the sidewalk, soaking up the sun, no shackles around my ankles or handcuffs on my wrists.

"Maybe that means I'm getting out in the summer," I told Jaime the next day. "You don't wear yellow dresses in the winter."

But July turned into August. Summer was running out. And still no word from the governor.

"Dang," Jaime said one day when our patience was running thin. "What is the holdup?"

Jaime has always been a man to step out on faith. But when he told me he'd bought us tickets to go to a Houston Astros game that August, I wanted to cry.

"I was hoping you could go," he said sadly.

"Baby, even if I got out, I don't even know if I'll be able to travel like that."

"But maybe you will," he said. "God can do it."

I could hear the disappointment in his voice as the day of the game drew closer. Finally he admitted defeat and invited a friend. But he didn't give up. Next thing I knew, he'd bought tickets for my entire family to go with us to a Houston Texans game against the Dallas Cowboys later in August. I sighed as I felt my heart being tugged. Hearing him get his hopes up only to be crushed just killed me inside.

The Houston trip went on without me. Jaime printed out pictures so I could see Mommy and Missy bonding with Jaime's mom and stepdad, along with his brother and sister. "Our families just fit perfectly together," he told me, grinning.

Jaime's just preparing the soil, I thought. He's laying the foundation for our family before I get out.

I had always dreamed of a great big family. I pictured everyone getting together for Sunday dinners, sitting down and ribbing each other over whether the Texans or the Cowboys were the better team. As much as I wished I was there for that game, I felt comforted knowing that big family I'd always wanted was waiting for me when I got out. *God already said it*, I thought. *Let him do what he has to do.*

September ended. Still no word from the governor. By then, the only words on our minds were "Now what?" We'd felt so sure I'd get out in the summer. Now summer was over, and nothing had happened.

When Mr. Bone told me he had a meeting scheduled for November with the governor's attorneys, I couldn't wait to tell Jaime.

"We have a meeting!" I told him excitedly. "This is great news!"

Jaime, however, was not thrilled. "A meeting for what?" he shot back. "How many meetings do they have to have? Everyone was at the hearing. They need to just do what they have to do. I am sick of these freaking meetings."

"But it's a step closer," I said gently. Jaime wasn't used to the excruciatingly slow pace of government. I, however, had lived it for more than a decade.

"I know the system," I said. "Everything is a process. It all happens in increments."

I could practically hear him shaking his head. "They just gotta free you."

A couple of months later, Jaime was ready for yet another leap of faith.

"My lease is up," he told me. "I prayed about what I should do. And you know what? I'm stepping out on faith. I'm moving to Nashville."

I couldn't believe what I was hearing. "Jaime, we have no idea what's going to happen. Why won't you just wait?"

"Are you going to believe what God said, or what?" he demanded. "God said it. He said you're getting out. And he said you're my wife. Ain't no wife of mine gonna stay in prison."

"But we don't—"

"I already started. I started taking pictures off the walls without even realizing it. I know this is what God wants me to do. So I'm gonna obey."

Jaime had barely begun packing his boxes when another round of clemency announcements came out. I wasn't among them. The fact that my case was well known only made the news more agonizing. I groaned when I saw the headlines, all announcing that I wasn't getting clemency yet. It felt like they were rubbing it in my face.

"I know what God said," I sobbed on the phone to Jaime and Tim. "But it's like every headline drags me down. Everybody wants to talk to me about it and I just can't."

"You've got to pray," Tim told me. "Focus on what God's doing. Don't get distracted."

Those were the moments, those make-or-break moments where I wondered if there was no hope for me. Jaime was the one pushing me over those hurdles, pointing me back to God, listening to my fears. He was the one person I could truly be vulnerable with, the only person who never made me feel like I had to be strong. As much as I knew Mommy was there for me, I didn't want her to see me in that position. She had her own fears and worries to deal with.

Sometimes, I told Jaime I didn't know where I'd be without him, that he was my everything. That didn't fly with him. "You can't put me up on a pedestal like that," he said. "Something could happen to me tomorrow. You have to rely on God and know you're okay as long as you have him."

It was the sexiest thing I'd ever heard him say. I knew right then and there he was the first and only man who had ever put my best interests first. He didn't want to be first in my life. He wanted God in that position.

Mr. Bone must have been feeling frustrated, too, because when I called him before his meeting with the governor's attorneys, he told me not to get my hopes up.

"Mm-mmm, I rebuke that in the name of Jesus," I told him. I didn't care if I sounded nuts. I wasn't letting him plant that doubt in my head. "Don't limit God. You don't know what he can do."

"Oh, you're right, you're right," Mr. Bone said, backpedaling. But I could tell what he really thought.

The gist of the meeting was, the governor wanted to know why he should let me out after fifteen years instead of twenty-five years, like two of the parole board members had recommended. I'd already anticipated that was coming and had told my attorneys to counter that with an offer for fifteen years served and ten years of parole, which they did.

No one but me seemed to grasp the weight of what had just happened. "Y'all don't get it," I told them. "We went into this thinking it was clemency or no clemency. Now we're looking at fifteen years or twenty-five years."

"Yeah, that's real good," Mr. Bone agreed.

"Would y'all just listen to how God moves?" I smiled. "This is confirmation for me to keep up my faith. I can see what God is doing."

The attorneys told my team that the governor wouldn't make a decision until right before he left office on January 19, 2019. That meant I had to wait until January to learn my fate. Two more months of living in limbo. I sighed. *This ain't gonna be easy*, I thought.

If I thought the months after the clemency hearing were the wilderness, December was a wildfire. I knew I was so close to the finish line, just a breath away from hearing what I knew had to be good news. And yet, it felt so far away.

Every day brought another headline, another disappointment, another reason to worry that maybe clemency wasn't God's plan, that maybe my freedom was years away.

Even my attorneys kept putting worst-case scenarios in front of me. "He could come back and tell you it's thirty-five years," Mr. Bone said.

"Mm-mmm, not today, Satan," I shot right back. "God's getting me out of here."

Everybody probably thought I was nuts, but I wasn't having it. They could keep their negative comments to themselves.

In those moments, I felt Jesus calling me closer to him. *Just ignore everything else*, he told me. *Come to me. I'll give you the rest you need.*

So I did. I got a job in the prison chapel, setting up for services, cleaning, and just soaking up God's presence every day. Working there became my new refuge, my safe haven. I could feel the Holy Spirit heavy when I closed the door behind me. Boring tasks like picking up bulletins the ladies had tossed aside or straightening up the Bibles took on an almost holy quality. Just being there felt like an act of worship. Sometimes, I got to worship in song too. I'd crank up gospel music as I worked or listen to sermons. Koryn Hawthorne's "Won't He Do It" became my theme song, and I belted out the lyrics any chance I got.

I sang at the top of my lungs to anything that came on Hallelujah FM. Now, I am not what you'd call a good singer. My voice sounds like a cat in heat yowling at the world. But I did not care who heard it. I sang in my cell, even when Crystal was around. It didn't bother me none when I saw her slip on her headphones or turn up the TV. Sometimes, somebody would walk by my cell and stick her head in my window, looking at me like I was crazy. I just smiled and kept right on singing. I was praising the Lord. That's all that mattered to me.

I kept on reading Psalm 71 seven times a day. I talked to Jaime throughout the day and prayed with him constantly.

Every once in a while, I'd get a little nugget. Like the day Captain Henry walked through the chapel, a smile on his face.

"How you doing?" I called out to him.

"It's been a good day," he said slyly.

"Oh, you get a promotion or something?"

He stopped and looked me in the eye. "Something like that. Somebody from the governor's office called me today. Wanted my opinion about you."

I could feel my pulse getting faster as I waited for him to finish.

"For the first time in my career, I've been proud to give my opinion about an inmate," he said. He grinned as he kept on walking out of the chapel.

Oh my god, I'm going home, I thought. If the governor's office was calling people here at the prison asking about me, he must be thinking about letting me go free.

I called Kathy that same day to check in. We always talked at least once a week.

"You're never going to believe this," she said in a hushed voice. "But I ran into Governor Haslam at a restaurant."

"You're kidding me."

"They seated me right next to him and his wife."

"And? What happened?"

"We prayed."

"You didn't talk to him?"

"No. But we prayed," Kathy said.

Well, I thought. *Who knows what God will do?*

It turned out, a lot. I learned Mr. Bone was called to Governor Haslam's office almost immediately after Kathy bumped into him at the restaurant. He'd been trying to meet with the governor for forever, but it hadn't worked out until that day.

Oh my god, I'm going home, I realized, my heart racing. *I'm fixing to go home.*

January took its sweet time arriving but it finally came. Jaime was up in Nashville, staying in temporary housing and waiting for the right house to come through. You've got to remember, he still wasn't allowed to see me, which made no sense. Normally, anyone who gets suspended has it lifted after three months. But with Jaime, the warden refused to let up. Even though he still hadn't been allowed to see me in prison, Jaime didn't care. He moved up here anyway. He sold his car—a Bentley, his dream car—and walked away from everything to wait on me. There was nothing in it for him. Nothing but obeying what God had said.

"But Jaime, what if they say it's twenty-five years?" I had protested.

"No. That's not what God brought me here for," Jaime said. "I came to get my bride."

Over the past few months, I'd dreamed over and over about getting out of prison. Every time, it was raining. I fully believed that dream meant it would rain on the day I got out of prison. I started checking the weather reports, looking for rain in the forecast. I wanted some kind of a sign to show me I wasn't wrong, that my good news was coming.

"Something's going on," Jaime said when I called him. "I can't put my finger on it but I can just feel it."

"I'll tell you what it is," I said with all the confidence in the world. "I'm going home."

Then, it was Monday. January 7, 2019. I was in my unit, on the phone with Jaime, the clock not even striking eight o'clock yet. Out of nowhere, I heard my name.

"Brown, down to VG."

VG was the visitation gallery. Since I worked in the chapel, I could be called to the VG at any time to pick up equipment or books. But somehow, I knew. This wasn't equipment. This was it.

The VG was in another building, so I pushed the door open and strolled onto the sidewalk. The sun shone brightly in spite of the brisk January temperatures. And then, I felt them. Raindrops.

I looked up and grinned, letting the cold pellets hit my face, the smell of fresh rain overtaking me. *Okay, God*, I prayed. *I know this is it. I know this is you.*

After all those years, when I was locked up and longing for a way out. I'd looked for God in textbooks and papers, like he was a topic to be researched. I thought if he was real, he'd give me what I wanted, when I wanted it. I thought if he didn't answer my prayers, then he wasn't the kind of God I wanted to serve. I didn't see what was really going on. For years, I didn't understand that my story was a gift. It was a platform, a way to speak out against trafficking, life sentences, exploitation of young girls. Now, as I felt that rain hit my body, yet another dream that came true, I knew he was here.

The VG was empty when I burst through the door. I took a seat by the window, a smile still plastered on my face. I closed my eyes and remembered that night curled up in my jail cell, crying out to a God I wasn't sure existed. *If you let me out of here, I'll tell the whole world about you,* I had prayed. I didn't know then I was making a covenant with him. If he'd let me out right then and there, I probably would have gone right back to my old life. I certainly couldn't have told many people about him. I never could have imagined the platform God created for me, a platform that very well could allow me to tell the world about the God who set me free.

I don't care what they throw at me next, I prayed. *I'm going to do this for you. I won't get caught up in the vanity. I know you're letting me out of here for a reason.*

I was still thanking God when I saw Mr. Bone cutting around the corner. He didn't sit down. He didn't even wait to cross the room. I could tell from the grin on his face what he was about to say.

"You go home in August," he blurted out.

In an instant I was in his arms, wrapped in a hug, soaking in his words. All this time, I had never stopped believing God would come through. I'd never stopped believing God would do what he said. To actually watch him do what he said was incredible. I felt his joy radiating through me, as if I were smiling with my entire body.

"Cool!" I said. It was all I could think to say. Nothing came anywhere close to expressing the relief, the peace, the excitement flowing through me.

The Lord was waiting for me this whole time. He waited for me through the write-ups and trips to seg. He waited for me even as I denounced him to anybody who would listen. He waited for me when I fell back into my old mistakes, when it seemed like I was powerless to stop myself from letting anger take control. And he opened my heart to the thing I desired the most.

Jaime thought clemency would mean I'd get out right away. He'd worked out a whole plan to surprise me with a Sprinter van. Without my knowing, he'd bought me a big diamond ring and asked Mommy for permission to marry me all the way back in April 2018. He'd planned to have Tim in the van waiting for us, so we could get married right then and there.

"Now we'll have to wait until August." He was so crushed you would think the governor had denied my request for clemency.

"Uh, no we don't." If marriage was on the table, I wanted it now. For most of my life, I'd lived under someone else's rules, under someone else's control. This was one thing I wanted on my own terms. My mind was already springing into action. "We can get married before that."

"And how are we gonna do that?"

"I don't know, but I will research and find out."

I wasn't kidding. I made myself an appointment to look up cases and statutes and marriage laws. I started with Tennessee. That one was a no-go. If I got married in the prison, I'd have to do four months of counseling, plus get Jaime approved to visit and fly Tim in to marry us. Seeing as the warden still hadn't agreed to let Jaime see me, that wasn't gonna work for me.

But then I looked into Texas laws. If you were in prison, all you needed was a notarized affidavit to be married by proxy. Basically, since Jaime still owned property in Texas, that meant we could be married over the phone.

"Are you sure about all this?" he asked.

"I'm telling you, I researched it," I said.

It took a call to the clerk's office in Jaime's hometown to convince him that it was all legal. After a trip to Kinko's to print out the affidavit and a visit with Mommy to get my birth certificate and Social Security card, we mailed in the paperwork and waited. Legal mail is so slow in prison, and you never know who's opening your envelopes. I fretted over the whole process.

"We gonna pray over it," Jaime said. "If it's God's will, it'll happen."

Sure enough, the marriage license arrived a few days later.

We waited for the day before my birthday—January 28, 2019. I called up Jaime, who was with Tim and his wife, Angie.

"You ready?" he asked.

"I'm ready."

We prayed together and Tim read the marriage vows. There was no sermon, no reading of 1 Corinthians 13, no music. It was short, sweet, and to the point. I barely paid attention to what Tim was saying, I was so anxious to say my part.

"Yes, yes, yes, I do!" I shouted when it was my turn.

"By the power vested in me by—" I swear Tim listed about every state in the union at this part.

If he doesn't get to the doggone point, I thought. I was just ready to be Jaime's wife.

Finally, he said it. "I now pronounce you husband and wife."

"Well, I guess we're good to go," Jaime said.

"Okay, well once we turn it in, I'll know it's real," I said. I'd been disappointed too many times in my life by now. I didn't trust anything until I could see it for myself.

Jaime laughed. "Girl, that marriage license is signed. We're married."

"Okay, but I just want to see it. Then I can breathe."

In the weeks that followed, I settled into my new, temporary home at the prison annex building. I got to wear khakis and a polo instead of the standard-issue jeans and baggy shirt. I didn't have as many guards breathing down my neck or people telling me where to go and what to do. It was still prison, but at least it had more freedom, the kind of place where ladies who are close to the end of their sentence are placed as they transition out. For the first time in over a year—and only for the second time in our relationship—Jaime and I saw one another again. We still had guards yelling at us if Jaime rubbed my back or I touched his shoulders, and we were only allowed to hold hands, but it was something. We were together, if only for a few hours.

As each day brought me closer to my release date, I couldn't help but think of all the ladies who might not ever be in my shoes. I thought of Erika, who was so busy helping other girls file their appeals that she missed her own. She's still locked up today, even though she was living an exemplary life. I thought of Tamika, who made one horrible mistake as a teenager that landed her in adult court. What hope did she have without mercy? The sad fact is, America's prisons are filled with men and women who deserve a second chance. They've owned up to their crimes and did exactly what they're supposed to do in prison—they rehabilitated themselves. They understand what I learned, that you can have a meaningful life right there in prison. And many of them will never step outside the prison walls.

BACK IN THAT OLD CHURCH WITH MOMMY, SITTING ON THE WOODEN pews, I had no idea what that salvation the preacher talked about really meant. God's power went beyond granting my wishes like a genie. God transformed me. He healed me from the pain of being used by men, of making mistakes too deep to take back. He covered my shame and gave me joy. He took my anger and replaced it with peace. And he gave me a story to tell the world. All I had to do was trust him. In an ocean of uncertainty, I grasped tightly to the life preserver he threw to me. I knew in that moment he was all I needed.

I closed my eyes for a moment, picturing the day I now knew was seven months away. I saw myself wearing a yellow dress, the sun warming the visitation gallery where I waited. When the guard gave me a signal, I'd push open the metal door, hearing it squeak and crash shut behind me for the last time. A car would be waiting for me, Mommy and Jaime standing outside it, their faces lit up with grins. Maybe we wouldn't even speak as I walked across the asphalt, no shackles or zip ties around my ankles and wrists. We wouldn't need to.

I'd open the door, feeling the cold blast of the air conditioner

Mommy always kept cranked up. Mommy would hit the gas, open road ahead of us. I knew I wouldn't ride off into the sunset. There would be new struggles ahead, new joys, new challenges. My life as a free woman might look nothing like I pictured. But I would be free. No chains. No locks. No guards. No anger.

Whatever you have for me, I receive it, I prayed. To God be the glory.

EPILOGUE

The clock read 1:15 a.m. when the moment I had waited fifteen years for finally came. No one had told me what time guards might wake me up and escort me from my bed for the last time. All they told me was that the details of my release were outlined in confidential papers that I was not privy to.

My last day in prison was filled with question after question. "Are you excited?" my friends asked me. "Is your family excited?" "Are you nervous?" The truth was, I was just ready. The excitement I'd felt back in January when the release date was set had given way to impatience as I anxiously watched the days on the calendar tick by. I'd heard women who were about to be released say they were nervous or scared about getting out. But I wasn't nervous at all. I didn't need to be. I knew the Lord was with me. Instead of anxiety, I felt peace. A peace the ladies around me couldn't understand. A peace so deep I slept like a baby my last night in prison, when everyone told me I wouldn't be able to even close my eyes.

The sound of an officer's voice snapped me out of my knocked-out haze in the wee hours of August 7, 2019. "It's time to go," the officer said. I smiled.

The officer led me to the Transition Center's Administration Building, where Unit Manager Carswell was waiting for me. She'd been a champion for my reentry into society for the past seven months, so it was only fitting that she was the one to see me off. I stepped into her office and closed the door behind me, then slipped off my prison uniform for the last time at 1:43 a.m. I sure didn't feel any nostalgia about saying goodbye to my polo shirt and prison-issued khakis. I sighed with relief as I pulled on the blue dress and tan heels I'd picked from the prison's donation closet weeks earlier. The dress felt cool on my skin as it hugged my curves, a far cry from the shapeless uniform I was used to. I felt like a woman, ready to take on the world.

Lightning flashed in the darkness outside the office window, illuminating the soaking wet sidewalk. I couldn't remember the last time I'd seen so much lightning. Instantly I remembered the dreams the Lord had shown me more than a year ago, dreams of me leaving prison when it was dark and raining. I wasn't surprised. It was far from the first dream that had come true.

I stood with Ms. Carswell waiting for the officers, reminiscing about our encounters over the last seven months.

"You keep on caring for the ladies here," I told her. "Care for them just like you did me."

She nodded emphatically. "You know I will. My heart wouldn't let me do anything else."

Finally, the radio next to Ms. Carswell sputtered to life. "The captain is on his way," a voice said among the static. I signed my release papers as I learned a tactical team was waiting outside, ready to spring on anyone who came too close.

"News crews are camped out on the street," Ms. Carswell said. "It's crazy out there. That security detail swarmed me on my way into work this morning. Everybody thinks you're gonna walk right out of the front gate in broad daylight."

After the tactical team made one final sweep to make sure no danger or media were lurking in the trees, and it was time. Ms. Carswell escorted me to the annex's checkpoint, where I was handed a packet of information on community resources, all my identifying documents from the records department, and a debit card with the remaining money in my prison account.

"There's been a change of plans," the assistant commissioner announced. Instead of my husband picking me up, they would drive me to another location, where Jaime would meet us.

"That's fine with me," I said. All I wanted was to be in my own home when the day broke through the night. I didn't care how I got there.

On my way out the door, I looked back at the prison staff, who stood behind me and smiled.

"Do y'all realize we're standing in the middle of a miracle of God?" I asked them. They all nodded with every fiber of their being. "Oh yeah," they said. "We sure do."

I stepped into the night, no shackles around my ankles, no handcuffs on my wrists. The storm had calmed, the night now quiet except for the music of crickets chirping away. The media vans were dark, the reporters clueless to the fact that the moment they'd camped out to capture was happening right under their noses.

I climbed into the back of an awaiting pickup truck as prison staffers communicated through their radios about where we were heading. We ended up at the historic Tennessee State Prison. I stared at the castle-like building in awe. I'd heard stories about this place, but it was my first time seeing it in person. *So this is where they filmed* The Green Mile, I thought. *I wonder what miles are waiting for me.*

The next thing I knew, four other vehicles pulled up. There was Jaime, lit in the darkness by headlights, storming toward me like he was coming to rescue me from my captors. In a way, he was. Just as God told him all those months ago, when he packed up and moved to Tennessee on faith, he was coming to get his bride.

In an instant, I was in the back seat of a van next to Jaime, his arm protectively around me as if he would never let me go. It was 3:18 a.m., August 7, 2019, and I was no longer a prisoner. I was free.

"Get us out of here," he told the driver. I closed my eyes and melted into Jaime as award-winning photographer and personal friend Flip Holsinger captured my first seconds of freedom.

The weight of the past fifteen years slid off my body in that moment. I felt my shoulders relax, the tension lift from my muscles, as I leaned into my husband's arms. The freedom that had once seemed like it would never be mine was finally here. I was leaving this prison as a new woman, a married woman, a woman of God, and a woman determined to use her experiences for the good of others.

As I stared at the dark highway illuminated by the van's headlights, humility washed over me. My future seemed as uncertain as the pitch-black road ahead of me. I didn't know what lay ahead or where the Lord might lead me. But everything about my release had God's stamp all over it. That was confirmed even further in May, when I had the opportunity to meet with Governor Bill Haslam and his wife, Crissy. Sitting before them, I could see the light of Christ shining through them. Their words confirmed what I already knew—just as the Lord spoke to me, he was also speaking to them. When Governor Haslam signed the commutation order, he had been acting in obedience to the Lord. God had brought me this far. He wouldn't abandon me now. I knew he'd continue to lead me as long as I stayed committed to his will.

I sat glued to the window as the van pulled into a neighborhood with its name etched in a stone setting. This was it. I was about to see my new home for the first time.

It was all I could do to keep from jumping up and down as the van slowed to a stop in front of a two-story brick house nestled in the cutest neighborhood I could have imagined. "This is ours?" I asked Jaime.

He grinned, squeezing my hand. "This is ours, baby."

As soon as I walked inside, my eyes zeroed in on the cleaning supplies in the laundry room. I'd dreamed of Pine-Sol for months and couldn't wait to get on my hands and knees cleaning my own home.

In the kitchen, I barely noticed the gleaming cabinets and shining granite countertops. I was too busy staring longingly at the bowl overflowing with every fruit I'd craved in prison—mangoes, kiwis, bananas, apples, and oranges. Suddenly, my stomach growled and I realized I was starving.

"You want me to order something?" Jaime asked as I opened cabinets, checking out the food Jaime had picked for me.

"You know what? I haven't had ravioli in a long time." I pulled a can of Chef Boyardee meat ravioli from the cabinet and grabbed a can opener. "This is all I want right now."

It wasn't what I had imagined as my first post-prison meal, yet somehow it was exactly right.

When I'd swallowed my last mouthful, Jaime took me on a tour of our new home. I felt like the queen of the castle as I saw the freshly painted walls with Bible verses stenciled on them. Each verse had meant something to us along our faith journey, each verse had carried us to this moment. It truly felt like a home built on faith. I took in the basket full of every beauty and hygiene product I'd ever mentioned to Jaime, the closet he'd stocked with stylish clothes and more shoes than I'd ever owned. I thought back to my cell, my home for half my life. I thought of the scratchy blue shirts that made up my wardrobe, my cubby stocked with prison-approved hygiene products, my thin pad that passed for a mattress. The reality that this house of plenty was all mine was almost too much to take in. Even in my wildest dreams, I'd never imagined God would bless me like this. I'd never dared to ask for it. I also knew this was far from the typical situation for most people newly released from prison. I thought of all the men and women released after years in prison with no safety net, no plan, no family to support them, no beautiful house to go home to. I knew I was beyond lucky. It hardly seemed fair.

I glanced at the clock. Only a few hours before I had to meet with my parole officer. I was a free woman, but not without strings attached. I hadn't been pardoned or declared innocent. My sentence had been commuted, and I'd been released because my time had been served. In the eyes of the law, I was still a convicted murderer. I was required to check in with my parole officer on a regular basis, and I had to do community service. But after everything I'd been through, those requirements felt easy. The parole officer was a far cry from the guards I'd had breathing down my neck for all those years. And community service? I'd already dedicated the rest of my life to helping other women and girls. I saw myself speaking out against trafficking, mentoring young girls and warning them of the fate that could await them if they didn't turn around. I saw myself sitting at the table as an advocate, pushing for laws that got juvenile inmates out of prison sooner, turning prison into a place of transformation, where men and women could truly turn their lives around.

But before I met with my parole officer, I wanted one thing. I turned on the bathtub faucet, lit a candle, and settled into the hot water. I hadn't had the luxury of a bath since I was a child. Now, soaking in my own tub, I felt like I'd made it.

Tomorrow, I want to clean my house from top to bottom, I thought. *I think I'll try on my clothes. Then maybe I'll fix us fried chicken and green beans, maybe even some corn bread. Maybe we can watch a movie.*

That's when it hit me. I'd never had the freedom to plan my day in prison. Every moment from the time I woke up to when I ate my meals to when I had to be in my cell was dictated by officers. Now I could make decisions. I could sleep in if I wanted, eat whenever the mood struck. *I could get used to this*, I thought.

The days that followed would be filled with discoveries. I'd learn that Jaime woke frequently throughout the night and wore the same do-rag and hoodie around the house. I'd learn to text with two thumbs after Jaime poked fun at me pecking at my iPhone keyboard with one finger. I'd don a baseball cap and sunglasses to pick up mixing bowls and baking sheets from Walmart without attracting any attention—after all, my release was still all over the news. I'd have the occasional "prison moment," where the sound of a radio would make me forget I was home, not in the corridors of the Tennessee Prison for Women.

Those days were also filled with greater joys than I could have expected. I celebrated my release with Mommy, Poppy, Missy, Jaime's family, and every man and woman who'd played a pivotal role in my life in these last few years. To sit in a room with people I had only known through the lens of prison the past fifteen years, now at home, knowing that more encounters like this were just a car ride away, was a more incredible feeling than I could ever put into words.

Sitting at home, with my husband sleeping on the couch beside me, I truly understood what freedom meant. Freedom is more than living on the other side of a locked door or razor- wire fence. Freedom is making my own decisions. It's living on my own terms and setting my own priorities. Freedom is sitting on my bedroom floor in my nightgown, a half-eaten plate of food before me, my husband's head on my lap as we watch movies together.

Until this point, I've been captive to so many unfulfilling roles—outcast Cyntoia, delinquent Cyntoia, convict Cyntoia, heathen Cyntoia. Now I am exactly who and what the Lord called me to be: free Cyntoia.

There is hope. Hope for everyone locked in prisons physical or spiritual. Hope for everyone who doubts they'll ever be free. No matter how far you may have fallen, that hope is still there for all who dare to believe their best days are not behind them.

ACKNOWLEDGMENTS

Had it not been for the grace, mercy, and guidance of our Heavenly Father, this book would have never been written. The Lord has been patient with me as he has led me to this point in my journey. I am so thankful to him for the way that he loves us—no matter how much I tried to run from him, he never gave up his pursuit. Thank you, Jesus, that I came to know our Father through you.

To my incredible husband Jaime, thank you for guiding me back into a relationship with God. I shudder at the thought of how truly lost I was without him. Thank you for your patience and obedience to the Lord—not to mention the countless hours you've spent ministering to me in my lowest moments. This book would not have been possible if it weren't for your tireless work managing everything when my own hands were tied. As you say, for many months, you were more Cyntoia Brown-Long than I was, period.

For years, people encouraged me to write. The words simply

wouldn't come together for me, though. It wasn't until one Sunday night in the TPW chapel that Lakethia from Spirit and Truth Fellowship in Nashville, Tennessee, delivered the word of the Lord that the words began to flow. "Write the book," you told me. Thank you for your obedience to the Lord, for delivering that word to me.

To my mother, Ellenette. You will always be the epitome of what motherly love is to me. Even when I was resistant, you insisted on introducing me to the Lord, and it took more than twenty years for me to truly appreciate it. During the darkest of my days, you were the voice of light and reason reminding me that God had a plan for my life. Thank you for never giving up on me, for your sacrifice, and your love.

Wes Yoder, your kind soul and devotion to the Lord has made this entire process a joy. It was important to Jaime and me to work with someone who could themselves hear the call of the Lord on this project. The fact that you are as thorough and efficient an agent as you are has been an added bonus. We are both grateful to you and Linda for your prayerful approach to this project and for the many times you went to the Lord on our behalf.

To Bethany Mauger. We did it! It was such a great experience working with you and writing this book. I will smile for years to come when I think of your three- and four-year-olds yelling "MORE CRACKERS PLEASE!!!" in the background as we dissected my most serious life crises over the prison phone line. Mostly, though, I appreciate that you truly *get it*. The way that we had to write this book was anything but conventional, but through God's grace, we did it.

Throughout my journey, the Lord has called people from all walks of life to come together in a myriad of ways in the crafting of this testimony of God's glory.

Thank you Pastor Tim McGee for being an on-call prayer warrior for my husband and me, and for helping us to stay focused on the Lord as we walked through the wilderness.

To the Old Man (Jacob E. Jhingree), and my in-laws Melvin and Jackie Hudnall, thank you for your unwavering support.

Thank you, Governor Bill Haslam and First Lady Crissy Haslam. God Bless you both! Charles W. Bone, J. Houston Gordon, Ed Yarbrough, and the entire "Team Free Cyntoia," thank you for your tireless work on my behalf. To everyone who has ever sent me a letter of encouragement, signed a petition to support my freedom, posted on social media, or had a conversation with another person advocating on my behalf—thank you for allowing God to soften your heart for me. To everyone who has been kind to me on this journey, and even those who played a role in some of my hardest lessons, know that the Lord was using you in turning something that was meant for my bad into something that resulted in a glorious testimony.

Finally, to everyone that I left behind in the Tennessee prison system serving life sentences, know that God is able.

To Erika East, Alisha Glisson, Toronda Williams, and Michelle Lockwood—know that God *can*. I will carry you in my heart. Thank you all for inspiring me with your grace in the face of uncertainty and stacked odds.

In the years that follow I will encourage all that I meet to educate themselves on the realities of prison sentences in America and to advocate for more compassionate approaches to justice.

TO GOD BE ALL THE GLORY!